Violence against Women and Mental Health

Key Issues in Mental Health

Vol. 178

Series Editors

Anita Riecher-Rössler Basel
Norman Sartorius Geneva

Violence against Women and Mental Health

Volume Editors

Claudia García-Moreno Geneva
Anita Riecher-Rössler Basel

5 figures and 9 tables, 2013

KARGER

Basel · Freiburg · Paris · London · New York · New Delhi · Bangkok ·
Beijing · Tokyo · Kuala Lumpur · Singapore · Sydney

Claudia García-Moreno, MD, MSc
Department of Reproductive Health and
Research
World Health Organization
20 Avenue Appia
CH-1211 Geneva (Switzerland)

Anita Riecher-Rössler, MD
Center for Gender Research and Early Detection
Psychiatric University Clinics Basel
University Hospital Basel
Petersgraben 4
CH-4031 Basel (Switzerland)

Library of Congress Cataloging-in-Publication Data

Violence against women and mental health / volume editors, Claudia García-Moreno, Anita Riecher-Rössler.
   p. ; cm. -- (Key issues in mental health ; v. 178)
   Includes bibliographical references and indexes.
   ISBN 978-3-8055-9988-7 (hard cover : alk. paper) -- ISBN 3-8055-9988-9 (hard cover : alk. paper) -- ISBN 978-3-8055-9989-4 (e-ISBN)
   I. García-Moreno, Claudia. II. Riecher-Rössler, Anita. III. Series: Key issues in mental health ; v. 178.
   [DNLM: 1. Battered Women--psychology. 2. Mental Health. 3. Stress, Psychological--therapy. 4. Violence--prevention & control. 5. Women's Health. W1 BI429 v.178 2013 / WA 309.1]

  616.89--dc23
                                                            2012044534

Bibliographic Indices. This publication is listed in bibliographic services, including MEDLINE/Pubmed.

Disclaimer. The statements, opinions and data contained in this publication are solely those of the individual authors and contributors and not of the publisher and the editor(s). The appearance of advertisements in the book is not a warranty, endorsement, or approval of the products or services advertised or of their effectiveness, quality or safety. The publisher and the editor(s) disclaim responsibility for any injury to persons or property resulting from any ideas, methods, instructions or products referred to in the content or advertisements.

Drug Dosage. The authors and the publisher have exerted every effort to ensure that drug selection and dosage set forth in this text are in accord with current recommendations and practice at the time of publication. However, in view of ongoing research, changes in government regulations, and the constant flow of information relating to drug therapy and drug reactions, the reader is urged to check the package insert for each drug for any change in indications and dosage and for added warnings and precautions. This is particularly important when the recommended agent is a new and/or infrequently employed drug.

All rights reserved. No part of this publication may be translated into other languages, reproduced or utilized in any form or by any means electronic or mechanical, including photocopying, recording, microcopying, or by any information storage and retrieval system, without permission in writing from the publisher.

© Copyright 2013 by S. Karger AG, P.O. Box, CH–4009 Basel (Switzerland) and
World Health Organization (chapters by Dr. Claudia García-Moreno et al.)
www.karger.com
Printed in Germany on acid-free and non-aging paper (ISO 9706) by Bosch Druck, Ergolding
ISSN 1662–4874
e-ISSN 1662–4882
ISBN 978–3–8055–9988–7
e-ISBN 978–3–8055–9989–4

Contents

VII Foreword
Bachelet, M. (New York, N.Y.)

X Preface
Sartorius, N. (Geneva)

XII Acknowledgments
García-Moreno, C. (Geneva); Riecher-Rössler, A. (Basel)

Violence against Women Worldwide

1 Violence against Women, Its Prevalence and Health Consequences
García-Moreno, C. (Geneva); Stöckl, H. (London)

12 Gender-Based Violence in the Middle-East: A Review
Madi Skaff, J. (Beirut)

24 Violence against Women in Latin America
Gaviria, S.L. (Medellin)

38 Violence against Women in South Asia
Niaz, U. (Lahore)

54 Violence against Women in Europe: Magnitude and the Mental Health Consequences Described by Different Data Sources
Helweg-Larsen, K. (Copenhagen)

65 Intimate Partner Violence as a Risk Factor for Mental Health Problems in South Africa
Jewkes, R. (Pretoria)

Special Aspects of Violence

75 Intimate Partner Violence and Mental Health
Oram, S.; Howard, L.M. (London)

86 Sexual Assault and Women's Mental Health
Martin, S.L.; Parcesepe, A.M. (Chapel Hill, N.C.)

96 Child Sexual Abuse of Girls
MacMillan, H.L. (Hamilton, Ont.); Wathen, C.N. (London, Ont.)

107 Sexual Violence and Armed Conflict: A Systematic Review of Psychosocial Support Interventions
Stavrou, V. (Bethesda, Md.)

118 Abuse and Trafficking among Female Migrants and Refugees
Kastrup, M. (Copenhagen)

129 Abuse in Doctor-Patient Relationships
Tschan, W. (Basel)

139 Workplace Harassment Based on Sex: A Risk Factor for Women's Mental Health Problems
Cortina, L.M.; Leskinen, E.A. (Ann Arbor, Mich.)

148 Violence against Women and Suicidality: Does Violence Cause Suicidal Behaviour?
Devries, K.M.; Seguin, M. (London)

159 Violence against Women Suffering from Severe Psychiatric Illness
Rondon, M.B. (Lima)

Conclusions

167 Violence against Women and Mental Health
García-Moreno, C. (Geneva); Riecher-Rössler, A. (Basel)

175 Author Index

177 Subject Index

Foreword

Violence against Women as a Public Health Priority

The silent pandemic of violence against women and girls leaves no country or community untouched.

Long accepted as a normal part of women's lives, violence against women has been declared a public health priority requiring urgent attention by the World Health Organization. This declaration built on the dedicated efforts of the international women's movement over the past several decades, raising awareness and demanding action to end violence against women. Today there is increasing political momentum by the international community to tackle one of the most pervasive human rights violations in the world.

Gender-based violence is increasingly recognized by decision-makers and the public at large – men, women and young people – as a priority concern, no longer acceptable in the 21st century. Pervasive violence against women and girls is not compatible with the values of equality, human dignity and democratic participation. This is especially relevant today in the current global context of political and social transitions and popular demands for inclusiveness and equity. Each and every act of violence against women violates and threatens the very principles upon which the United Nations was founded – human rights, human dignity and the equal rights of men and women. These values provide a unifying platform across geographic, cultural and linguistic boundaries.

Yet despite progress in many countries of the world, the reality of violence in women's and girls' lives, and the rampant trampling of their basic freedoms and well-being, chart us on a challenging road ahead. Based on analysis carried out by UN Women of surveys from 86 countries, including WHO's landmark study of 2005, between 9 and 76% of women report having experienced physical and/or sexual violence by any perpetrator, partner or non partner at some point in their lifetime. The majority are assaulted by men they know, often their own husbands or partners.

This violence takes many forms, from domestic abuse and sexual assault, to sexual harassment and the humiliation of women and girls in public spaces, to harmful practices such as child and forced marriage or female genital mutilation. Today sexual trafficking constitutes a form of modern day slavery, and rape and sexual torture are routinely used as a tactic of warfare. The list goes on and includes all the women and girls who have been murdered, been victims of femicide, so-called honor killings and abandoned as newborns, their main risk factor simply being female.

While the most commonly identified damages of violence against women are physical injuries, the unseen damage penetrates deeper. Those working on these issues have seen bruises and broken bones heal. But if you ask a woman what is the greatest and lasting harm inflicted from an incident of rape or years of abuse by her life partner, she will tell you: the psychological, emotional and mental impacts. There is also the social stigma – the sense of being alone, of being silenced by a society that questions and blames *her*, and seeks excuses for the men who perpetrated the crimes against her – 'what did *you* do wrong to provoke him?' – instead of holding abusers accountable.

Most women who experience abuse will never report it to anyone, neither their friends nor the police, nor are they likely to consult a physician. Yet women and girls tend to be impressively resilient, perhaps more so because of the discrimination they face and the need to overcome the barriers to equality that they encounter. In the end, women survive violence and continue as active and productive members of societies, as heads of households and family breadwinners, food gatherers and caretakers, *despite* the social and political neglect they may encounter.

The mental health needs of women and girls who experience gender-based violence is an area that has been overlooked and needs urgent attention. This is especially important given the lack of specialized services for the millions of women and girls who suffer from depression, anxiety, post-traumatic stress disorder, attempted suicide, poor social functioning, eating disorders, social isolation and marginalization as a result of the cruel and inhumane treatment and violence they have experienced.

Economic strains have been found to exacerbate violence against women. In fact, rising unemployment increases the risk of violent behavior by men who may already be predisposed to abusive attitudes and actions. The disempowerment of losing the ability to fulfill their socially ascribed role as provider is an affront to their identity and manhood. This has been reported from the United States to Japan and Europe, where, in the context of the current global economic crisis, more women are seeking refuge in shelters. Under fiscal and belt-tightening pressures, programmes that address domestic violence and sexual assault services are often among the first national cuts in social budgets – even as the needs and risks of violence to women increase.

Ultimately, violence against women is an unnecessary and preventable burden on societies and economies. It costs women and girls their lives, their health and wellbeing. It costs society the loss of the benefits of women's full participation and contributions. It fuels the inter-generational cycles of harm, malaise, violent behavior and diminished prospects for children who are witness to or targets of the abuse. It undermines international goals (such as, the Millennium Development Goals adopted by Heads of State and Government in 2000) to keep girls in school, improve maternal and child health, halt the spread of HIV and overall, reduce poverty and improve the quality of life of the world's inhabitants, especially for those living in poverty.

It actually costs public budgets *more* to stand by and let women alone bear the brunt of the violence than to take a determined political stand and take action to prevent it. In the US, for example, it was found that the Violence against Women Act not only saved lives, it also saved money. In its first 6 years alone, VAWA saved taxpayers at least USD 14.8 billion in net averted social costs. A recent study found that civil protection orders saved one state (Kentucky) on average USD 85 million in a single year.

What Is the Way Forward?

Lifting the costly and avoidable burden of violence against women is no simple challenge. It has been deeply ingrained socially and culturally throughout the history of humankind, an expression of the underlying discrimination, unequal treatment and undervaluation of women and girls. Nonetheless, it is a learned behavior and social norm and, as we know from modern history, rapid shifts in social orders and power structures are possible even within our own lifetimes, accompanied by the fast pace of medical and technological breakthroughs.

As a human rights priority, we should aspire in the coming years to ensure universal access to prompt, quality care and services for the safety, health and justice of women and girls who have experienced gender-based violence. Violence against women needs to be acknowledged as the global emergency that it is, requiring universal access to emergency and basic services, including psychological support. The United Nations and countries around the world have mobilized emergency services for other priority health issues – such as reducing maternal mortality and the spread of HIV – and the same attention and accountability is needed to address violence against women.

Ending violence against women also requires increased investment in prevention – especially engaging strategic groups such as men and young people and through the prevention of child abuse. Socialization of boys and girls since childhood and throughout adolescence on values of gender equality and nonviolence is key – at home, in schools and in their communities. Fathers and mothers should be supported and motivated to promote norms and behaviors based on equality and respect between women and men, boys and girls, that can lead to healthy and nurturing relationships and thus contribute actively to social transformation. The mass media has a tremendous role to play, through awareness raising, educational campaigns, and setting public norms of what is and is not acceptable.

This book is to be commended for bringing to the forefront the often neglected but critically important issue of mental health and violence against women.

Michelle Bachelet, MD, Executive Director of UN Women,
New York, N.Y.

Preface

Violence against Women as a Risk Factor for Mental Ill Health

This is a book about violence against women as a risk factor for mental disorders. It demonstrates, convincingly, that violence against women is widespread and that it is contributing to the occurrence of mental disorders. It is a valuable contribution to the literature on the impact of violence and aggression on health, wellbeing and productivity of women and it should be read and remembered when addressing public health problems related to violence against women and to help victims. The fact that violence against women contributes to the occurrence of mental disorders which have far reaching consequences for the life of those who have suffered them underlines the need to do whatever is possible to prevent it or to attenuate its impact.

This and other books, meetings and articles that examine the effects of violence against women on their health in general, on their working capacity, on their family relationships – are informative and enlarge our knowledge not only about the consequences of violence against women but also about the impact of trauma on various forms of human functioning. The presentation and discussion of these facts is of great importance and can be of immediate use in practice, in orienting research and in teaching the variety of professionals who are likely to have to deal with the problem in various roles.

And yet, the attention given to the fact that violence against women can contribute to the incidence of mental disorders and create a host of other problems for the women affected may obscure the much more fundamental issue – which is that violence against women is wrong, that it is a transgression against one of the most important ethical rules which states that aggression against another human being is evil and must be stopped – regardless of the immediate or long-term consequences which the evil act may have. In other words, even if it were true – and it is certainly not true – that violence against women will make them more resilient, not harm them or enhance their capacity to fight for their goals, it would never be justified to perpetrate it.

There are women who experience violence (in one or more of its various forms) yet continue to live without apparent mental disorders and perform admirably well in their social and personal roles. This has, not infrequently, been used by those who do not feel that more attention should be given to the prevention of violence as an argument to let things be as they are. The opponents of resolute action against violence argue that the consequences of violence against women are a problem of lesser public health importance than many other health problems. This, they say, should be reflected in deciding about the priority that the prevention of violence against women and its consequences should have. When fighting against this notion it is essential that we remind or convince all concerned that stopping violence is an act against the intrinsic evil that characterizes the acts of violence in general and violence against vulnerable groups such as women, the elderly, children and the disabled in particular. The justification of giving high priority to the prevention of violence does not reside only in its consequences such as, for example that there will be damage to victims' health or that victims of abuse are at risk to become perpetrators of violence later on: its power is derived from the ethical imperative which recognizes that in addition to its immediate consequences violence also erodes the structure of society and diminishes the probability that the human societies will survive.

It is a pleasure to see this book in print. It will certainly help many to think about and deal with mental disorders and other psychological consequences of violence. I hope that it will also enlarge the numbers of those who will abhor violence in all its forms and who will devote at least a part of their professional and civilian life to its prevention.

Norman Sartorius, MD, PhD, FRCPsych,
Geneva

Acknowledgments

This book would not have been possible without the combined effort of many people. First and foremost our thanks go to the staff of Karger publishers. We would like to specially mention Gabriella Karger for her enthusiasm in publishing a book on a topic with a truly global dimension, Sandra Braun for her thorough guidance during its completion, Esther Bernhard for the meticulous editing of and insightful comments on the chapters, and Angela Gasser for her commitment to making this book a success. We would also like to thank Claudine Pfister from the Center of Gender Research and Early Detection at University of Basel Psychiatric Clinics for copyediting of the manuscripts, and Catherine Daribi from the Department of Sexual Health, Gender, Reproductive Rights and Adolescence (GRR) at the WHO Geneva for assistance during the review process. The commitment of all those working behind the scenes is also gratefully acknowledged.

Claudia García-Moreno, MD, MSc, Geneva
Anita Riecher-Rössler, MD, Basel

Violence against Women, Its Prevalence and Health Consequences

Claudia García-Moreno[a,1] · Heidi Stöckl[b]

[a]Department of Reproductive Health and Research, WHO, Geneva, Switzerland; [b]Gender Violence and Health Research Centre, London School of Hygiene and Tropical Medicine, London, UK

Abstract

Violence against women in its many forms has been recognized as a highly prevalent social and public health problem with serious consequences for the health and lives of women and their children, and also a serious violation of women's human rights. This chapter provides a global overview of the most common forms of violence against women, which include intimate partner violence, sexual abuse by non-intimate partners, human trafficking, female genital mutilation and conflict-related sexual violence. Furthermore, it discusses the prevalence of intimate partner violence, one of the most widespread forms of violence against women, among both the general population as well as among women who may be more at risk of violence, such as pregnant women, adolescent girls, women with disabilities or abusing substances. It provides a brief overview of the health consequences of violence against women which include fatal outcomes, such as homicide, suicide and maternal mortality to nonfatal health consequences such as physical and chronic health problems, mental health and sexual and reproductive health problems. The high prevalence and serious physical and mental health effects of violence against women outlined in this overview highlight the necessity for implementing policies and strategies in the health sector and educating healthcare providers on the problem, guided by a human rights framework.

Copyright © 2013 WHO*

'I suffered for a long time and swallowed all my pain. That's why I am constantly visiting doctors and using medicines. No one should do this.'

Woman interviewed in Serbia and Montenegro, WHO Multi-Country Study on Domestic Violence against Women, p. 26 [1].

---

[1] The author is a staff member of the World Health Organization. The author alone is responsible for the views expressed in this publication and they do not necessarily represent the decisions, policy or views of the World Health Organization.

*All rights reserved. The World Health Organization has granted the publisher permission for the reproduction of this chapter.

The quote above reflects the situation of many women across the world, as violence against women, also called gender-based violence, because of its roots in gender inequality, is highly prevalent. This is a major concern given the strong evidence of the serious consequences violence against women can have on women's physical, mental, sexual, and reproductive health and wellbeing, as well as on other aspects of their lives.

The 1993 Declaration on the Elimination of Violence against Women defined violence against women as:

'any act of gender-based violence that results in, or is likely to result in, physical, sexual or psychological harm or suffering to women, including threats of such acts, coercion or arbitrary deprivation of liberty, whether occurring in public or in private life' [2].

This definition shows that violence against women comprises various forms of violence. It can include, although it is not limited to, physical, sexual and psychological violence, including battering, sexual abuse, dowry-related violence, rape including marital rape, female genital mutilation, sexual harassment and intimidation at work, trafficking and forced prostitution and violence related to exploitation. Violence against women can occur in the family, the general community and it can also be perpetrated or condoned by the State [2]. This definition also highlights the many perpetrators who commit violence against women, which include spouses and partners or ex-spouses and ex-partners, parents, other family members, neighbors, and men in positions of power or influence. It can occur in the home but also in the community, institutions like prisons and mental health institutions and is particularly prevalent in situations of displacement, armed conflict and other crises [3]. Violence against women, particularly that by intimate partners, is often not restricted to one single, isolated incidence, but can be long lasting and may continue for more than a decade.

Many forms of violence against women are often experienced by women as an extremely shameful and private event. Because of this sensitivity, violence is almost universally under-reported. Nevertheless, existing data of the prevalence of such violence suggests that globally, millions of women are experiencing violence or living with its consequences.

The following overview will focus on providing information on the prevalence and health consequences globally of the most common form of violence against women, namely violence by intimate partners. Information on other forms of violence, such as nonpartner violence and trafficking of women is also provided.

Prevalence

Research over the last decade has demonstrated that violence against women by male partners and ex-partners is common worldwide. For example, a national representative survey from the United States of America found that 21% of women reported having ever experienced physical or sexual intimate partner violence or both in their lifetime [4]; nationally representative surveys from Europe report a lifetime prevalence of between 25% in Germany [5] and 27% in Finland [6]. However, the fact that different measures and methodologies have been used in each study makes it difficult to compare prevalence across settings. One of the few studies that produced comparable data across urban and rural sites in 10, primarily low and middle income, countries was the World Health Organization (WHO) Multi-Country study on violence against women, which used a standardized questionnaire and standardized training and implementation procedures to measure the population-based prevalence of different forms of violence, in particular partner violence [1]. The WHO Multi-Country study, which interviewed over 24,000 women between the ages of 15 and 49 found the prevalence of physical and/or sexual intimate partner violence to range between 15% in Japan and approximately 70% in Ethiopia and Peru, with most sites reporting prevalence of between 29 and 62%. Physical abuse by a partner at some point in life up to 49 years of age was reported by 13–61% of interviewees across all study sites, and sexual abuse by 6–59%. Physical and sexual violence or both, by a nonpartner any time after the age of 15 was reported by 5.1–64.6% of interviewees. Sexual violence by a nonpartner any time after 15 and up to 49 years of age was reported by 0.3–11.5% of interviewees. New Zealand which replicated the WHO Multi-Country study methodology found that 33% of women in Auckland and 39% in Waikato, a more rural province, had experienced at least one act of physical and/or sexual violence by an intimate partner in their lifetime [7]. More recent studies, using the same instrument, have found prevalence of partner violence of 34% in Vietnam [8] and above 60% in the Solomon Islands and Kiribati [9].

As can be seen in table 1, the prevalence of nonpartner violence seems to correspond with the prevalence of intimate partner violence in some of the countries, for example in Japan, where both are comparatively low. However, there are stark differences in other countries, such as Bangladesh or Thailand, where the prevalence of intimate partner violence is notably higher. The only country where the prevalence of non-partner violence is higher than the prevalence of intimate partner violence is Samoa, where it exceeds it by nearly 20%.

Studies on special populations reveal even higher rates of intimate partner violence. Clinical surveys, for example, especially those conducted in emergency rooms yield much higher rates of intimate partner violence [10]. For example, a study of 24 Emergency Departments and Primary Care Clinics in the Midwest of the United States found higher rates of physical (58.1 vs. 40.7%), severe physical (34.8 vs. 16.4%), emotional (67.7 vs. 51.3%) and sexual abuse (33.9 vs. 18.2%) in emergency departments than in clinics where no university teaching took place. Rates in clinics with university teaching were slightly higher than in those without [11]. High prevalence rates are also found among pregnant and adolescent women as well as among women abusing substances.

Among women who had ever been pregnant, the WHO multi-country study found the lowest prevalence of physical intimate partner violence during pregnancy

Table 1. Physical and sexual violence against women by an intimate partner in the WHO Multi-Country study on Domestic violence against women [1]

Site	Physical or sexual or both nonpartner violence		Physical or sexual violence or both partner violence		Physical or sexual violence or both by nonpartners or partners or both	
	number of respondents	%	number of ever partnered women	%	number of respondents	%
Bangladesh City	1,603	22.0	1,373	53.4	1,603	58.5
Bangladesh Province	1,527	11.0	1,329	61.7	1,527	59.9
Brazil City	1,172	24.5	940	28.9	1,172	38.7
Brazil Province	1,472	15.9	1,188	36.9	1,473	38.8
Ethiopia Province	3,016	5.1	2,261	70.9	3,016	55.9
Japan City	1,365	7.5	1,276	15.4	1,370	18.5
Namibia City	1,498	21.9	1,368	35.9	1,499	42.5
Peru City	1,413	33.7	1,086	51.2	1,414	56.9
Peru Province	1,837	37.8	1,534	69.0	1,837	70.8
Samoa	1,640	64.6	1,204	46.1	1,640	75.8
Serbia & Montenegro City	1,453	11.9	1,189	23.7	1,453	26.2
Thailand City	1,534	12.1	1,048	41.1	1,535	35.0
Thailand Province	1,280	11.3	1,024	47.4	1,281	43.8
Tanzania City	1,816	26.7	1,443	41.3	1,816	49.9
Tanzania Province	1,443	22.1	1,256	55.9	1,443	60.2

to be one percent in Japan city and the highest to be 28% in Peru Province, with the majority of sites reporting a prevalence between 4 and 12% [1]. Similarly, prevalence ranging between 2% in Australia, Denmark, Cambodia and Philippines and 13.5% in Uganda were found in an analysis of Demographic and Health Surveys and the International Violence against Women survey, also with a majority between 4 and 9% [12]. As with intimate partner violence among the general population, clinical studies find much higher prevalence. A systematic review of clinical studies from sub-Saharan Africa reports prevalence of 23–40% for physical, 3–27% for sexual and 25–49% for emotional intimate partner violence during pregnancy [13].

Adolescents are another group who seemed to have a high risk of intimate partner violence. As the WHO Multi-Country study showed, the prevalence of lifetime experiences of physical or sexual violence or both among women aged 15–24 was around 50% or higher in many sites. The lowest prevalence of 19% was found in the Serbian city of Belgrade and the highest of 66% in rural Peru. In nearly all sites, except rural Ethiopia, the prevalence of intimate partner violence decreased as women got older [unpubl. paper]. A review of different studies in the US showed varied prevalence of intimate partner violence among adolescents, ranging from 9 to 49% [14]; a South African study of 928 males and females aged 13–23 years found that 42%

of females reported experiencing physical dating violence at some point in their life [15]. The comparisons across studies however, even within the review of American studies, are difficult due to different sampling strategies and definitions of what constitutes an intimate partner, which in Western studies often includes short-term dating relationships.

The WHO Multi-Country study has also found that 3–24% of women reported that their first sexual experience was forced, and that for a majority of respondents their first sex occurred during adolescence [1]. This finding is supported by nationally representative surveys of 12- to 19-year-old girls from Burkina Faso, Ghana, Malawi, and Uganda conducted in 2004, which found that 38% of girls in Malawi reported that they were 'not willing at all' at their first sexual experience; the same was reported by 30% in Ghana, 23% in Uganda and 15% in Burkina Faso [4]. Embedded qualitative interviews revealed that this coerced sex was a result of force, pressure through money or gifts; flattery, pestering, threats of infidelity or passive acceptance [4].

The prevalence of intimate partner violence seems to be especially high among substance abusing women or women with known mental illnesses. For example, a study of a random sample of 416 women in methadone treatment in the United States found lifetime experiences of intimate partner violence of 89.7% and a prevalence in the last 6 months of 78.4% [16]; while a study of 715 drug-dependent pregnant women attending a multidisciplinary perinatal substance abuse treatment program in the United States found a lifetime prevalence of physical abuse of 71.3% and 44.5% for sexual abuse. Their rates of abuse remained high during their current pregnancy, ranging from 20.0% for physical abuse to 7.1% for sexual abuse [17].

Few studies exist on the prevalence of violence among women with disabilities. Evidence from a population-based survey of 5,326 women in North Carolina, USA, shows that women who had any type of disabilities had more than 4 times the odds of experiencing sexual assault in the past year compared to women without disabilities [18]. A representative sample of 7,027 Canadian women with a current partner found that women with disabilities also face a higher risk of intimate partner violence. They not only have 40% greater odds of violence in the last 5 years, they also seem at higher risk of experiencing severe violence [19, 20].

Health Consequences

Intimate partner violence has been associated with fatal outcomes and a broad range of adverse health effects.

Fatal Outcomes
Fatal health outcomes include homicide, suicide and maternal mortality. In the United States of America, women are nine times more likely to be murdered by an intimate partner than by a stranger and the Supplemental Homicide Reports

suggest that approximately 30% of murdered women are killed by an intimate partner compared to 5.5% of men who are killed by an intimate partner [20]. This rate is expected to be even higher in less-industrialized countries, where data on the perpetrators of female homicide victims are still sparse [10]. Evidence also suggests that violence during pregnancy may be an indicator for women's increased risk of intimate partner homicide, at least in high income countries, as a study of police and medical examiner records in 11 US cities found [21].

Regarding suicide, a recent analysis of the WHO Multi-Country study found that the most consistent risk factors for suicide attempts were intimate partner violence, nonpartner physical violence, ever being divorced, separated or widowed, childhood sexual abuse and having a mother who had experienced intimate partner violence, after adjusting for probable common mental health disorders [22]. Evidence on the association between maternal mortality and intimate partner violence was summarized by a systematic literature review that found that the risk for maternal mortality is three times as high for women who are abused and that intimate partner violence is also responsible for increased fetal deaths in affected pregnancies [23].

Physical Health

Physical health consequences of intimate partner violence include injuries, such as broken bones, cuts, burns, hemorrhages and broken teeth. Being punched in the face with a fist can result in blunt trauma-related injuries, particularly maxillofacial injuries which are commonly reported among women who experienced intimate partner violence, as is strangulation, especially manual strangulation [24]. A literature review found that the prevalence of traumatic brain injury in women seeking emergency shelter or care in the emergency department for intimate partner violence ranges from 30 to 74% [25]. Another systematic review of physical injuries associated with intimate partner violence among women presenting to emergency room departments found head, neck or facial injuries to be significant markers for intimate partner violence [26]. Blunt physical trauma resulting from hits, kicks and pushes can be especially problematic during pregnancy, when abusive partners often target the abdomen, and thereby harm the health of the mother and their unborn child [27].

In addition to blunt force trauma, other chronic or nonchronic physical health problems have also been found to be associated with intimate partner violence. A cross-sectional survey of 14,100 Australian women aged 45–50 years found that women who experienced intimate partner violence were more likely to have allergies or breathing problems, pain or fatigue, bowel problems, vaginal discharge, eyesight and hearing problems, low iron, asthma, bronchitis or emphysema, or cervical cancer, even after adjusting for demographic and health behavior characteristics and menopause status [28].

Mental Health

Intimate partner violence is a significant risk factor for depression, anxiety and stress among women. A literature review of studies conducted before 1999 found that the weighted mean prevalence of mental health problems among women experiencing intimate partner violence was 47.6% for depression, 17.9% for suicide attempts or thoughts, 63.8% for post-traumatic stress disorder, 18.5% for alcohol abuse, and 8.9% for drug abuse. While this review highlighted the huge discrepancies across studies, it still concluded that intimate partner violence increases women's risk for mental health problems [29]. A systematic review published in 2012 supports this claim, suggesting a 2- to 3-fold increased risk of major depressive disorder and 1.5- to 2-fold increased risk of elevated depressive symptoms and postpartum depression among women exposed to intimate partner violence relative to nonexposed women. It further argues that 9–28% of major depressive disorder, elevated depressive symptoms, and postpartum depression can be attributed to lifetime exposure to intimate partner violence [30]. In addition, violence against women and girls has been associated with sleeping disorders, eating disorders and psychosomatic disorders [31, 32].

The literature also shows that women with severe mental disorders (bipolar disorder, schizophrenia and other psychotic disorders) are very vulnerable to intimate partner violence and sexual violence [28, 29, 33]. The relationship between violence against women and mental health is bidirectional, and therefore mental health professionals (who mainly see severe mental disorders in psychiatric services) as well as primary care providers (who are more likely to see depression and commoner disorders) need to be aware of this and be competent in this area.

Reproductive and Sexual Health

Intimate partner violence often affects the sexual and reproductive choices a woman can make, either through direct exposure to forced or coerced sex, their inability to control or negotiate the use of condoms and other forms of contraception consistently or at all or because they are not allowed to seek health care for themselves and their children without their partner's permission. This puts them at greater risk of early and unwanted pregnancy and induced abortion, sexually transmitted infections, including HIV, sexual dysfunction and poor reproductive health outcomes, especially during pregnancy [34, 35].

For example, physical and sexual intimate partner violence during pregnancy has been associated with mother's insufficient weight gain, bleeding, preeclampsia, anemia, urinary tract infections and low birth weight, and preterm labor and delivery [27, 36], in addition to increased risk of miscarriage, stillbirth and abortion [37, 38]. It also has an effect on their ability to breastfeed [39] and to refrain from unhealthy behavior, such as smoking and drinking during pregnancy [40].

Analyses using the Demographic and Health Survey showed an increase in mortality of children under two among mothers who experienced any form of intimate partner violence in Kenya, Malawi and Honduras [41]. In Haiti and Kenya they also found that children of abused mothers had an increased risk of malnutrition, being stunted and being underweight [42]. Other studies from India [43] and Brazil [44] have also found an association between intimate partner violence and child malnutrition.

A longitudinal analysis from the Eastern Cape Province in South Africa among 1,099 women aged 15–26 years who were HIV negative at baseline and had at least one additional HIV test over 2 years of follow-up provides the strongest evidence to date on the link between intimate partner violence and HIV. This study found that in rural South Africa, women who experienced intimate partner violence and who had high gender inequity in their relationships had increased incidence of HIV infection [45].

In addition to intimate partner violence, female genital mutilation or cutting (FGM) is also known to seriously affect women's reproductive and sexual health. FGM is a harmful traditional practice that is generally performed on girls before they reach the age of 10 years and often takes place under unhygienic conditions. A prospective study in six African countries showed that many girls who underwent FGM, especially those who were severely cut, suffer from chronic morbidity, including recurrent urinary tract and reproductive tract infections. Women who experienced severe FGM are significantly more likely to have a caesarean section, postpartum hemorrhage, and a long stay in hospital after delivery. Furthermore, their babies were more likely to need resuscitation, to be stillborn or to die of early neonatal death [46].

Very little research has been conducted on the health consequences of human trafficking, with the majority of studies focusing on women and girls trafficked for sexual exploitation. A multisite study of more than 200 women entering post-trafficking services in Europe found that these women suffer from multiple concurrent physical and mental health problems following their trafficking experience. The most prominent of them are fatigue, headaches, sexual and reproductive health problems (e.g. STIs), memory difficulties, back pain, and significant weight loss. Later interviews underlined that mental health symptoms persisted longer than most physical health problems [47].

Conclusion

This brief overview highlights that violence against women, especially intimate partner violence, but also other froms of violence such as FGM and trafficking, operates as a risk factor for a wide range of women's health problems, including mental health problems. It impacts also on neonatal, infant, and child health.

In addition to its serious health effects, intimate partner violence affects all aspects of a woman's life and her overall well-being. It also carries severe human, social and economic costs that have not been discussed here, such as the time abused women miss at work, the economic burden on the health care system, the psychological effect it has on their children and the gross infringement of women's right to live a life free of violence and fear. The high prevalence and the human and social costs of violence make it necessary that healthcare providers, including mental health care providers, educate themselves on the problem and that health systems develop and implement relevant prevention and response policies and strategies that are guided by a human rights framework. Health policies and healthcare delivery, particularly those related to sexual and reproductive and women's mental health, need to include violence in their agenda and address it systematically in order to reduce the burden of this important public health problem.

References

1 García-Moreno C, Jansen HAFM, Ellsberg M, Heise L, Watts C: WHO Multi-Country Study on Women's Health and Domestic Violence against Women: Initial Results on Prevalence, Health Outcomes and Women's Responses. Geneva, World Health Organization, 2005.

2 United Nations General Assembly: Declaration on the Elimination of Violence against Women. A/RES/48/104. 1993.

3 Watts C, Zimmerman C: Violence against women: global scope and magnitude. Lancet 2002;359: 1232–1237.

4 Moore AM, Awusabo-Asare K, Madise N, John-Langba J, Kumi-Kyereme A: Coerced first sex among adolescent girls in Sub-Saharan Africa: prevalence and context. Afr J Reprod Health 2007;11: 62–82.

5 Mueller U, Schroettle M: Health, well-being and personal safety of women in Germany: a representative study of violence against women in Germany. Baden-Baden, Federal Ministry for Family Affairs Senior Citizens Women and Youth, 2004.

6 Nerøien AI, Schei B: Partner violence and health: results from the first national study on violence against women in Norway. Scand J Publ Health 2008;36:161–168.

7 Fanslow J, Robinson E: Violence against women in New Zealand: prevalence and health consequences. NZ Med J 2004;117:1–12.

8 Nga NTV, Jansen H: Keeping Silent Is Dying. Domestic Violence in Viet Nam: A Hidden Issue. Sexual Violence Research Initiative Conference 2011, Cape Town, South Africa: http://www.svri.org/forum2011/KeepingSilentisDying.pdf; 2011.

9 Honiara, SI: Ministry of Women, Youth and Children's Affairs and National Statistics Office, 2009 and the Secretariat of the Pacific Community for Ministry of Internal and Social Affairs and Statistics Division, Ministry of Finance and Economic Development, Kiribati Family Health and Support Study: A study on violence against women and children. Tarawa, Republic of Kiribati, 2010 in: http://www.spc.int/hdp/index.php?option=com_docman&task=cat_view&gid=46&Itemid=44.

10 Campbell JC: Health consequences of intimate partner violence. Lancet 2002;359:1331–1336.

11 Kramer A, Lorenzon D, Mueller G: Prevalence of intimate partner violence and health implications for women using emergency departments and primary care clinics. Women's Health Issues 2004;14: 19–29.

12 Devries K, Kishor S, Johnson H, Stöckl H, Bacchus L, Garcia-Moreno C, et al: Intimate partner violence during pregnancy: prevalence data from 19 countries. Reprod Health Matters. 2010;18:1–13.

13 Shamu S, Abrahams N, Temmerman M, Musekiwa A, Zarowsky C: A systematic review of African studies on intimate partner violence against pregnant women: prevalence and risk factors. PLoS One 2011;6:e17591.

14 Glass N, Fredland N, Campbell J, Yonas M, Sharps P, Kub J: Adolescent dating violence: prevalence, risk factors, health outcomes, and implications for clinical practice. J Obstet Gynecol Neonatal Nurs 2003;32:227–238.

15 Swart LA, Seedat M, Stevens G, Ricardo I: Violence in adolescents' romantic relationships: findings from a survey amongst school-going youth in a South African community. J Adolesc 2002;25:385–395.

16 Engstrom M, El-Bassel N, Go H, Gilbert L: Childhood sexual abuse and intimate partner violence among women in methadone treatment: a direct or mediated relationship? J Fam Violence 2008;23:605–617.
17 Velez ML, Montoya ID, Jansson LM, Walters V, Svikis D, Jones HE, et al: Exposure to violence among substance-dependent pregnant women and their children. J Subst Abuse Treatm 2006;30:31–38.
18 Martin SL, Ray N, Sotres-Alvarez D, Kupper LL, Moracco KE, Dickens PA, et al: Physical and sexual assault of women with disabilities: violence against women. 2006;12:823–837.
19 Brownridge DA: Partner violence against women with disabilities: prevalence, risk, and explanations. Violence Against Women 2006;12:805–822.
20 Campbell JC, Glass N, Sharps PW, Laughon K, Bloom T: Intimate partner homicide: review and implications of research and policy. Trauma Violence Abuse 2007;8:246–269.
21 Campbell JC, Webster D, Koziol-McLain J, Block C, Campbell D, Curry MA, et al: Risk factors for femicide in abusive relationships: results from a multisite case control study. Am J Public Health 2003;93:1089–1097.
22 Devries K, Watts C, Yoshihama M, Kiss L, Schraiber LB, Deyessa N, et al: Violence against women is strongly associated with suicide attempts: evidence from the WHO multi-country study on women's health and domestic violence against women. Soc Sci Med 2011;73:79–86.
23 Boy A, Salihu HM: Intimate partner violence and birth outcomes: a systematic review. Int J Fertil Women's Med 2004;49:159–164.
24 Sheridan DJ, Nash KR: Acute injury patterns of intimate partner violence victims. Trauma Violence Abuse 2007;8:281–289.
25 Kwako LE, Glass N, Campbell J, Melvin KC, Barr T, Gill JM: Traumatic brain injury in intimate partner violence: a critical review of outcomes and mechanisms. Trauma Violence Abuse 2011;12:115–126.
26 Wu V, Huff H, Bhandari M: Pattern of physical injury associated with intimate partner violence in women presenting to the emergency department: a systematic review and meta-analysis. Trauma Violence Abuse 2010;11:71–82.
27 Bacchus L, Mezey G, Bewley S: Domestic violence: prevalence in pregnant women and associations with physical and psychological health. Eur J Obstet Gynecol Reprod Biol 2004;113:6–11.
28 Loxton D, Schofield M, Hussain R, Mishra G: History of domestic violence and physical health in midlife. Violence Against Women 2006;12:715–731.
29 Golding JM: Intimate partner violence as a risk factor for mental disorders: a meta-analysis. J Fam Violence 1999;14:99–132.
30 Beydoun HA, Beydoun MA, Kaufman JS, Lo B, Zonderman AB: Intimate partner violence against adult women and its association with major depressive disorder, depressive symptoms and postpartum depression: a systematic review and meta-analysis. Soc Sci Med 2012;75:959–975.
31 Howard LM, Trevillion K, Agnew-Davies R: Domestic violence and mental health. Int Rev Psychiatry 2010;22:525–534.
32 Rasmussen B: No refuge: an exploratory survey of nightmares, dreams, and sleep patterns in women dealing with relationship violence. Violence Against Women 2007;13:314–322.
33 Oram S, Trevillion K, Feder G, Howard LM: Systematic review of the prevalence of domestic violence victimisation amongst psychiatric patients. Br J Psychiatry. In press.
34 Glasier A, Gülmezoglu AM, Schmid GP, Moreno CG, Van Look PFA: Sexual and reproductive health: a matter of life and death. Lancet 2006;368:1595–1607.
35 Coker AL: Does physical intimate partner violence affect sexual health? Trauma Violence Abuse 2007;8:149–177.
36 Dunkle KL, Jewkes RK, Brown HC, Yoshihama M, Gray GE, McIntyre JA, et al: Prevalence and patterns of gender-based violence and revictimization among women attending antenatal clinics in Soweto, South Africa. Am J Epidemiol 2004;160:230–239.
37 Fanslow J, Silva M, Whitehead A, Robinson E: Pregnancy outcomes and intimate partner violence in New Zealand. Aust NZ J Obstet Gynaecol 2008;48:391–397.
38 Pallitto CC, García-Moreno C, Jansen HAFM, Heise L, Ellsberg M, Watts C: Intimate partner violence, abortion, and unintended pregnancy: results from the WHO Multi-Country Study on Women's Health and Domestic Violence. Int J Gynecolo Obstet 2012 Sep 5, Epub ahead of print.
39 Lau Y, Chan KS: Influence of intimate partner violence during pregnancy and early postpartum depressive symptoms on breastfeeding among Chinese women in Hong Kong. J Midwifery Women's Health 2007;52:e15–e20.
40 Bailey BA, Daugherty RA: Intimate partner violence during pregnancy: incidence and associated health behaviors in a rural population. Matern Child Health J 2007;11:495–503.
41 Rico E, Fenn B, Abramsky T, Watts C: Associations between maternal experiences of intimate partner violence and child nutrition and mortality: findings from Demographic and Health Surveys in Egypt, Honduras, Kenya, Malawi and Rwanda. J Epidemiol Commun Hlth 2011;65:360–367.

42 Hindin MJ, Kishor S, Ansara DL: Intimate Partner Violence among Couples in 10 DHS Countries: Predictors and Health Outcomes. Calverton, Macro International Incorporated, 2008.

43 Ackerson LK, Subramanian SV: Domestic violence and chronic malnutrition among women and children in India. Am J Epidemiol 2008;167:1188–1197.

44 Hasselmann M, Reichenheim M: Parental violence and the occurrence of severe and acute malnutrition in childhood. Paediatr Perinat Epidemiol 2006;20:299–311.

45 Jewkes RK, Dunkle K, Nduna M, Shai N: Intimate partner violence, relationship power inequity, and incidence of HIV infection in young women in South Africa: a cohort study. Lancet 2010;376:41–48.

46 Banks E: Female genital mutilation and obstetric outcome: WHO collaborative prospective study in six African countries. Lancet 2006;367:1835–1841.

47 Hossain M, Zimmerman C, Abas M, Light M, Watts C: The relationship of trauma to mental disorders among trafficked and sexually exploited girls and women. Am J Publ Health 2010;100:2442–2449.

Dr. Claudia García-Moreno
Sexual Health, Gender, Reproductive Rights and Adolescence
Department of Reproductive Health and Research, World Health Organization
20 Ave Appia, CH–1211 Geneva 27 (Switzerland)
E-Mail garciamorenoc@who.int

Gender-Based Violence in the Middle-East: A Review

Josyan Madi Skaff

The Lebanese Hospital, Geitawi, Beirut, Lebanon

Abstract

The present work is a review of the available data on gender-based violence (GBV) as experienced by girls and women in the Middle East region. Its purpose is to examine the different forms of GBV, which are most specific to the region: certain forms of domestic violence, female genital mutilation/cutting, honor killing, and violence in times of war. It will attempt to define their prevalence, social background, and complications as they occur in the Middle East. This review shows that the systematic denial of women's human rights throughout the Middle East and the ancestral collusion between Law, State and Religion have led to the increase of women's vulnerability to violence. It highlights the considerable social and political forces behind the underreporting, and reviews the attitudes concerning GBV especially by the women themselves. In conclusion, there is a need for more research on the attitudes of men and women regarding gender-based violence and how these attitudes may be changed; also, researchers, advocates and health care professionals must work together to develop culturally sensitive interventions. Above all, long-term change will only be possible through access to education, civil and political rights for all the women in the region.

Copyright © 2013 S. Karger AG, Basel

Violence against women is increasingly being recognized as a problem in many countries throughout the Middle East. In those countries for which at least some studies exist, the high prevalence of gender-based violence (GBV) is quite apparent; yet the limited available evidence suggests that GBV is a severe, chronic and widespread problem across the region.

The data reported in this review are the first wave of studies on GBV in the region and should be viewed as initial estimates. Given the sensitive nature of the subject and that of women's rights in the Middle East, some underreporting is expected.

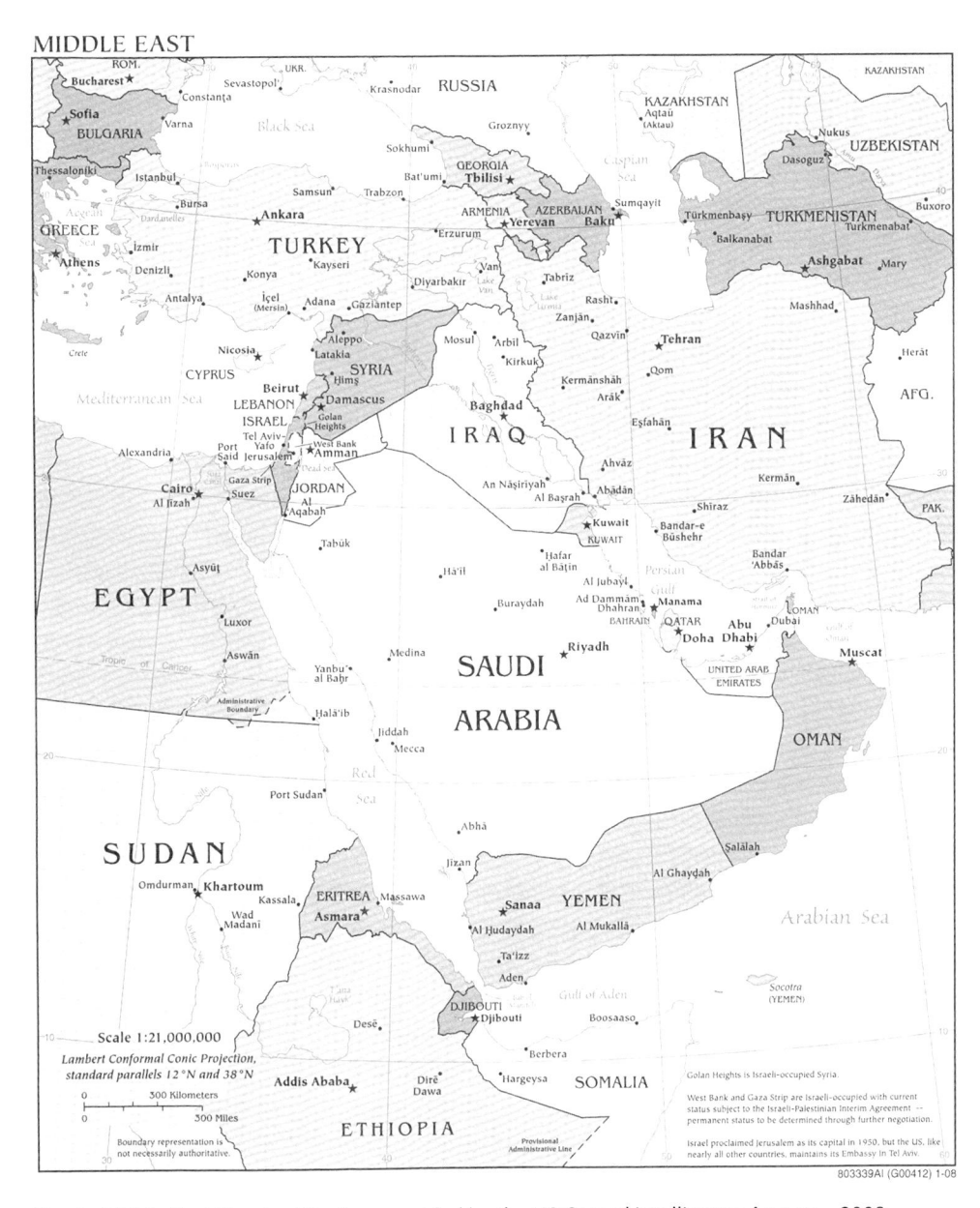

Fig. 1. Middle East Map (political) as provided by the US Central Intelligence Agency – 2008.

Middle East: Definition and Map

The Middle East defines a geographical area, but does not have precisely defined borders. The modern definition of the region includes: Bahrain, Egypt, Iran, Iraq, Israel, Jordan, Kuwait, Lebanon, Oman, the Palestinian territories, Qatar, Saudi Arabia, Syria, the United Arab Emirates (a federation of seven emirates), and Yemen.

In June 2011, the population of the Middle East area was a little over 336 million, representing 3% of the population of the world [1].

The Middle East map (political) as provided by the US Central Intelligence Agency in 2008 is shown in figure 1.

Women's Rights in the Middle East

The human rights of women throughout the Middle East are systematically denied by each of the countries in the region, despite the diversity of their political systems.
1. In the Middle East the relationship between women and the state is essentially mediated by men. Throughout the region, family, penal and citizenship laws treat women essentially as legal minors under the eternal guardianship of their male family members: women's right to vote, to acquire an identity card or passport, to marry, to work, or to travel is granted only with the consent of a spouse or other male family member.
2. In most countries family matters are governed by religion-based personal status codes: they deny women equal rights with men with respect to marriage, divorce, child custody and inheritance. Governments routinely join forces with religious figures in order to curtail women's rights, including their sexual autonomy.
3. Women's inferior legal status also acts as a deterrent to their full participation in public life and puts women at an increased risk for violence: women in the Arab sub-region, for example, occupy only 9.7% of all seats in parliament – as opposed to 18.5 in the rest of the world [2].
4. While occurring frequently in the region, violence and insecurity resulting from war have had particularly detrimental effects on women: in times of military conflicts, women's unequal legal status and feeble participation in economic, professional, and political life, increase their vulnerability to military and social violence [3].

Valid Statistics?

The World Health Organization's *World Report on Violence and Health* could cite only three studies for the Eastern Mediterranean Region [4]; a review article on intimate partner violence (IPV) in the Middle East by Boy and Kulczycki [5], published in 2008, found only 10 studies reporting on the prevalence of IPV. There are two main reasons for thinking that many of these studies may underestimate the true prevalence of violence against women:
1. The strength of family ties in this region makes it more likely that some proportion of women will not report being physically assaulted by a relative, let

alone by their intimate partner; violence against women is often not reported or is hidden by the victims because of their fear of social rejection and family isolation.
2   A female victim will usually seek police assistance only in the most extreme cases, and even then, her report may be ignored by the police. Under Islamic law, which exerts a dominant influence over issues of family life, a wife has no legal right to object to any form of domestic violence [6]; in 1995, the Egypt Demographic and Health Survey (DHS) found that less than half of abused women sought help [7]; in the Israeli Negev only 8% of abused Bedouin women sought help from outside agencies [8].

Violence against Women: Physical and Psychological Abuse

Prevalence
Results from systematic research show that the most common form of reported violence against women is physical violence in the form of beating, slapping and kicking.

In Egypt, the Demographic and Health Survey (DHS) indicated that around one in three (34%) ever-married women aged 15–49 had been beaten by their spouse since they were married [7].

In May 2006, the United Nations Development Fund for Women (UNIFEM) and the Syrian General Union of Women released the first-ever comprehensive field study of violence against women in Syria; it concluded that nearly one in four married women surveyed had been beaten [9].

In Israel reported prevalence rates of abuse during the past 12 months or current year ranged from 6% among women in the general population to 52% among Palestinian women living in the West Bank and Gaza [10].

Although psychological abuse is harder for women to recognize and to report, the El-Sheik Zayed village study in Ismailia (Egypt) reports that 10.8% of the women in the sample have suffered from severe psychological violence such as verbal abuse, fear, abandonment, or unfaithfulness [11].

Complications

1   Studies among Palestinian women have found higher rates of psychological distress and higher levels of anger and fear among abused than nonabused women [12].
2   Among Egyptian women who reported being beaten at least once since their first marriage 10% said they needed medical attention as a result of the beating [7].
3   A more recent study conducted by the Land Center for Human Rights shows that out of the 300 cases of domestic violence monitored in Egyptian national

newspapers, 140 (almost 50%) were cases of wife abuse ending in the death of the wife [13].
4   In Egypt, battered women were more likely to have unwanted or mistimed pregnancies, to commence antenatal care later (or not at all), and to terminate a pregnancy [7].
5   A study of Saudi women found higher risk of abruptio placenta, fetal distress, and preterm birth among abused pregnant women than among their nonabused counterparts [14].

Violence against Women: Honor Killing

Social Background
In the Middle East as a whole, family status is largely defined by its 'honor', much of which is determined by the respectability of its daughters: it is dependent on the girl's virginity which is the property of the men around her, first her father, later a gift for her husband. Honor killing emerged in the pre-Islamic era: 'it stemmed from the men's interest to seek control of women's reproductive power and to prevent women from having sexual freedom or the right to use their sexual powers the way they want' [15].

Prevalence
Given that honor killings often remain a private family affair, no official statistics are available on the practice or their frequency and most estimates are little more than guesses that vary widely. In 2000, the United Nations estimated that the annual worldwide number of 'honor killing' victims may be as high as 5,000 women [16]. During the summer of 1997, Khaled Al-Qudra, then Attorney General in the Palestinian National Authority (PNA), told Sout Al-Nissa' (Women's Voices), that he suspects that 70% of all murders in Gaza and the West Bank are honor killings.

Legal Background
In regular judicial settings, full or partial extenuation of the sentence may be granted to perpetrators of intentional homicide: the Jordanian Penal Code – legislated in 1960 – considers murder a legitimate act of defense when 'the act of killing another or harming another is committed as an act of defense of oneself, or somebody else's life or honor'. Only males (i.e. husbands and male blood relatives) can be exempted from penalty or benefit from reduced sentences: a woman who kills her spouse after she 'catches' him committing adultery cannot be considered to have had a 'justifiable excuse' when she committed the crime [17].

In tribal settings, the priority is to ensure that a woman suspected or perceived of committing sexual transgressions is not subjected to scandal, either through forced marriage often to the offender or by killing the woman: the family awaits for an opportune moment to take the life of the woman under the pretext that she fell from the roof or accidentally ingested poison.

Violence against Women: Female Genital Mutilation/Cutting

Female genital mutilation comprises all procedures involving partial or total removal of the external female genitalia or other injury to the female genital organs for non-medical reasons [18]. Every year, three million girls and women are subjected to genital mutilation/cutting, a dangerous and potentially life-threatening procedure that causes unspeakable pain and suffering.

The majority of girls and women at risk of undergoing female genital mutilation/cutting (FGM/C) live in Africa. In Egypt, the 2005 Demographic and Health Survey [7] found that 96% of the ever-married women interviewed had been circumcised and about 90% of girls were cut between the ages of 5 and 14 years. In northern Iraq, it was only in 2005 that the German nongovernmental organization WADI proved the existence of female genital mutilation: of 1,554 women and girls over 10 years old interviewed by the WADI local team, more than 60% said that they had had the operation [18].

That no first-hand medical records are available for Saudi Arabia or from any other countries in that region such as Syria and Jordan does not mean that these areas are free of FGM, it is only that these societies are not free enough to permit a formal study of societal problems.

Social Background
FGM/C is an important part of girls' and women's cultural gender identity: the procedure may impart a sense of pride, of coming of age, and a feeling of community membership. Social convention is so powerful that girls themselves may desire to be cut, as a result of social pressure from peers and because of fear – not without reason – of stigmatization and rejection by their own communities if they do not follow the tradition: FGM/C ensures a girl's or woman's status, marriageability, chastity, health, beauty, and family honor [19].

Religious Background
FGM/C is not prescribed by any religion: the Koran and the Bible contain no text that requires the cutting of the female external genitalia.

'There is no text in Shari'a, in the Koran, in the prophetic Sunna, addressing FGM.'
The Grand Imam, *Sheikh Mohammed Sayed Tantawi*, Sheikh of Al-Azhar University, the foremost institution in the Islamic world for the study of the Islamic law, 2003

'There is not a single verse in the Bible or the Old or New Testaments, nor is there anything in Judaism or Christianity – not one single verse speaks of female circumcision.'
Bishop *Moussa*, Representative of Pope *Shenouda III*, Patriarch of the largest Christian Community in the Middle East 2003

Complications and Consequences

Severe pain, bleeding and infection are common consequences; the mortality rate is not known, since few records are kept and deaths due to FGM/C are rarely reported as such. For many girls and women, FGM/C is an acutely traumatic experience that leaves a lasting psychological mark and may adversely affect their emotional and psychological development.

Violence against Women: War-Related Violence against Women

Iraq
Today, many Iraqi women are worse off after the invasion by the US and its allies: they suffer the daily loss of loved ones, food shortages, and increased levels of violence [20]. Behind the wave of insurgent attacks, the violence against women who dare to challenge the Islamic orthodoxy is growing: women are subjected to verbal abuse on the streets if they are not wearing a hijab (Muslim dress) and in extreme cases face being abducted by unknown gunmen, who sexually abuse and then kill them [21]. According to a United Nations report in 2007, police in Basra registered 44 cases of women who were killed with multiple gunshot wounds after being accused of committing 'honor crimes'.

The Iraqi Red Crescent reported in December 2007 that since the beginning of the Iraq war over four million people have been displaced, and more than 82% of those displaced are women: without job experience or opportunities, women turn to prostitution, and sexual violence and domestic violence are on the increase [22].

Palestine
In 2000, a research conducted in Palestinian refugee camps, particularly in Gaza, showed that refugee women and girls do bear the brunt of increased physical, mental, psychological, and sexual domestic violence, including incest and rape [23]. The conflict, curfews, and check-points also have adversely affected girls' access to schooling. Women also face the violence of the occupation: they may be 'killed, targeted for arrest, detained and harassed for being related to men suspected of being linked to armed groups, and may be displaced as a result of house demolitions' [24].

Lebanon
In the aftermath of the war of Israel on Lebanon in July 2006, the United Nations Population Fund (UNFPA), in collaboration with the Lebanese Ministry of Social Affairs, conducted a study to explore the extent to which the violence associated with the conflict was affecting the lives of Lebanese women and girls. During the conflict,

women were pushed, threatened with weapons, deprived of food, and prevented from seeking medical care mostly by soldiers, whereas their husbands were the most common source of hitting, kicking, or sexually abusing them. One of the most traumatic experiences that women reported during and after the war was dealing with their husbands [25].

Attitudes Regarding Violence

Women's Attitudes
A major concern regarding intimate partner violence and other forms of violence against women in this region is that many women have been conditioned to believe that violence is not only justified but also is their fault:
- In Egypt, 86% of ever-married women believed that husbands were sometimes justified in beating their wives, with the highest specified reason (70%) being the refusal of sexual intercourse [7].
- Reporting spousal abuse in Egypt is still shrouded by the idea that this is a private family issue that should not involve outsiders: the National Population Council survey conducted in 1995 shows that among those wives who have been beaten, fewer than half have ever sought help or reported the abuse. Attitudes varied little by age, more by level of education with less educated women more likely to justify wife abuse [7].
- In Jordan, as many as 87% of ever-married women of childbearing age agreed with at least one justification of physical abuse: overall, 83% of respondents agreed that betraying one's husband gave him a right to use violence against his wife [26].
- An analysis of the first Israeli national survey on domestic violence held in 2000–2001 reported that 18% of women accepted the use of violence if the woman was sexually unfaithful toward the man; 49% of women agreed that the violent man should not be held solely responsible for violence committed against a woman. Three of five Palestinian women in Israel agreed that nagging or insulting the husband constituted legitimate grounds for a husband to beat his wife [27].

Men's Attitudes
Research on the beliefs of men regarding justification for physical abuse of wives is much more limited: only four studies report such data and all of these studies indicate that significant proportions of men hold that wife beating is appropriate in certain situations.

In Palestinian refugee camps in Jordan, 60% of married men agreed that wife beating was sometimes justified, in cases such as neglecting the children, refusing sex, and dishonoring the family [28]. Two small-scale studies conducted in southern Iraq and in Palestinian refugee camps in Jordan revealed that every second man considered that a husband had the right to beat his wife if she disobeyed him [29]. The Israeli national survey on domestic violence showed that three in 10 men agreed that a man had a right to use violence against a woman if she was violent with him, if she cheated on him with another man [27].

Judicial System
Law enforcement authorities, ranging from police to judges, tend to dismiss spousal abuse as a private matter between husband and wife because the 'integrity of the family' is more important than the well-being of the woman.

Another concern for the various service providers is whether the victim's welfare could be addressed without it being in contradiction with the welfare of society at large: representatives of social control agents are very reluctant to deal with abuses inflicted upon women, especially sexual abuses.

Judges apply different standards in assessing the behavior of men and women. In Egypt a study of 50 battering cases adjudicated by the courts during the year 1994 showed that 80% of the women who beat their husband received prison sentences, compared with only 50% of the men being convicted for wife battering.

Future Directions

Research
One of the most disturbing issues highlighted in this review concerns the dearth of research on violence against women in the Middle East where the status of women is among the poorest in the developing world [30]. As a matter of priority, future research should expand the knowledge base to consider the situation in countries for which studies do not currently exist. For all countries, more research is needed on the attitudes of men and women regarding gender-based violence, how those attitudes developed, and how they may be changed. Also, research is needed on developing culturally sensitive solutions that could be successfully offered to victims and perpetrators of violence in this region.

Interventions

In the Middle East interventions for women victims of violence are limited: few countries have enacted laws against gender-based violence, let alone implemented them, and social services have restrictions on the help they can offer. A further problem is that many Arab countries tend to limit and control the activities of nongovernmental organizations that offer hotlines, information, and counseling for abused women.

1. Empowerment of women is an essential first step: it is a lengthy process that requires cooperation from governments, religious leaders, community members, and nongovernmental agencies.
– It requires the removal of laws that discriminate against women, especially in the family realm, and this has proved difficult in many parts of the Middle East.
– Governments must work to ensure that women and girls have the same educational opportunities afforded to men and boys.
– Improving access to health information and health care is another vital step toward empowerment because it allows a woman to have greater control over her own body and health choices.

2. Services such as shelters, counseling and legal assistance are critical for victims: however, shelters may not always be appropriate because of high maintenance costs and a victim's unwillingness to leave familiar surroundings.

Local community involvement is also an important step in serving victims: community members must be involved in reporting violence and speaking out against abusive husbands.

3. Education about gender-based violence, along with training on how to assist victims, must be offered to a variety of professionals, including police, lawyers, health care providers, and social workers.

For there to be a coordinated response, education efforts should include victims themselves, their partners, the family members, and the community at large.

Victims must be convinced that gender-based violence violates their human rights and that the abuse does not have to be accepted.

Men must be sensitized to the harmful effects of intimate partner violence and taught how they can interact safely with their intimate partner.

Family members should be taught that violence is not the fault of the victim, who deserves love and support rather than ostracism and further abuse.

The community-at-large must move toward a situation in which violence is not tolerated.

Health care workers at all levels must be sensitized to the problem and given the means to identify and help violence victims.

4. Prevention activities must focus on developing broad partnerships representing all areas of public life: advocates must work with religious and political leaders, legal authorities and law enforcement officials, school teachers, and the health care field to effect change.

In conclusion, there may be limits on how much change may occur in the short term, both because education levels of women are significantly inferior to those of men throughout the region and because many civil and political rights for women are widely denied in most countries of the Middle East.

However, change is possible in the long term, but it will require more sustained research and intervention efforts as well as the development of broad-based coalitions of concerned individuals and groups to force recalcitrant governments and complacent societies to address the issue of gender-based violence and make the necessary reforms.

References

1 World Development Indicators database. World Bank, 2011.
2 The Arab Human Development Report: United Nations Development Program, Regional Bureau for Arab States (RBAS). New York, 2005.
3 Inter-Agency Standing Committee Guidelines for Gender Based Violence. Interventions in Humanitarian Settings. 2003.
4 Krug EG, et al: World Report on Violence and Health. Geneva, World Health Organization, 2002.
5 Boy A, Kulczycki A: What We Know about Intimate Partner Violence in the Middle East and North Africa. Violence against Women, 2008, vol 14, pp 53–70.
6 Douki S, Nacef F, Belhadj A, Bouasker A, Ghachem R: Violence against women in Arab and Islamic countries. Arch Women's Ment Health 2003;6:165–171.
7 El-Zanaty F, Hussein EM, Shawkey GA, Way A, Kishor S: Egypt Demographic and Health Survey. Cairo, National Population Council: Macro International, 1996.
8 Cwikel J, Lev-Wiesel R, Al-Krenawi A: The physical and psychosocial health of Bedouin Arab women in the Negev region of Israel. Violence against Women, 2003, vol 9, pp 240–257.
9 United Nations Development Fund for Women (UNIFEM) – Violence against Women in Syria. Report 2006.
10 Haj-Yahia M: Wife abuse and its psychological consequences as revealed by the First Palestinian National Survey on Violence against Women. J Fam Psychol 1999;13:642–662.
11 Ramiro LS, Hassan F, Peedicayil A: Risk makers of severe psychological violence against women: a world SAFE multi-country study. Injury Control Safety Promotion 2004;11:131–137.
12 Women's Centre for Legal Aid and Counselling, Al Haq NGO: Alternative Pre-Sessional Report on Israel's Implementation of the United Nations Convention on the Elimination of All Forms of Discrimination against Women (CEDAW) in the Occupied Palestinian Territories (OPT). January, 2005.
13 Ammar N: *Al-unf did al-mara' fi al-sahafa al-misriah* (Violence against women in Egyptian newspapers). Land Center for Human Rights. Report 40. Cairo, 2005.
14 Rachana C, Suraiya K, Hirsham A, Abdulaziz A, Haj A: Prevalence and complications of physical violence during pregnancy. Eur J Obstet Gynecol Reprod Biol 2002;103:26–29.
15 Ruggi S: Commodifying Honour in Female Sexuality: Honour Killings in Palestine. Middle East Report, 2008.
16 United Nations Population Fund: Ending Violence against Women and Girls. State of the World Population. New York, 2000.
17 Shalhoub-Kevorkian N: Mapping and Analyzing the Landscape of Femicide in Palestinian Society. Report Submitted to UNIFEM, 2000.
18 WHO: Eliminating Female Genital Mutilation: an Interagency Statement. HCHR, UNAIDS, UNDP, 2008.
19 Von der Osten-Sacken T, Uwer T: Is Female Genital Mutilation an Islamic Problem? Middle East Q 2007.
20 Mackie G: A Way to End Female Genital Cutting. Female Genital Cutting Education and Networking Project, 2003.
21 Susskind Y: One Year Later: Women's Human Rights in 'Liberated' Iraq'. Madre Articles and Factsheets, 2004.
22 Judd T: For the Women of Iraq, the War Is Just Beginning. The Independent (UK), 2006.
23 Iraqi Red Crescent Organization – Disaster Management Department: the Internally Displaced People in Iraq. 2008.
24 Abdo N, Engendering Compensation: Making Refugee Women Count! Ottawa, Expert and Advisory Services Fund, International Development Research Center, 2000.
25 UNIFEM: Afghanistan: Women in the News. Kabul, New York, 2004.
26 United Nations Population Fund: Assessment of Psychosocial and Mental Health Needs of Women in War Affected Regions. Institute for Development, Research, Advocacy and Applied Care (IDRAAC) – Lebanon, 2007.

27 Government of Jordan & ORC Macro: Jordan Population and Family Health Survey 2002. Calverton, 2003.
28 Eisikovits Z, Winstok Z, Fishman G: The first Israeli National Survey on domestic violence. Violence against Women, 2004, vol 10, pp 729–748.
29 Khawaja, M: Domestic violence in refugee camps in Jordan. Int J Gynecol Obstet 2004;86:67–69.
30 Amowitz L, Kim G, Reis C, Asher J, Iacopino V: Human rights abuses and concerns about women's health and human rights in southern Iraq. J Am Med Assoc 2004;291:1471–1479.
31 Nazir S: Challenging Inequality: Obstacles and Opportunities towards Women's Rights in the Middle East and North Africa. New York, Freedom House, 2005.

Josyan Madi Skaff, MD
The Lebanese Hospital
Geitawi Beirut (Lebanon)
Tel. +961 1 577 177, E-Mail Josyan.Madiskaff@Gmail.com

Violence against Women in Latin America

Silvia Lucía Gaviria

Department of Psychiatry, CES University, Medellin, Colombia

Abstract

It is estimated that more than 50% of the women in Latin America and the Caribbean suffer some type of family violence, in addition to other forms of violence affecting women and children in other settings. Gender-based violence (GBV) is a phenomenon occurring in all Latin American countries, at all social levels and in every sphere of society. In the Latin American region there is great cultural diversity; there is also a great variety of norms, systems, sexual division of labor, distribution of sexual power, gender social norms and public representations regarding violence and honor that are influencing the manifestations of violence against women. This violence attempts against life, dignity and the human rights of the victims in private and public spaces since it has consequences ranging from mental and physical health, consequences to reduced economic, political and social participation; even homicides and suicides, as shown by the indicators of income, labor participation, morbidity and mortality, education, nutrition, and years of healthy life lost by the affected women. There is a substantial body of research on violence against women in Latin America and the Caribbean, but studies have defined and measured violence in such diverse ways that it has often been difficult to compare findings across studies and settings. Furthermore, most research has centered on the experiences of female victims; few studies have focused on boys or men either as victims or perpetrators. It is noteworthy that relatively few published studies from the Latin American and the Caribbean region mention ethical issues relevant to conducting research on such a sensitive topic.

Copyright © 2013 S. Karger AG, Basel

Violence against women has become recognized as a public health issue with serious implications for the physical and psychological well-being of women and children [1]. The last three decades have been accompanied by considerable progress in Latin America, albeit not sufficient, in improving women's access to support and services for violence from the health sector [2].

The United Nations provides a broad framework for understanding violence against women [3], also referred to as gender-based violence (GBV) because of its link to gender inequality. It defines it as any act 'that results in, or is likely to result in, physical, sexual or psychological harm or suffering to women, including threats of such acts, coercion or arbitrary deprivation of liberty, whether occurring in public or private life'.

GBV is a phenomenon occurring in all Latin American countries, at all socioeconomic levels and in every sphere of society. In the Latin American region there is great cultural diversity [4]; there is also great variety of norms, rules systems, sexual division of labor, distribution of sexual power, gender social norms and public representations regarding violence and honor, all of which are influencing the manifestations of violence against women [5].

Evidence indicates that violence occurs differently in men and women. The risk factors as well as the consequences of violence vary according to sex, largely as a result of gender inequality. Men are more exposed to violence related to armed conflict, criminal activity and suicide, while women are more likely than men to experience violence and injury inflicted by people close to them, such as intimate partners or ex partners. Girls and women are also more likely than boys or men to experience sexual violence generally [6], although several studies are finding the sexual abuse of boys to also be a problem. In addition, physical and sexual violence against women and girls has a host of sexual and reproductive health consequences that are different to the consequences of violence against men [7].

This chapter will review the subject of gender-based violence in the Latin American context; the magnitude of the problem, historic background, and relevant aspects will be discussed.

Magnitude of the Problem

It is estimated that more than 50% of women in Latin America and the Caribbean suffer some type of family violence, and this does not include other forms of violence affecting women and children in other scenarios [8].

Regarding gender-based violence research, there is still a limited number of well-designed and executed studies that can provide sound data on the magnitude and nature of the problem and its determinants and consequences, although this is improving. There are difficulties in the theoretical models and methods used which result in many studies not being published [9]. The data provided by the services where women are cared for are incomplete as there are many barriers to women reporting and seeking help [10].

There are specific groups of women that are more vulnerable to violence: ethnic and other minority groups, indigenous, temporary workers, refugees, women in areas of armed conflicts, residents in institutions, handicapped women, girls and elderly women from whom we have less information and for whom there is a real underestimation about the violence they experience [11, 12].

Background

During the colonial period, the model of the 'perfect wife' was transported from Spain to Latin America. This model entered in conflict with the traditional concepts from native Indians which by virtue of their marriage and family ways, organized from a more collective rather than an individual perspective, and where the possibilities of women controlling their own communities and having better resources, protected them from violence [5, 13].

Despite the patriarchal model of colonial times, reinforced by the Judeo Christian values and further promoted by the Catholic Church, which is still in force in the majority of Latin American societies, many efforts have been made by women. Many resisted, since those early days, assuming in an unconditional manner the patriarchal family model of a submissive, passive and dependent woman [5].

At the end of the 1960s, women's associations in Latin America reappeared to contribute in a decisive manner to giving visibility to the phenomena of violence against women as a social problem (not just an individual one), of public character (not just private); of relevance to the courts and which demands public policies with specific obligations for institutions, including the health institutions [5, 11].

The growing attention to gender-based violence grew from the felt need of some women caring for gender-based violence victims, to highlight the social and political importance of the problem, and the need to promote adequate legal frameworks and public policies to address the problem. Social and health sciences lagged behind, but eventually the academic world also began to pay attention to violence against women, amidst doubts and questions about its legitimacy [11].

It is pertinent to point out how, in the patriarchal culture, women are associated with the private or domestic space, reproduction, emotions and unpaid work; while men are associated with the public sphere, culture, rational thinking and productive economic work [14]. These stereotypes generate barriers and difficulties concerning women's participation in the social sphere, limiting enjoyment of their rights and their autonomy and increasing their vulnerability to GBV.

The Situation of Women in Latin America

The prevalence of violence in a particular setting is influenced by a web of interrelated factors. GBV has deep social and cultural roots and is based on the ancestral belief that a woman is a man's property. It is linked to the imbalance in power between men and women in the social, economic, religious and political spheres, regardless of all the national and international legislation and efforts to promote equal rights [15].

Both the 1993 UN Declaration and the Convention of Belém do Pará used the phrase 'gender-based' violence to acknowledge that the risk factors, consequences, and community responses to violence against women are heavily influenced by women's subordinate social, economic and legal status in many settings. Women's vulnerability to violence may be heightened by gender inequality within relationships and economic dependence on intimate partners [2]. Latin American women's social determinants and health situation that could increase their vulnerability to violence and limit their ability to protect themselves are described below.

Education

The differences in illiteracy rates between males and females have been reduced during the last decades, reaching equality now in several Latin American countries. However, some countries still maintain important differences between males and females. In Guatemala, for example, in 2002 the illiteracy rate was 36% for females and 21% for males [12]. Likewise, there is evidence of disparity by sex among groups of lower social economic level, rural residence and indigenous peoples as compared to those who are more privileged. In Ecuador, in 1998, the illiteracy rate was 12% for females and 8% for males, but when the place of residence was considered, a larger gap was observed in the rural areas, where illiteracy rates were 21% for females and 15% for males [16].

It is important to note that several studies have demonstrated a positive relationship between female's level of education and the exercising of their rights, including their reproductive rights.

Work Load

For the past several years there have been important social changes, such as an increase in the educational level of females, in some cases reaching levels of enrollment equal to or higher than males in the basic and intermediate educational levels; increased participation of women in the workforce, which has given place to better access to and control over resources and a change in the power relationship between women and men; improvements in socioeconomic structures and policies such as the construction of legal frameworks to promote gender equality and equal opportunities between men and women and exercise of their sexual and reproductive rights.

Regarding remuneration, it was found that on average women generally receive a lower salary than males. In several countries of the region, the average income gap of women with respect to men is bigger among those with higher education [17, 18].

Among the countries for which information is available for the year 1999, Colombia and Paraguay show the highest rates of work participation of women in urban areas, reaching 55%; in rural areas, the country with the highest female participation is Bolivia, with 77% [12].

According to data from CEPAL, for the year 2003, close to 227 million inhabitants of the region lived in poverty and 102 million were indigent; these numbers represented 44.4 and 20% of the population, respectively. Women are over-represented among the poor in both rural and urban areas, and this is particularly the case among those aged 20–59 years [19].

Environmental Conditions

For women, who carry the main responsibility for the health of family members and domestic work, the access to drinking water in their homes is one of the basic elements for improvement in the health conditions of people and the control of certain diseases. Likewise, the access to water suitable for human consumption at home represents a decrease in the domestic work load. In 1998, Paraguay was able to cover with potable water 44% of the population and Haiti, 46%. The population which is most affected by lack of water concentrates in the rural areas, reaching differences like in Paraguay where 13% of the rural population had access to water in contrast to 70% of the urban population [12, 20, 21].

Health Status

In all the Latin American countries women outlive men; however, this does not mean that they enjoy better health than men during the different stages of their life-cycle. Given the same environmental conditions and the same level of care, the higher life expectancy of women is due to biological and other factors which make them more resistant to health risks [22].

Risk factors related to the roles socially assigned to men play an important role in avoidable mortality; for example, for young adult males, external causes of mortality are more important than for females. Likewise, pregnancy, delivery and puerperium complications are the main causes of death of females of reproductive age in underdeveloped countries [23]. In the comparative study carried out by Diaz-Granados et al. [24], regarding health indicators by gender in Canada, Colombia and Peru, the biggest difference observed among the countries was in maternal mortality. Peru has a rate that is 27 times higher than Canada's and twice the rate of Colombia's maternal mortality rate.

With regard to HIV transmission, it is known that it is higher from male to female than vice versa. In countries that have information, the male:female ratio of the numbers of deaths due to AIDS ranges from 10:1 in Costa Rica to 1:1 in Haiti [12].

Regarding avoidable mortality in spite of the limited information, the increasing prevalence of smoking among women has increased lung cancer in women. The increase in cigarette consumption can be due to a greater women's social and labor participation, as well as to higher stress levels.

Many countries are experiencing a marked increase in the prevalence of overweight and obesity. There is evidence that obesity is more frequent in females and the highest incidence is found among the lower income groups [17]. In situations of extreme poverty, women recur to a higher ingestion of carbohydrates of different types depending on their habits or the region. Besides the health problems, self-physical image affects women more than men, since they have to face more limitations regarding opportunities, especially in the labor market in which employers demand certain stereotypes of beauty. Also, there are several factors associated with fashion standards that demand certain beauty profiles and which have a higher impact in urban than in rural areas, which in turn is translated into a higher prevalence of eating disorders [25].

Lifestyle, economic factors, eating habits, social fashion parameters and female stereotypes influence weight, and combined with biological vulnerability are expressed in different pathologies.

Intimate Partner/Intrafamily Violence

Domestic violence has been defined as any act committed within the family by one of its members that seriously harms the life, body, psychological integrity and/or freedom of any of the other members of the family. Most frequently, this violence is committed by male intimate partners (whether married or co-habiting) or ex-partners against women and this is referred to as intimate partner violence [26].

The traditional conservative context in the Latin-American region is characterized by social representations of heterosexual couples as the only successful form of adult life that must be preserved at any cost in order to build a family. Violence in a couple's relationship, whether physical, sexual or psychological/emotional, is considered a private and individual problem, present in tormented relationships of jealous people ('crimes of passion'). It is also characterized as a problem affecting only some women, particularly of low social class and low educational level, rather than as a collective phenomenon with a social meaning and which reinforces the underlying gender inequality. This violence is often seen as the victim's fault because in some way, she 'provokes' the aggressor either by tolerating it or because of her economic and emotional dependency [5].

The studies on the topic point to women as the main victims of domestic violence, and children in second place. It is challenging to obtain representative and precise data regarding the actual dimension of the problem in the region, due in part to the complexity of the subject. Cultural, economic, family and personal factors make it difficult for women to report this violence, in this manner perpetuating its social invisibility [9]. A growing number of surveys, however, have been carried out in the region.

The Pan-American Health Organization (PAHO) and the Centers of Disease Control and Prevention (CDC) have produced a comparative analysis of population level data on violence against women for 12 countries in the Latin American and Caribbean region. In the Latin American and Caribbean region [2], over 75 population-based health surveys have been conducted in 19 countries over the past 35 years. The most common are the Demographic and Health Surveys (DHS) supported by MACRO International and the Reproductive Health Surveys supported by the Centers for Disease Control in the USA. In recent years, many of these surveys have included an optional module on violence against women that has generated an

Table 1. Surveys in the comparative study

RHS Surveys			DHS Surveys		
Country	Year	N	Country	Year	N
Ecuador	2004	9,576	Bolivia	2003	14,679
El Salvador	2008	9,717	Bolivia	2008	14,900
Guatemala	2008/9	16,582	Colombia	2005	37,597
Jamaica	2008/9	8,259	Dom. Rep.	2007	10,140
Nicaragua	2006/7	14,165	Haiti	2005/6	3,568
Paraguay	2008	6,526	Honduras	2005/6	19,948
			Peru	2007/8	16,648

Source: Bott S et al. [2].

important body of evidence on the issue. The PAHO/CDC publication [2] provides a regional comparative analysis of these data.

Table 1 shows the 13 surveys in 12 countries that are part of this comparative analysis, alongside the total sample sizes.

Some key findings of this study are the following [2]:

Among women ever married or in union:

- In all 12 countries, a substantial percentage of women reported physical violence by an intimate partner ever, though reported prevalence varied widely, ranging from 13.4% in Haiti in 2005/2006 to 52.3% of women in Bolivia in 2003. In four countries the prevalence was less than 20%, in six countries it fell between 20 and 40%, and in Bolivia in 2003, it exceeded one-half (52.3%) (fig. 1).
- The reported prevalence of physical intimate partner violence in the past 12 months ranged from 6.5% in Jamaica in 2008/2009 to 24.5% in Bolivia in 2008, with a majority of countries falling within the 6–11% range (fig. 1).

Among women who reported physical violence by an intimate partner *ever*:

- In three DHS surveys (Colombia 2005, the Dominican Republic 2007, and Haiti 2005/2006), a majority of women who reported physical violence by an intimate partner ever also reported physical violence in the past 12 months. Haiti 2005/6 was a particular outlier, with approximately nine out of 10 women who reported physical partner violence *ever* also reporting violence in the past 12 months. (When considering these data, however, note that these DHS surveys asked specifically about violence by the current or most recent partner only, whereas Reproductive Health Surveys asked about violence by any partner in life.)

The comparative analysis also documented widespread emotional and mental health consequences of intimate partner violence, including fear, anxiety,

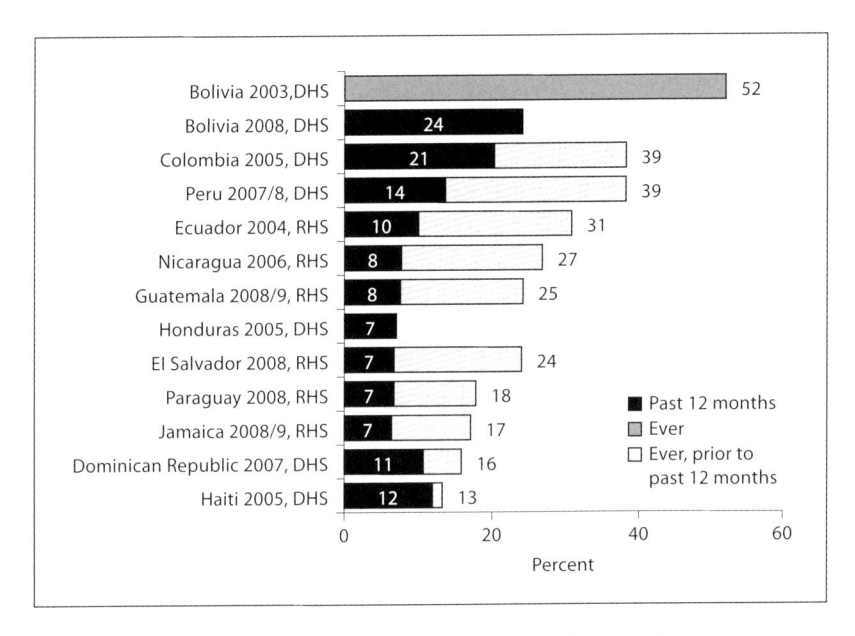

Country/Survey	Past 12 months	Ever
Bolivia 2003, DHS		52
Bolivia 2008, DHS	24	
Colombia 2005, DHS	21	39
Peru 2007/8, DHS	14	39
Ecuador 2004, RHS	10	31
Nicaragua 2006, RHS	8	27
Guatemala 2008/9, RHS	8	25
Honduras 2005, DHS	7	
El Salvador 2008, RHS	7	24
Paraguay 2008, RHS	7	18
Jamaica 2008/9, RHS	7	17
Dominican Republic 2007, DHS	11	16
Haiti 2005, DHS	12	13

Fig. 1. Prevalence of physical violence against women by an intimate partner, ever and in the past 12 months for selected countries in Latin America. DHS = Current/most recent partner only. Source: Bott S et al. [2].

depression, and suicidal thoughts. In the five surveys that measured this indicator, between 50% and more than 75% of women who experienced partner violence in the past 12 months said they had experienced anxiety or depression severe enough that they could not carry out their usual work as a result of the violence. Two studies (Guatemala 2008/2009 and Paraguay 2008) gathered data that allowed an examination of suicidal thoughts according to history of intimate partner violence. In those surveys, women who had experienced physical or sexual partner violence in the past 12 months were significantly more likely to have contemplated or attempted suicide in the past 4 weeks compared with those who had never experienced partner violence.

In all 12 countries, large proportions of women who experienced partner violence ever and/or in the past 12 months reported being physically injured as a result, including 'minor' injuries such as bruises and pain as well as more 'severe' injuries such as broken bones, burns and knife wounds. Between 41 and 82% of women who are abused by their partner experience injuries as a result. In addition to the consequences to each individual woman, this has direct consequences in terms of the costs to the health sector for caring for such injuries.

While the prevalence of intimate partner violence against women is not known for every country in the region, the existing studies provide an insight into the forms of abuse, the response of women, the characteristics of aggressors and the prevailing culture in the region regarding this problem [27].

The most frequently cited factors associated with partner violence in said studies are: socioeconomic level, level of schooling and age (in all cases, the lower is the age, the higher the risk), marital status (separated or divorced women are at more risk), having been the victim of abuse or violence during childhood or having been a witness to it (both the woman, as well as her partner), the employment status of the couple (if unemployed the risk increases), and of the woman (if she is working outside the home, the risk decreases); the number of children, the number of years being married and alcohol consumption (in the three cases, the higher it is, the higher the risk of violence) [8]. Finally, other factors are the presence of a marked power asymmetry in the couple as well as the existence of rigid ideology regarding gender roles [28].

A substantial minority of women and girls experience sexual abuse by nonpartners, as indicated by a review of studies from Latin America and the Caribbean region that found that between 8 and 27% of women report having experienced sexual violence by a nonpartner [29].

Unintended and unwanted pregnancy is more common among women who had partner violence; between 3 and 13% of women reporting intimate partner violence during pregnancy from countries such as Mexico, Brazil and Peru [2, 29].

The links between HIV/AIDS and GBV are becoming increasingly apparent based on the findings of various studies. Findings show an increased risk of HIV/AIDS among women victims of GBV and also that being HIV-positive can lead to violence against women. This relationship has grave consequences for global health and human development, especially with regard to adult women, adolescents and girls, who are most affected by sexual violence and are consequently more vulnerable to HIV/AIDS [29]. The global proportion of HIV-positive women has increased significantly over the last 10 years, and this process is most visible in countries where the virus spreads mainly through heterosexual intercourse, as is the case in most parts of the Caribbean and Central America. By the end of 2004, 440,000 people in the Caribbean and 1,700,000 people in Latin America were estimated to be living with HIV. Among female sex workers, HIV prevalence ranges from less than 1% in Nicaragua and 2% in Panama, to 5% in Guatemala and more than 10% in Honduras [2, 29].

According to published data, forced sexual relations are also frequent. However, these data are usually not comparable since there are large differences in the definition of rape and sexual abuse. In Mexico City, for example, rape and intimate partner violence against women was estimated to be the third most important cause of morbidity and mortality, accounting for 5.6% of all disability-adjusted life years lost [30].

It is noteworthy that studies conducted in Brazil, Haiti, Mexico, Nicaragua and Peru have all found considerable overlap between sexual and physical violence by intimate partners [29]. In Nicaragua, for example, 36% of women reported that they were commonly forced to have sex while being beaten [31]. Research from Haiti found that in that setting, women were equally likely to experience physical violence and sexual violence [32].

Data regarding sexual abuse, especially during childhood, are even more difficult to obtain. However, there are some indications that this is more frequent than is usually thought. In Barbados, for example, in a study carried out in a representative sample of men and women between the ages of 20 and 45, it was observed that 33% of the females and 2% of the males admitted having been the object of sexually abusive behaviors during childhood or adolescence [26].

In a case-control study carried out in the city of Medellin, Colombia, in a clinical population of women that consulted the psychiatric outpatient consultation service of two general hospitals, it was found that in the sample of 117 women with unipolar depression, 53 (45%) had a history of sexual abuse during childhood. Of these, 26 (49%) told their experience to someone at the time they were facing the abuse and only 5 (19%) received some type of help [33]. This finding shows the negligence and lack of attention experienced by children who suffer sexual violence and reinforces the need to educate the caregivers and take necessary measures for the prevention of child abuse.

Violence against women can lead to death. The mortality rate for women from homicides is usually much lower than for men. In the Americas, external causes are responsible for 51.7% of men's and 24.5% of women's deaths. For men, the main external cause is homicide representing 39.5% of the total, while female homicides constitute the second external cause of death with 23.2% of the total. However, it is known that homicide in women is associated with intimate partner violence. A large proportion of women's murders are carried out by persons known to the victim, especially their partners or former partners. Many of these deaths happen when the woman decides to look for help or leave her aggressor [26].

Political and Social Violence

In areas of conflict, the violation of human rights is accentuated. Young girls are kidnapped by illegal groups and forced to work as sexual slaves, combatants, informants, guides and messengers. Some of these young girls, former combatants, admit to having been victims of intra family violence or sexual abuse. According to the People's Rights Office of Colombia, the special envoy of the United Nations received testimonies in which the majority of young girls that have left the guerrillas in one of the mountain areas, were sexually active, some of them had intrauterine devices implanted and, about 70% of them had sexually transmitted diseases. Also, forced abortion is a common practice within armed groups [34]. If a woman wants to keep her child she has to escape.

In situations of conflict, forced displacement is a phenomenon represented mostly by women and children. Displacement produces a breakdown of traditional family structures, especially when men of the family have disappeared, been forced to look for job security elsewhere, or have died [27].

Situations of conflict, postconflict and displacement may exacerbate existing violence and present new forms of violence against women.

Discussion

In the Latin America region, there is the Convención Interamericana to prevent, sanction and eradicate violence against women (Inter American Convention, Belem Do Pará, 1994) [35], that is the only legal instrument in the world specifically directed to eliminate violence against women. However, as well as numerous national laws dealing in a specific manner with this subject, there is still a lot to be done regarding the implementation and achievement of effective prevention and attention to gender-based violence. This requires coordinated efforts at all levels: municipal, regional and national, with the purpose of achieving the implementation of existing laws and creating awareness about this problem.

The prevention of any form of violence against women has been among the social goals of many countries in Latin America and the Caribbean. However, it is well known that women are underrepresented in political positions and in decision-making bodies in the majority of the countries in the region. This existing inequality in power distribution means that women have fewer possibilities to see their rights transformed into better opportunities, and to harness the political will to carry out prevention programs against GBV.

Prevention of all forms of violence is everyone's problem. The presence of human resources in the health sector through a large network of primary health care facilitates the implementation of a comprehensive model for the prevention and care of intra-family and sexual violence that uses the health sector as the vehicle for the identification, detection, assistance and rehabilitation of survivors of intra-family violence. At the same time, this comprehensive model requires the involvement of women´s associations, educational institutions, mental health services, legal medicine institutes, the Attorney General, police, legal and other actors that have been trained in responding adequately to this problem.

The coherence among the different professionals attending victims of GBV must be such that the persons requiring their services leave the place strengthened and not revictimized after receiving professional help.

Considering that GBV is a widely prevalent phenomena and public health problem, the attention to such a scourge has not been given sufficient attention in Latin America and the Caribbean. The health problems, the disabilities, the impact generated in the family, work, society and culture continue at alarming rates.

Some of the factors influencing the lack of attention are the perception of the problem as a private matter; the existing inequality in couple's relationships and the poor participation of women in positions of power, as well as the strong social and cultural norms that promote a model of masculinity based on aggression and control ('machismo'). Another relevant aspect is the ignorance women have of their rights contributing to the fact that they do not claim them, and even justify the abuse of which they are victims.

In the case of some Latin American countries, GBV has been over shadowed by other forms of violence, specially political and social ones.

It is necessary to create comprehensive programs with the different sectors involved, to sensitize the population and ensure information and knowledge regarding the problem is shared across sectors, as the problem requires a comprehensive response.

From the perspective of health services, it is known that women's participation in health is generally greater than men's; however, in the medical and health care systems, their participation is also not equitable since the decision-making, research and direction of health services usually lies in men's hands. The region has made very important advances regarding women's participation in decision-making and political bodies, but in the majority of the cases it is due to the assignment of quotas. While this is an advance, this participation still needs to be assimilated in the collective consciousness and result from popular election.

Conclusions

Violence against women is a complex and multidimensional social, political and public health problem, in which underlying structural conditions such as gender inequality and cultural norms regarding women-men relations play an important part. This violence attempts against life, dignity and the human rights of the victims in private and public spaces; its affects range from mental and physical health problems to decreased participation in economic, political and social affairs, as shown by the indicators of income, labor insertion, morbidity-mortality, education, nutrition, and years of healthy life lost by the affected women.

Violence against women has serious consequences to women's health and also affects the well-being of their children and families. It is also an important cause of morbidity related to multiple mental, physical, sexual and reproductive health problems. It is also linked with known risk factors for poor health, such as alcohol and drug use, smoking and unsafe sex, and with female homicides and suicides.

Intimate partner violence during pregnancy is more common than some maternal health conditions routinely screened for in antenatal care. Global initiatives to reduce maternal mortality and improve maternal health must devote increased attention to violence against women, particularly violence during pregnancy.

IPV prevention programs should increase the focus on transforming gender norms and attitudes, addressing child abuse, and reducing harmful drinking. Development initiatives to improve access to education for girls and boys can also have an important role in violence prevention. It is necessary to analyze women's subjective obstacles in order to accede in their couple relations to the rights stated in national and international laws and legislations. The inter-sectoral attention to the problem of violence will contribute to the reduction of risks and damage to persons living in violent situations.

Most research has centered on the experiences of female victims; few studies have focused on boys or men either as victims or perpetrators.

More recently, the problem of violence against women has been receiving the attention and is on the working agendas of many Latin American governments. However, there is still a long way to go since in many Latin American societies, violence against women continues to be considered as a private act and is socially tolerated or condoned.

References

1 UN (United Nations): Declaration on the Elimination of Violence against Women. UN Document A/48/49. New York, 1993.
2 Bott S, Guedes A, Goodwin M, Mendoza J: Violence against Women in Latin America and Caribbean: A Comparative Analysis of Population-Based Data from 12 countries. Washington, PAHO, 2012.
3 World Health Organization: Violence against Women: A Priority Health Issue. Geneva, WHO, 1997.
4 Blichtein Winicki D, Reyes-Solari E: Factores asociados a violencia física reciente de pareja hacia la mujer en el Perú, 2004–2007. Rev Perú Med Exp Salud Publica 2012;29:35–43.
5 Ariza Sosa GR: De inapelable a intorelable: violencia contra las mujeres en sus relaciones de pareja en Medellín, ed 1. Bogotá, Universidad Nacional de Colombia, 2012.
6 Ellsberg M, Jansen HA, Heise L, et al: Intimate partner violence and women's physical and mental health in the WHO multi-country study on women's health and domestic violence: an observational study. Lancet 2008;371:1165–1172.
7 Ellsberg M: Violence against women and the millennium development Goals: Facilitating women's access support. Int J Ginecol Obstet 2006;94:325–332.
8 Organizacion Panamericana de la Salud: Indicadores básicos para el análisis de la equidad de género en salud. Washington, Organizacion Panamericana De La Salud, 2004.
9 Castro R, Riquer F: La investigación sobre violencia contra las mujeres en América Latina: entre el empirismo ciego y la teoría sin datos. Cad Saúde Públ 2003;19:135–141.
10 Colombini M, Mayhew S, Watts C: Health-sector responses to intimate partner violence in low and middle-income settings: a review of current models, challenges and opportunities. Bull WHO 2008;86:8.
11 Larrain S, Rodríguez T, Gómez E: Los orígenes y el control de la violencia doméstica en contra de la mujer. Género, mujer y salud en las Américas (Internet). 1993, p 541. Habilitado en: http://www.amro.who.int/Spanish/DD/PUB/PC541-202-209.pdf.
12 OPS: Unidad Género, Etnia y Salud. Indicadores básicos para el análisis de la equidad en género y salud. Washington, OPS/Paltex, 2004.
13 Rondon MB: From Marianism to terrorism: the many faces of violence against women in Latin America. Arch Womens Ment Health 2003;6:157–163.
14 Amorós C, de Miguel A: Introducción. Teoría feminista y movimientos feministas, p 78.
15 Heise LL: Violence against women: an integrated ecological framework. Violence Against Women 1998;4:262–290.
16 Instituto Nacional de Educación Católica, Consejo Nacional de la Mujer: Mujeres y hombres de Ecuador en cifras. Quito, CONAMUC, INEC, 2000.
17 Gaviria SL, Rondon MB: Some considerations on women's mental health in Latin America and the Caribbean. Int Rev Psychiatry 2010;22:363–369.
18 Diaz-Granados N, Pitzul KB, Dorado LM, Wang F, McDermott S, Rondon MB, et al: Monitoring gender equity in health using gender-sensitive indicators: a cross-national study. J Women's Health 2011;20:145–153.
19 CEPAL: Capital social y reducción de la pobreza en América Latina y el Caribe: en busca de un nuevo paradigma. 2003 ene;Habilitado en: http://www.eclac.org/publicaciones/xml/6/11586/Indice.pdf.

20 Stewart DE: La salud mental de la mujer en el mundo; in Correa E, Jadresic E (eds): Psicopatología de la mujer. Santiago de Chile, Mediterráneo, 2005.
21 Browner: Women, household and health in Latin America. Soc Sci Med 1989;28:461–473.
22 WHO: The World Health Report 2000. Health Systems: Improving Performance. Geneva, Word Health Organization, 2000.
23 Gómez EG: Equidad, género y salud: retos por la acción. Rev Panam Salud Publ 2002;11:454–461.
24 Diaz-Granados N, McDermott S, Wang F, Posada-Villa J, Saavedra J, Rondon MB, et al: Monitoring gender equity in mental health in a low-, middle-, and high-income country in the Americas. Psychiatr Serv 2011;62:516–524.
25 Belleza LI: Mujer y psicopatología; in Correa E, Jadresic E (eds): Psicopatología de la mujer. Santiago de Chile, Mediterráneo, 2005, pp 60–61.
26 García Moreno C: Violencia contra la mujer. Género y equidad en la salud OPS/OMS. Harvard, Harvard Center for Population and Development Studies, 2000. Habilitado en: http://www.paho.org/english/DPM/GPP/GH/Moreno.pdf.
27 Bunch C, Carrillo R: Violencia de género: Un problema de desarrollo y derechos humanos. Estados Unidos, Targum Productions, 1995. Habilitado en: http://www.cwgl.rutgers.edu/globalcenter/publications/genderspanish.pdf.
28 Jewkes R: Intimate partner violence: causes and prevention. Lancet 2002;359:1423–1429.
29 Ellsberg M: Sexual violence against women and girls: recent findings from Latin America and the Caribbean; in Jejeebhoy SJ, Shah I, Thapa S (eds): Sex without Consent. Young People in Developing Countries. London, Zed Books, 2005.
30 Garcia Moreno C, Watts C: Use violence against women: an urgent public health priority. Bull World Health Organ 2011;89:2.
31 Ellsberg M: Candies in hell: women's experiences of violence in Nicaragua. Soc Sci Med 2000;51:1595–1610.
32 Hindin MJ, Kishor S, Ansara DL: Intimate partner violence among couples in 10 DHS countries: predictors and health outcomes. DHS Analytical Studies No. 18. Calverton, Macro International, 2008. Available at: http://www.measuredhs.com/pubs/pdf/AS18/AS18.pdf (Accessed April 2012).
33 Correa Saldarriaga J, Almario Hernandez AF, Gaviria SL: Características de pacientes deprimidas que reportan abuso sexual en la infancia versus pacientes deprimidas que no lo reportan, 2006.
34 ACNUR: Derechos de las mujeres. Bogotá, Alto comisionado de las Naciones Unidas para los Refugiados.
35 ACNUR: Convención interamericana para prevenir, sancionar y erradicar la violencia contra la mujer «Convención de Belem do Para». 1995 mar 5 (citado 012 feb 17); Habilitado en: http://www.acnur.org/t3/fileadmin/scripts/doc.php?file=biblioteca/pdf/0029.

Dr. Silvia Lucía Gaviria
Head Department of Psychiatry, CES University
Calle 5c # 36 b 20
El Poblado, Medellin (Colombia)
E-Mail sgaviria1@une.net.co

Violence against Women in South Asia

Unaiza Niaz

University of Health Sciences, Lahore, Pakistan

Abstract

In South Asia, the rigid cultures and discriminatory attitudes towards women have led to the exploitation of women, from individual to community levels. Women and girls in this region are exposed to biased, inequitable practices and violent behaviors at all stages of life. The high incidence of female infanticide in India, the frequent incidence of culture-specific types of violence like honor killings, acid attacks, and stove burnings in Pakistan and Bangladesh, trafficking of women from Nepal, Sri-Lanka and India to other regions of world, forced into prostitution and other forms of sexual violence, as well as the high prevalence of domestic violence in all countries of the region, all constitute examples of violence against women in this region. The deeply entrenched cultural norms, lead to acceptance of violence as 'normal life experiences for a woman' and to dispel such cultural myths and norms is a formidable task. In the family unit the man is the undisputed ruler of the household. The ineffective legislations encourage abusers to commit abusive acts against women without any repercussions. To eradicate violence against women in this region there are some fundamental challenges which include: changing existing social and individual attitudes, both at the family and societal levels, as well as implementation of policies for equity and sustaining of the political will to achieve significant results.

Copyright © 2013 S. Karger AG, Basel

Violence against women remains a problem of pandemic proportions. It is prevalent globally at both regional and national levels, as well as at the social, interpersonal and family levels. It is recognized as a global public health and human rights problem affecting women's physical and mental health and well-being. The globally accepted definition considers as violence 'any act that results in, or is likely to result in, physical, sexual, or psychological harm or suffering to women, including threats of such acts, coercion or arbitrary deprivation of liberty, whether occurring in public or private life' [1]. Rates of women experiencing physical violence by an intimate partner at least once in their lifetime vary from several percent to over 59% depending on where they live [2].

Presently, there is still no universal agreement on the terminology referring to violence against women. The most commonly used terms are derived from diverse theoretical perspectives and disciplines and hence have different meanings in various regions. WHO's World Report on Violence and Health defines violence as the international use of physical force or power, threatened or actual, against oneself, another person or against a group or community, that either results in or has a high likelihood of resulting in injury, death, psychological harm, mal development or deprivation [3].

According to the United Nations geographical region classification. Southern Asia comprises the countries of Bangladesh, Bhutan, India, Maldives, Nepal, Pakistan, and Sri Lanka [4]. Afghanistan, Burma, and Tibet are also sometimes included in the region. In South Asia 400 million people are affected by hunger and it has nearly 40% of the total number of people living in poverty. Key statistical indicators for human development for health and education are poor [5]. Besides, in this region gender-based violence has relentlessly narrowed women's choices in virtually all spheres of life, and has consistently eroded the fundamental rights of women to, for example, bodily integrity, health, security, work, food, shelter and participation in political affairs. This leads to poor gender-related development indices in crucial areas like health, nutrition, education, employment and political participation. The World Bank regional report for South Asia as mentioned in Oxfam (2004) reports that women of these countries, especially Pakistan, are in crisis. According to this report 56% of South Asian women are illiterate, and one third of all maternal deaths in the world occur in the region [6].

Education is a basic tool for the empowerment of women and for the elimination of gender related violence [7]. But the majority of girls in South Asia are deprived of this opportunity. In South Asia only 45% of adult women are literate. About 250 million illiterate women live in South Asia, constituting 47% of the illiterates of the developing world. Women's work in South Asia is also distinguished by job and income insecurity, as they work mainly in the informal sector characterized by low wages and unsafe and hazardous working conditions. Employer's mostly prefer women workers as they are 'easier to handle', and less demanding in terms of wages or job security. In 2003, less than half the women of the age group 15–64 were economically active in the South-Asian region.

Types of Violence against Women in South Asia Communities

Intimate Partner Violence
The most common form of violence experienced by women globally is physical violence inflicted by an intimate partner, with women beaten, coerced into sex or otherwise abused.

Studies have found that rates of women suffering physical violence perpetrated by a current or former intimate partner range from 6% in China and 7% in Canada to over 48% in Zambia, Ethiopia and Peru [2].

Several global surveys suggest that half of all women who die from homicide are killed by their current or former husbands or partners [8].
- In Australia, Canada, and Israel 40–70% of female murder victims were killed by their partners, according to the World Health Organization [3].
- In the United States, one-third of women murdered each year are killed by intimate partners [Krug et al., WHO, 2002].
- In South Africa, a woman is killed every 6 h by an intimate partner [Mathews et al, 2004].
- In India, 22 women were killed each day in dowry-related murders in 2007.
- In Guatemala, 2 women are murdered, on average, each day [3].
- Violence before and during pregnancy has serious health consequences for both mother and child. It is associated with pregnancy-related problems, including miscarriage, preterm labor and low birth weight.

Sexual Violence

Sexual violence refers to any sexual act without the consent of the woman as well as attempted or completed sexual acts with a woman who is ill, disabled, under pressure or under the influence of alcohol or other drugs. Sexual violence can thus be described as any sexual act, attempt to obtain a sexual act, unwanted sexual comments or advances, or acts to traffic, or otherwise directed, against a person's sexuality, using coercion, threats of harm or physical force, by any person regardless of relationship to the victim, in any setting, including but not limited to home and work [9].

Rates of sexual violence are difficult to establish because in many societies sexual violence remains an issue of deep shame for women and often their families. Statistics on rape from police records, for example, are notoriously unreliable because of significant underreporting.

According to the World Health Organization, the proportion of women suffering sexual violence by nonpartners after the age of 15 varies from less than 1% in Ethiopia and Bangladesh to between 10 and 12% in Peru, Samoa and the United Republic of Tanzania [8].

In Switzerland, 22.3% of women experience sexual violence by nonpartners in their lifetime [3].

In Canada, a study of adolescents aged 15–19 years found that 54% of girls had experienced 'sexual coercion' in a dating relationship [10].

Forced and unregistered marriages can increase the vulnerability of women to violence, including sexual violence [11]. The practice of early marriage – a form of sexual violence – is common worldwide, with more than 60 million girls worldwide married before the age of 18, primarily in South Asia (31.1 million) and Sub-Saharan Africa (14.1 million) [12]. According to UNICEF's 'State of the World's Children – 2009' report, in India 56% of girls were married before the age of 18 and 45% were married by the age of 15 in Bangladesh. In Afghanistan, half of the marriages involve females under 16 years and in Pakistan the average age of a married girl is 16 years [Child Marriage Restraint Act, 1929].

Young girls forced into marriage and into sexual relations may suffer health risks, including exposure to HIV/AIDS, and limited school attendance. One effect of sexual abuse, particularly of girls and young women is traumatic gynecologic fistula: an injury resulting from severe tearing of the vaginal tissues, often rendering the woman incontinent and socially undesirable.

Dowry Murders
Dowry murder is a brutal practice where a woman is killed by her husband or in-laws because her family cannot meet their demands for dowry — a payment made to a woman's in-laws upon her marriage as a gift to her new family. While dowries or similar payments are prevalent worldwide, dowry murder occurs predominantly in South Asia [2].

Murders in the Name of Honor ('Honor Killings')
In many societies, rape victims, women suspected of engaging in premarital sex, and women accused of adultery have been murdered by their relatives because the violation of a woman's chastity is viewed as an affront to the family's honor. The United Nations Population Fund (UNFPA) estimates that the annual worldwide number of so-called 'honor killing' victims may be as high as 5,000 women [13].

Human Trafficking
Although the global scale of human trafficking is difficult to quantify, it is estimated that as many as 2.5 million people are trafficked annually into situations including prostitution, forced labor, slavery or servitude. Women and girls account for about 80% of the identified victims [14].

Violence during Pregnancy
Violence before and during pregnancy has serious health consequences for both mother and child. It leads to high-risk pregnancies and pregnancy-related problems, including miscarriage, preterm labor and low birth weight. Female infanticide, and systematic neglect of girls are widespread in South and East Asia, North Africa, and the Middle East [12].

In India and Pakistan, joint family systems are still fairly common, and mother-in-laws often deprive young daughter-in-laws of rest and nutritious food during pregnancy. Physical and verbal abuse is often reported in lower socioeconomic groups. In clinical practice, the author has observed such maltreatment and abuse of women who attend psychiatric outpatient clinics for the treatment of depressive illness or anxiety states, during pregnancy.

Discrimination and Violence
Many women face multiple forms of discrimination and increased risk of violence. Factors such as women's ethnicity, caste, class, migrant or refugee status, age, religion, sexual orientation, marital status, disability or HIV status will influence what forms of violence they suffer and how they experience it.

- Indigenous women in Canada are five times more likely than other women of the same age to die as the result of violence.
- In India, Dalit women experience high rates of sexual violence committed by men of higher caste.
- In Europe, North America and Australia, over half of women with disabilities have experienced physical abuse, compared to one-third of nondisabled women [15].

Female infanticide, gender-biased sex selection and systematic neglect of girls are widespread in South and East Asia, North Africa, and the Middle East as a result of son preference.

Sexual Harassment
Small surveys in Asia-Pacific countries indicate that 30 to 40 per cent of women workers report some form of harassment – verbal, physical or sexual [15].

VAW Facts and Figures of Pakistan in 2011 [Report by Daily Times]
Pakistan has been highlighted because the women in this region in the past few years have gained some attention internationally. For example, the Muktarra Mai UK Aid program has focused on 15 countries to help women to improve their health, address violence issues and education, and Pakistan is one of the 15 countries.

It is also pertinent to report on the cultural aspects of violence against women in Pakistan. For example in Pakistan, domestic violence is generally considered a private matter, as it occurs in the family, and therefore not an appropriate focus for assessment, intervention or policy changes [16]. Women have to face discrimination and violence on a daily basis due to the cultural and religious norms that Pakistani society embraces [17]. According to an estimate, approximately 70–90% of Pakistani women are subjected to domestic violence [18].

According to a survey conducted on 1,000 women in the Punjab, 35% of the women admitted in the hospitals reported being beaten by their husbands. The survey reported that on average, at least 2 women were burned every day in domestic violence incidents and approximately 70–90% of women experience spousal abuse. In 1998, 282 burn cases of women were reported in only one province of the country. Of the reported cases, 65% died of their injuries [19].

As many as 8,539 women became victims of violence in 2011 and there was an overall 6.74% increase in reported cases of violence against women (VAW) in the country, as compared to those in 2010, according to a report [20].

A 2011 report on VAW, conducted by the Aurat Foundation (AF) was launched at a local hotel in the federal capital.

According to the report, 8,539 women became victims of violence in 2011, out of which, 6,188 incidents were reported in the Punjab, 1,316 in Sindh, 694 in Khyber Pakhtunkhwa, 198 in Balochistan, and 148 in Islamabad. The figure was 8,000 in 2010; in 2009, the incidents of violence against women were 8,548, and in 2008, these incidents were 7,571.

The report revealed that a large number of incidents were not reported to police, which reflected lack of public trust on the department.

Among the total 8,539 incidents, FIRs (First Investigation Report) were registered in 6,745 cases whereas no FIR was registered in 911 cases and no information was available in 883 cases. The highest number of unregistered cases was noted in Sindh where FIRs were not registered in 605 cases and no information was available in 75 incidents among the total of 1,316 reported cases.

The annual statistics revealed that 2,089 women became victims of abduction, 1,575 victims of murder, 610 victims of domestic violence, 758 victims of suicide, 705 victims of honor killing, 827 victims of rape/gang rape, 110 sexual assault, 44 acid throwing, 29 burning and 1,792 victims of miscellaneous violent incidents.

Cases of abduction top the list with 2,089 such cases reported in 2011, representing 24.4% of reported cases for crimes against women. Murder combined with 'honor' killings total to another ugly figure of 2,280, constituting 26.70% of the total crimes against women, with 1,575 murders (18.44%) and 705 'honor' murders (8.25%).

There were 827 reported incidents of rape and gang rape in 2011 representing 9.68%, while 758 (8.87%) cases of suicide were reported by women in 2011. There were 110 reported cases of sexual assault (1.28%), 29 each of burning and acid throwing (0.33%), and offences of miscellaneous nature were 21% of the total with 1,792 cases in four provincial regions.

In the process of collecting data, the Aurat Foundation staff observed some emerging trends that, if allowed to continue, would further aggravate the situation of violence against women in the country. One such trend was noticed in Balochistan where, in most of the cases of honor killing, the women were killed on the orders of a Jirga but the same Jirga let the men live after an exchange of heavy amount in terms of compensation.

The report stated that in some forms of violence, there had been a notable increase in reporting, from the period 2010 to 2012 for instance, sexual assault increased by 48.65%, acid throwing increased by 37.5%, 'honor' killings by 26.57%, and domestic violence increased by 25.51%. However, with an overall 6.74% increase in violence cases from 2010 to 2011, the number of incidents decreased 8.03% from the first half to the second half of 2011.

Addressing the occasion, AF official Waseem Waghoo said that most of the perpetrators of violence against women were found to be the relatives of the survivor or the victim such as husband, brother, cousin, father, uncle, father and mother-in-law, brother-in-law, son or step-son. Honor killing was almost always committed by male members against female members who were accused of having brought dishonor upon the family.

He said at the same time, it was heartening that 2011 witnessed some landmark women-related legislations being unopposed in the National Assembly and Senate. The AF believed that the establishment of an independent and autonomous National Commission on Women (NCW) and the passing of an Anti-Women Practices (Criminal Law Amendment) Bill from parliament were some of the major achievements of the present government and would go a long way in protecting women from violence and discrimination in future.

Risk Factors Common to All Forms of Domestic Violence
At a global level, the most common risk factors for domestic violence include: coming from violent households, poverty, rigid gender roles, social isolation, income inequality and substance abuse. Besides, individual characteristics, such as low self-esteem and poor impulse control.

- At the individual level: factors such as being abused as a child or being exposed to parental conflict and violence at home, an absent/rejecting father, and history of frequent alcohol and drug abuse.
- At the family and relationship level: several cross-cultural studies reported male control of wealth and decision-making within the family, and marital conflict as strong predictors of abuse.
- At the community level: isolation of women, lack of social support, along with the male peer groups which condone and legitimize men's violence, predict higher rates of violence.
- At the societal level: globally, multiple research studies have found that violence against women is most common where gender roles are inflexibly defined and imposed and violence is rampant in cultures where the concept of masculinity is linked to toughness, and male honor, or dominance. The tolerance of the physical punishment of women and children, acceptance of violence as a means to settle interpersonal disputes, and the perception that men have 'ownership' of women are other cultural norms associated with VAW.
- And lastly at the State level, studies indicate that derisory legislation and lack of policies to prevent and punish acts of violence are linked to a higher incidence of violence. Low levels of sensitivity/awareness in the law enforcement agencies and social services are proportionately related to the incidence of violent practices in the community.

Specific Risk Factors for Domestic Violence against Women in South-Asian Countries
The low socioeconomic status and educational levels of women, as described in the first section of this chapter, are common risk factors for domestic violence against women in the South Asian region. Among the demographic factors, young age and low income were found to be factors linked to the likelihood of a man committing

physical violence against a partner. In South-Asian countries, research has shown that societal and cultural factors also add to higher levels of violence in this region [3, 21]. In Levinson's anthropological analysis of many cultures, wife beating occurred more often in societies in which men had economic and decision-making power in the household. Particularly, when women do not have easy access to divorce, and where people routinely resort to violence to resolve their conflicts [21].

Other than the mentioned risk factors there are various culturally and traditionally entrenched factors that interact to increase the risk of violence against women in this region. These can be grouped as the traditional, cultural, and religious factors that promote subordinate gender roles, privacy of violence, the lower status of women and seeming inability of states to prevent violence against women. VAW is usually veiled under the cultural norms and religious and traditional tenets and, therefore, the exact number of women and girls facing violence has always been underreported and underestimated. For instance, officially reported cases are likely to be the tip of the iceberg in showing the real incidence of VAW due to the tendency of women not to report the violence because of shame, fear and/or cultural acceptance of violence in South Asia. On the other hand, most of the surveys conducted to determine the prevalence of violence against women are usually small scale, except for a few surveys in India and Bangladesh. Thus the prevalence numbers available do not represent the national levels of violence. Also definitions of violence differ in different studies. Furthermore, none of the countries of South Asia has a system to collect data and monitor progress in this area. In spite of this, available data give us some idea of the disturbing extent of violence perpetrated against women in South Asia. The criminal reports, which can be used as an indication of incidence, demonstrate that in India during 2003 at least 140,603 crimes were committed against women's dignity and personal security. More than one third of these cases were cruelty perpetrated by husbands of women or relatives (36%), followed by molestation of women or girls by others (23%) [22].

Often the factors that contribute to violence related to attitude and behavior are connected to larger social, economic, political and cultural contexts, and while these can be changed with awareness and education, this is often a long-term process and requires action at multiple levels.

Core Challenges to Stop Violence against Women in South-Asian Countries
The fundamental challenges in the prevention of violence against women are:
1 To confront and modify existing social and individual attitudes that accept violence against women as 'normal'.
2 To mobilize family and society to work together to prevent violence against women.
3 To muster popular pressure to put into action policies that promote equality between women and men and equity and to help sustain the political will to accomplish them.

4. To draw together diverse local, national, regional, and international efforts to work towards ending violence against women.

Indeed, it is a formidable task to attempt a change in the deeply entrenched community norms that accept violence against women as 'normal'. The community plays a crucial role in perpetuating and endorsing gender inequality and violence. Attitudes and biases that support violence against women are created, sustained, and played out at the community level [23].

The acceptance of and support for the laws, programmes and policies must be achieved at the community level, or else they can be a easily undermined. Often in societies where class, caste, and religious dictates overrule other laws, women's rights are lost in the larger goal of community rights. The key to change, then, is to sway a shift in popular opinion. Community structures that promote opinion-change and positive collective action to prevent or combat violence against women need to be strengthened. State policies and programmes would be better received and easier to implement as a result.

This task is far from easy. A recent United Nations Population Fund (UNFPA) study of male attitudes to violence against women in Bangladesh found that an overwhelming majority of men felt that a wife was accountable to her husband for her behavior and that violence was an acceptable form of corrective punishment. Only 30% of men opposed general (not marital) violence against women [22]. Studies from other South Asian countries echo the same male attitudes [24].

Both at the cultural and social levels, massive efforts are required, as most forms of violence against women are still considered by a mainstream of the population as 'private matters' to be tolerated, and certainly not seen as a crime. To tackle violence against women, it is pertinent to challenge and change unequal power relations between men and women to the extent that it means dealing with issues of gender inequality in relation to resources, benefits and political power.

The lives of millions of women in Pakistan are restricted by customs and traditions, which impose extreme seclusion and obedience to men, many of whom enforce their control over women with violence. Generally, women bear with stoicism, the traditional male control over every aspect of their bodies, speech and behavior. According to the Human Rights Commission of Pakistan, it is estimated that a woman is raped every 2 h; a gang rape occurs every 8 h, and about 1,000 women die annually as a result of honor killings.

Violence against women, predominantly domestic violence, is largely unreported. According to a study carried out in 2009 by the Human Rights Watch [25]. About 70–90% of Pakistani women in rural areas are subjected to domestic violence [26]. The distinctive violent acts are: murder in the name of 'honor', rape, spousal abuse (including marital rape), acid attacks, and being burned by family members (often labeled an accident by family members).

The tragedy of Pakistan is that it is the influentially empowered people and policy makers that blatantly commit breach, therefore most people are scared to testify or report such cases. The passage of this bill is a mere paper document unless an appropriate plan is devised to implement the same. The rural population needs to be empowered and educated about their rights. No clear strategy for implementing these laws has been provided. These reforms will be of little practical benefit until federal and provincial authorities create mechanisms for compensating and rehabilitating victims of gender-based violence. Authorities must establish immediate benchmarks for assessing the implementation of these new laws.

Individual acts are supported overtly or in the guise, through social institutions such as the family and the community, and by the State, either through normative rules or by impunity towards acts of violent domination. Acts of violence are often committed by a group of individuals acting collectively. These groups could be family-based, or share other forms of identity such as political ideology, religious ideology, or membership of a gang. And within these groups, violence can be promoted through ritual, symbolism, or ideological expression. In South Asia, even acts of domestic violence are quite often not family-based acts, as they involve more than one perpetrator. Likewise, women are often targeted in times of war, communal conflict, political struggle, and in caste-based violence.

Hence, the measures to end violence against women in South Asia must deal with a series of issues, from women's unequal access to resources and decision-making in the family to concepts of masculinity and femininity. The male 'right' to domination and to be in command in all societal institutions, ranging from community-level groups to the education system and state structures, wherever these ideas are cultivated and effective, need to be queried.

The state also plays an important role in sustaining gender inequalities and male dominance and violence. Women are often targeted in state-sponsored violence in conflict situations in South Asia. Legal systems are overwhelmed by reticence and strong gender bias. Additionally, the legal assistance is expensive, and often women lack independent access to resources, though family courts have been set up to facilitate access to justice. Women are often unable to approach the courts because of legislation based on religious and customary laws such as the Hadood Laws in Pakistan and various other laws in India and Sri Lanka.

The male dominance in the judiciary, with the gender bias in society, adds to the biased decisions in the courts. 'A study of judicial attitudes to women in India found that 48% of judges agreed that it was justifiable for a man to hit his wife on certain occasions; 74% endorsed the view that preservation of the family should be the primary concern for women, even within a violent marriage' [26, 27]. It is vital to introduce human rights into the legal discussions, so that these are reflected in the policy making at the government levels.

The governments in South Asia are keen to narrow the extent of the definition of violence against women. The argument against violence breaches current cultural practices or the violence by private actors is a criminal offence rather than the violation of human rights in the society [28]. For instance, the Indian government often uses the argument that action against violence will 'conflict with existing culture and traditions and family structures' in order to freeze legislation on domestic violence. It is of vital importance that both those who exercise the law or are responsible for promoting the legislation understand women's rights. Sensitizing the state machinery (particularly the judiciary), police, planners, policy makers, and parliamentarians to gender issues is needed urgently [24].

In some instances where the State has accepted responsibility for protecting women against violence, it has been met by social unrest. Communities consider it as interference in family and cultural matters, and mostly agitation is to retract the laws. Such reactions are the greatest demotivator for the governments. In Pakistan, a variety of Islamist groups have been in arms against the elimination of the draconian Islamic penal law, Hudood, which, among other discriminatory clauses, requires that a women must produce four Muslim male witnesses to prove rape, failing which she faces the charge of adultery (an act that is defined as a crime against the state and is punishable with death by stoning).

The Senate, in Pakistan in December 2011 passed two private member bills, the Acid Control and Acid Crime Prevention Bill 2010 (makes acid throwers causing disfigurement, liable to 14 years' imprisonment with a minimum fine of Rs 1 million). The new law would also prohibit forced marriage, punishment being imprisonment for 7 years but not less than 3 years and a fine of Rs 0.5 million. They also passed the Prevention of Anti-Women Practices (Criminal Law Amendment) Bill 2008, which prohibits forced marriage, gives women the right to get their share in inheritance and gives severe punishment to anyone physically harming women with corrosive substances. The Prevention of Anti-Women Practices Act 2011 remained stuck for 3 years, first in various National Assembly committees and then the house itself so the fact that it has finally been passed is definitely a milestone. But the question is will these bills really be implemented practically? In a society where feudal lords, influential ministers and senators advocate killings, where tradition is not allowed to be questioned, will women in Pakistan have access to a fair judiciary, which will ensure their protection and rights to live as an individual? [29].

The judicial action to reform Muslim personal laws, in India, to increase protection and rights for women gave rise to huge protest from some sections of the Muslim community, who described it as a threat to their religious identity and practice.

In Sri Lanka, efforts by women's groups to reform the Muslim personal laws, especially those relating to the age of marriage for girls, have been thwarted by the government for fear of a voter reaction and opposition from fundamentalist groups who can easily mobilize public opinion in their favor.

Social scientists understand that dominant groups in society maintain their power not only by controlling resources but also by defusing any potential challenge to their power by making certain that ideas and beliefs sustain their interests through popular culture into the 'common sense' [30]. Disapproval and public protests of women's organizations appear as contradicting the conventional 'wisdom' or 'common sense' [31] and 'destructive' to culture and family. For instance, the actions of the team members of the Indian Council of Child Welfare to prevent female infanticide being greeted with hostility in villages [27]. Thevar and Kallar communities were resentful of women activists or pottachinga (contemptuous term for women) who came and corrupted their women with evil ideas. Therefore, to bring cultural and political change, it must be stressed that a beginning has to be made at the community level. Communities' perception of the world must be questioned, exposed and substituted by a new awareness.

Achievements at the Global Level
Internationally violence against women has received a tremendous attention, in the last few decades. Thanks to persistent struggles of women's organizations in the last three decades, violence against women is clearly defined and recognized as a public and mental health concern and a human rights violation. A range of international agreements have enabled signatory States to introduce legal measures and services to combat such violence and to support women affected by it.

As of 2000, 118 countries have developed national action plans to implement their commitments to the Platform of Action of the Fourth World Conference on Women (Beijing, 1995), which outlines violence against women as one of the key areas for action. Several crucial international and regional coalitions have also surfaced, assisted by international meetings and conferences. As a consequence, ground-breaking conventions, such as the South Asian Association for Regional Cooperation (SAARC) Convention on Preventing and Combating Trafficking of Women and Children for Prostitution, 2002, have taken place in the region. Generally speaking, however, these gains have not been translated into action by the states in the region to make women's lives free from violence. According to the recent United Nations Development Fund for Women (UNIFEM) report [32], the 'gaps between norms and practices remain'. Until now, the task for tackling violence against women has mostly been done by the women's nongovernmental organizations actively working in South-Asian countries.

Attempts of Some Nongovernmental Organizations to Change Current Opinions and Beliefs
A network of 17 organizations and women's human rights groups in the Sindhupalchock district of Nepal encourages affected communities and families to organize themselves for action, and mobilizes local councilors on village development committees to punish local traffickers.

Polli Sree, working in the northern part of Bangladesh, works with students and teachers in 60 different schools and colleges to generate awareness about gender discrimination and violence against women. They mobilize students as change agents in their families and community.

Ain-O-Salish Kendra in Bangladesh attempts to challenge and change attitudes at the community level by encouraging the use of gender-aware 'traditional' salishes (people's councils) to deal with cases of violence.

The Women's Development Centre in Sri Lanka runs awareness programmes on abuse and violence against women, targeting both children and teachers. They also provide counseling and training to teachers so that they can identify victims of abuse. The programme also trains students as 'peer counselors'.

Organizations in Bundelkhand (north India) and Orissa (east India) have mobilized a network of rural and urban women's groups to challenge social norms that foster violence against women. They work to prevent domestic violence and to provide support to women facing domestic and other violence.

In Pakistan, Amal in Punjab, Roots Work in Balochistan, and Pirbhat Development Society in Sindh are tackling violence against women issues by organizing women and men to work as pressure groups. A couple of groups have already attained effective results on domestic violence.

Organizations working in this field must highlight how violence against women affects the entire community, and that it should be the onus on both men and women, to tackle this grave societal menace. It is essential that women's documentation, and experience of violence, must be named as 'violence' by the community at large, it must be defined as unacceptable [33]. Globally statistics show that too often women view domestic violence as their own fault and an acceptable punishment for poor behavior [34], while men consider their behavior as an expression of masculinity and maintenance of male honor [35]. Obviously, effective strategies are needed to challenge the commonly accepted attitudes, beliefs, and behavior, where these support or condone violence.

Efforts of Women's Organizations [36]

In spite of the recent state constitutional and statutory safeguards, women continue to remain disadvantaged in their endeavors for a violence-free life. The usefulness of State legislation and programmes is also limited by the strong culture of patriarchy. Still the legislation, policy measures, national programmes, institutional mechanisms, and the allocation of resources have not led to a gender-impartial environment.

South Asian women's organizations have made tremendous progress, particularly in creating awareness in women of their fundamental rights as human beings. By taking on a human rights-based approach, they have managed to develop a range of services and programmes to empower women. Even though they have attained a measure of success at the policy and programme level, the resistance to change in the community has also multiplied. Their efforts to challenge existing community attitudes have been made to appear to be in conflict to the conventional attitudes, culture and wisdom.

Women activists in different organizations maintain that women will be less safe in the future if priority is not given by the State to a range of policy plans and public campaigns to bring about change in community perceptions, assumptions and beliefs.

The Way Ahead

Public education and awareness raising alone cannot achieve the desired goals to eradicate violence against women. The major challenge for the individuals, groups or organizations working on this issue is to change the prevalent gender-biased attitudes, practices and customs in South Asian societies. A popular campaign is required that engages people at all levels, at home, family, community, society, and the State levels, simultaneously raising awareness and mobilizing women and men to work towards preventing violence.

Such campaigns must also be linked to a multifaceted and wider social change process related to other aspects of gender inequality and women's economic and political empowerment. Community efforts should enable the implementation of positive state interventions and support the efforts of women's organizations and other groups to promote women's rights and to activate effective change.

For public education campaigns [36], use of mass media and other innovative means of communication, are important, and the focus of attention must be to:

1. Remove the stigma experienced by women facing violence and modify the common perception of the problem as a 'private' matter.
2. Expose and counter-existing myths, so as to make the prevalence of violence against women visible and unacceptable, in the community.
3. Encourage alternative and more equitable attitudes, gender relations, and behavior.

Such campaigns [37] would support and work in synergy with the national, regional, and international efforts to end violence against women, in particular those focusing on policy advocacy and state responsibility. To achieve a paradigm shift in the social attitudes and beliefs that support gender inequality and violence against women, these efforts must be combined to sustain a long-term commitment to a process involving a wide range of actors, in order to reach all segments of society.

Acknowledgement

Thanks to Ms Qudsia Tariq, Assistant Professor of Psychology at the Karachi University, for research articles.

References

1. García-Moreno C, et al: WHO Multi-Country Study on Women's Health and Domestic Violence against Women. Geneva, WHO, 2005.
2. United Nations Statistics Division (2010), United Nations Statistics Division (2010): The World's Women 2010: Trends and Statistics. United Nations Publication ST/ESA/STAT/SER.K/19, p 131.
3. Krug EG, et al (eds): (2002) World Report on Violence and Health. Geneva, World Health Organization, 2002.
4. Farmer BH: An Introduction to South Asia. London, Routledge, 1993.
5. UNDP: Human Development Report 2003. New York, UNDP, 2003.
6. Oxfam Briefing Paper: Towards Ending Violence against Women in South Asia. August, 2004.
7. For South Asia, see ICRW (2002), op. cit.; Bangladesh CARE and UNFPA (2003): Male Attitudes towards Violence against Women in Bangladesh. Dhaka, 2002.
8. Garcia-Moreno C, Heise L, Jansen H, Ellsberg M, Watts CH: Public health. Violence against women. Science 2005;310:1282–1283.
9. Jewkes R, et al: Rape perpetration by young, rural South African men: prevalence, patterns and risk factors. Soc Sci Med 2006;63:2949–2961.
10. General Assembly: In-depth study on all forms of violence against women. Report of the Secretary-General, A/61/122/Add. 1, 2006.
11. Manjoo R: Report of the Special Rapporteur on Violence against Women, Its Causes and Consequences A/HRC/14/22/Add.2, paragraph 48. Geneva, United Nations, 2010.
12. UN Women: Facts and Figures on Violence against Women, 2011. www.unwomen.org.
13. UNFPA: The State of the World's Population, 2000, chap 3.
14. United Nations Office on Drugs and Crime: Report, 2009.
15. General Assembly: In-depth study on all forms of violence against women. Report of the Secretary-General, A/61/122/Add. 1. Paragraph 148, 2006.
16. Fikree FF, Bhatti LI: Domestic violence and health of Pakistani women. Int J Gynaecol Obstet 1999; 65:195–201.
17. Bettencourt A: Violence against women in Pakistan. Human Rights Advocacy Clinic; Litigation Report Spring 2000 [online] 2000 [cited 2005 November 3, 2000. Retrieved November 3]. Available from URL: www.du.edu/intl/humanrights/violencepkstn.pdf.
18. Human Rights Watch: 'Crime or Custom? Violence against Women in Pakistan. Report of Human Rights Watch, 1999.
19. Pakistan – Report on the State of Women in Urban Local... – ESCAP. http://www.unescap.org/huset/women/reports/pakistan.pdf Aug 14, 2000.
20. Human Rights Commission of Pakistan (HRCP): State of Human Rights in 1999. Lahore, HRCP, 2000.
21. Heise L, Garcia-Moreno C: Violence by intimate partners; in Krug E, Dahlberg LL, Mercy JA, et al (eds): World Report on Violence and Health. Geneva, World Health Organization, 2002, pp 87–121.
22. HSDA: Canadian Community Health Survey 3.1. 2005.
23. HSDA: Health Service Delivery Area boundaries provided by BC Stats Human Development in South Asia: Human Security in South Asia, 2005. The Mahbub ul Haq Human Development Centre. London, Oxford University Press, 2006.
24. Cited in highlights of a speech by Radhika Coomaraswamy, UN Special Rapporteur at the 47th session of the Commission on the Status of Women, in her final report on 'Violence against Women' submitted to the CHR. See www.hindu.com/thehindu/mag/2003/04/13/stories/2003041300290400.htm.
25. Human Rights Watch Pakistan: Halt Execution of Lawyer's Killer. http://www.hrw.org/news/2012/05/15/pakistan-halt-execution-lawyer-s-killer
26. Gosselin DK: Heavy Hands: An Introduction to the Crime of Intimate and Family Violence, ed 4. New York, Prentice Hall, 2009, p 13.
27. Aravamudan G: Born to Die. Report on Rediff Special, 24 October, 2001. Retrieved from http://www.rediff.com/news/2001/oct/24spec.htm.
28. Adapted from 'A Framework for Understanding Partner Violence', Population Reports, Ending Violence Against Women, XXVII(4), December, 1999.
29. Prevention of Anti-Women Practices Act, 2011. Retrieved from http://us.oneworld.net/article/view/68164/1/.
30. The analysis and concept was first proposed by Antonio Gramsci in the 1930s-40s. See Simon R: Gramsci's Political Thought: An Introduction. London, Lawrence & Wishart, 1991, endnote 10, p 26.
31. In Gramscian terms, this 'commonsense' represents the uncritical and often unconscious way in which people perceive the world, cited in Simon R: Gramsci's Political Thought: An Introduction. London, Lawrence & Wishart, 1991.
32. UNIFEM South Asia: Say No to Gender Based Violence. Responses from South Asia. New Delhi, UNIFEM, 2003.
33. Degni-Ségui R: Report on the situation of human rights in Rwanda, 1994. E/CN.4/1996/68 paragraph 16. Geneva, UN, 1996.

34 Pickup F: Ending Violence against Women: A Challenge for Development and Humanitarian Work. Oxford, Oxfam GB, 2001.

35 Studies from various parts of the world show that a significant percentage of women hold such beliefs. ICRW 2000 survey for India, op. cit.

36 Mehta M: Towards Ending Violence against Women in South Asia. Oxford, Oxfam Publishing, 2004. Retrieved from www.oxfam.org/sites/www.oxfam.org/files/violence.pdf.

37 Oxfam Briefing Paper 66: Towards Ending Violence against Women. See www.mifumi.org/sitemap.htm, for an example.

Further Reading

Schuler M (ed): Freedom from Violence: Strategies from Around the World. UNIFEM, 1992.

Marcus R: Violence against Women in Bangladesh, Pakistan, Egypt, Sudan, Senegal and Yemen. Report prepared for Special Programme WID, Netherland Ministry of Foreign Affairs. Brighton, Institute of Development Studies, 1993.

Atai Y: Violence against Women: Reports from India and the Republic of Korea. Bangkok, UNESCO Principal Regional Office for Asian and the Pacific, 1993.

Rahman S: Domestic Violence in Pakistan: The Current Proposal, 2006.

Human Rights Commission of Pakistan (HRCP): Violence against women rose 13 pc in 2009. Feb 2010.

Adapted from 'A Framework for Understanding Partner Violence', Population Reports, Ending Violence Against Women, XXVII(4), December, 1999.

Human Development in South Asia: Human Security in South Asia, 2005. The Mahbub ul Haq Human Development Centre. Oxford, Oxford University Press, 2006.

Mehta M: Towards Ending Violence against Women in South Asia. Oxford, Oxfam Publishing 2004. Retrieved from www.oxfam.org/sites/www.oxfam.org/files/violence.pdf.

Degni-Ségui R: Report on the situation of human rights in Rwanda, 1994. E/CN.4/1996/68 paragraph 16. Geneva, United Nations, 1996.

UNAIDS, UNFPA and UNIFEM: Women and HIV/AIDS: Confronting the Crisis, 2004, chap 6. Available at http://bit.ly/sq7eKw.

UNICEF, UNAIDS and WHO: Young People and HIV/AIDS: Opportunity in Crisis, 2002, p 5.

UNAIDS: Global Report: UNAIDS Report on the Global AIDS Epidemic, 2010, p 121.

World Health Organization: An Update on WHO's Work on Female Genital Mutilation (FGM). Progress Report. Geneva, WHO/RHR/11.18, 2011, p 1.

United Nations Office on Drugs and Crime: Global Report on Trafficking in Persons. Human Trafficking. A Crime That Shames Us All, 2009.

Ali PA, Gavino MI: Violence against women in Pakistan: a framework for analysis. J Pak Med Assoc 2008; 58:198–203.

Mathews S, Abrahams N, Martin LJ, Vetten L, van der Merwe L, Jewkes R: 'Every six hours a woman is killed by her intimate partner': a national study of female homicide in South Africa. MRC Policy Brief, 5. Cape Town, Medical Research Council, 2004.

World Health Organization: World Report on Violence and Health. October 3, 2004.

General Assembly: In-depth study on all forms of violence against women. Report of the Secretary General, A/61/122/Add. 1. Paragraph 148, 2006.

Daily Times Report on Mukhtaran Mai.

UNIFEM South Asia: Say No to Gender Based Violence. Responses from South Asia. New Delhi, UNIFEM, 2003.

UN Office of the High Commissioner for Human Rights: Report of the Mapping Exercise documenting the most serious violations of human rights and international humanitarian law committed within the territory of the Democratic Republic of the Congo between March 1993 and June 2003. 2010. Available at: http://www.unhcr.org/refworld/docid/4ca99bc22.html.

Unaiza Niaz, MD, DPM, FRCPsych
Psychiatric Clinic and Stress Research Center
5A/11, West Avenue, Phase-1, Karachi 75500 (Pakistan)
E-Mail unaizaniaz@gmail.com

Violence against Women in Europe: Magnitude and the Mental Health Consequences Described by Different Data Sources

Karin Helweg-Larsen

National Institute of Public Health, Copenhagen, Denmark

Abstract

Data from a number of different data sources can illustrate the magnitude and nature of violence against women. Some European countries have access to nationwide register data that complement the information obtained by surveys. Danish data on intimate partner violence (IPV) are presented to demonstrate how different data sources may complement each other and serve to monitor the trends in IPV. Traditionally, many countries report lifetime prevalence of IPV even though figures reveal an important difference in the prevalence in younger and elder age groups and, thus, obscure variations and are of limited reliability. The lack of reliable and comparable European data on IPV calls for uniform and repeated data collection in all European countries to identify the magnitude, risk factors and consequences of IPV and to monitor the effect of national policies to combat violence against women. Countries that since the early 2000s have had national action plans tend to report a decline in last year prevalence of IPV. Cross-sectional studies show a strong correlation between violence and mental health problems. A few longitudinal studies point to mental problems as a causal factor for IPV exposure, other studies to bidirectional associations. There is a need for further follow-up studies to enhance our knowledge about how violence acts as a risk factor for mental health problems, and how the risk can be reduced.

Copyright © 2013 S. Karger AG, Basel

It is well documented that exposure to violence may result in physical and mental health problems, and that sex differences exist in correlations between violence and self-reported health problems and health care contacts [1–3]. Since the early 1990's it has been reported that violence is one of the major causes of loss of healthy years among women [4] and is a heavy cost to the society [5–7].

In 1997, the World Health Organization (WHO) Regional Office for Europe chaired a meeting on European strategies to combat violence against women. Among others, the scope was to improve data sources for epidemiological studies on prevalence, risk factors and health consequences of violence against women. It was recommended to include standardized questions on violence exposure in the national health interview surveys (NHIS) that are regularly conducted in most European countries [8]. Fifteen years later, data collection on violence exposure is only integrated in a few NHIS, and an easy accessible tool for describing the public health aspects and monitoring the trends in intimate partner violence (IPV) in different European countries is still missing.

It is essential to have access to reliable and comparable data to conduct analyses of health consequences of violence and to monitor trends in violence in relation to the European policy to combat violence against women.

During the last 10–20 years, various studies have been conducted to document the prevalence and nature of violence against women in several European countries. This includes both general victimization surveys [9, 10] and surveys that specifically target gender-based violence or IPV. The International Violence Against Women Survey, IVAWS, was conducted in Italy, Czech Republic, Denmark, Greece, Poland and Switzerland during 2003–2006 [11]. National surveys have collected data on gender-based violence, for example in Iceland [12], Finland [13, 14], Sweden [15], Norway [16], France [17], Ireland [18] and Spain [19]. Through the EU supported Daphne program, principles have been listed for data collection that could facilitate international comparisons: http://ec.europa.eu/justice_home/daphnetoolkit.hts.

While a number of European countries have conducted national surveys, the results are either not internationally comparable or they are outdated. Figures on the prevalence of violence against women in various European countries are based on very different data sources, different methods for data collection and various definitions of IPV (table 1). These differences may explain why the reported prevalence of violence against women vary in socioculturally similar countries in the European region [20].

In some countries, national surveys on IPV have been conducted repeatedly to describe the trends in violence against women and thereby monitor the impact of national prevention strategies. Such data are also crucial for NGOs and governments to optimize means and resources to cover the needs of survivors of gender-based violence.

Regular data collection on the magnitude and character of IPV in different cultural and socioeconomic settings could also facilitate the identification of modifiable risk factors for IPV. However, it is costly to conduct nationwide surveys, and, hence, few countries have conducted repeated surveys on IPV and thus lack data for trend analyses. A simple and not costly way to get access to trend data is to implement, in the regular NHIS, a few, standardized questions on violence exposure during a well-defined period (last 12 months) and on the relationship to the perpetrator. Since 2000, those questions are included on exposure to physical violence and threats of violence in accordance to Straus' Conflict Tactics Scales [32] in the Danish NHIS.

Table 1. Prevalence of IPV during the last 12 months in selected European countries.

Country	Time period	Number of respondents and age group	IPV, %	Physical violence, %	Sexual abuse/assault, %
England and Wales [1]	2004/2005	13,451	6	5	3
Sweden [2]	2006/2007/2008	18,000 16- to 79-year-olds	1.2	1.1	
Finland [3]	2005	4,464 18- to 74-year-olds	8.6	7.0	2.5
Spain [4]	2006	30,000 18 years +	2.1		
Poland, IVAWS [5]	2004	2,009 18- to 70-year-olds	3	3	1
Denmark; IVAWS	2003	3,589 18- to 70-year-olds	1	1	0.5
Switzerland, IVAWS	2003	1,973 18- to 70-year-olds	1	1	
France [6]	2001	5,908	5.5	2.5	0.9
Ireland	2006	1,483 18 years and older		Severe physical violence 1.4	Severe sexual abuse 0.7
Norway [7]	2006	2,407 20- to 55-year-olds	5.5		1
Denmark [8]	2010	7,500 16- to 79-year-olds	1.6	1.5	1.4

[1] Finney A: Domestic violence, sexual assault and stalkin: findings from the 2004/05 British Crime Survey. London, 2006.
[2] Selin KH: Våld mot kvinnor och män i nära relationer. Våldet karaktär och offrens erfarenheter av kontakter med rättsväendet. Stockholm, Brottsörebyggande rådet, 2009.
[3] Heiskanen M, Piispa M: Violence against women in Finland. Results from two national vitimisation surveys; in Aromaa k, Heiskanen M (eds): Victimisation Surveys in Comparative Perspective. Helsinki, HEUNI, 2008, pp 136–159.
[4] Gobierno de Espana: Annual Report of the National Observatory on Violence against Women. Madrid, Ministerio de Trabaj y Asuntos Sociales, 2007.
[5] Johnson H, Ollus N, Nevala S: Violence against Women. An International Perspective. New York, Springer, 2008.
[6] Jaspard M, Brown F, Condon S: Les violences envers les femmes en France. Une enquete nationale. Paris, La Documentation Francaise, 2003.
[7] Neroien AI, Schei B: Partner violence and health: results from the first national study on violence against women in Norway. Scand J Publ Health 2008;36:161–168.
[8] Helweg-Larsen K: Violence in intimate relationship. The extent, nature and trend in intimate partner violence agaisnt woem and men in Denmark 2010. Copenhagen, National Institute of Public Health and Ministry of Gender Equality, 2012.

At present, the European Union Agency for Fundamental Rights (FRA) is preparing a gender-based violence against women survey based on personal interviews with a random sampling of women in the 27 European Union Member States. The aim is to obtain EU-wide reliable and comparable data on violence against women that can be used for the development of policies and other measures to combat violence against women.

IPV and Mental Health

While it is widely agreed that violence is a strong risk factor for mental health problems among women, few studies have explored the causality between mental problems and exposure to violence. Findings from the WHO Multi-country study report a strong association between exposure to violence and the occurrence of mental problems [21]. However, few studies have explored if mental problems could be an independent risk factor for intimate partner violence [22] or explored the possible bidirectionality in the association between violence exposure and mental problems.

Violence against Women: A Hidden Public Health Problem

For many years, it was obvious that few European countries had access to reliable and comparable data that enabled an assessment of the magnitude and characteristics of violence against women in the region of Europe. In 1999, the European Women's Lobby published an overview, 'Unveiling the hidden data on domestic violence in the European Union', that drew attention to domestic violence against women as the most frequent of all forms of violence, and emphasized that official statistics including crime statistics, revealed very little on the issue of domestic violence. An exception at that time was Spain [23].

In the beginning of the 2000s, it was announced that France, Belgium, Denmark, Germany, Sweden and Finland would implement systematic data collection on victims as well as the ongoing data collection on alleged offenders in police reported cases of violence and register these data in the crime statistics. It would strongly facilitate analyses of police reported violence against women. By the end of 2006, a total of 28 out of 35 European countries had implemented a systematic recording of the sex of the victim in the crime statistics, and 23 countries recorded the relationship between the victim and the alleged offender of violence [24].

In 2002, the Council of Europe adopted the Recommendation on the protection of women against violence as the first international legal document to frame a comprehensive approach towards overcoming violence against women. It expresses a consensus on general principles in services for victims, legislation, policing, intervention with perpetrators, awareness-raising, education, and training as well as data collection.

The recommendation was followed by an overview of national statistics and of nationally representative survey data on violence against women in the different member states up to 2006. The review found that systematic data collection of emergency department contacts due to violence was implemented in 11 European countries. Twenty countries had conducted nationally representative surveys that provided figures on the prevalence of different forms of violence against women, but 14 countries had no data [24].

Few European countries have access to crime statistics, nationwide data on emergency department contacts and national survey data that can be merged and thus describe different aspects of violence against women. Denmark is one of those countries. The Danish experiences of utilizing different data sources are reported in this chapter to illustrate how various aspects of gender-based violence may be better understood by the combination of register and survey data.

In Denmark, all data in the national health and population registers, which also include police reported victim statistics and the National Patient Register of all hospital contacts, are linked to the unique personal identification number. The regular NHIS also record each respondent's personal identification number. This number makes it possible to link information in different data sources at the individual level for research questions [25]. Danish legislation permits, on strict conditions, to merge register-based and survey-based data and, thus, allows researchers to conduct cross-sectional and follow-up studies on encrypted data from various register databases linked to survey data [26]. This possibility has been used in a number of recent studies to describe the socio-demographic and psychosocial profiles of victims of violence and the cost of violence against women [7, 27–30].

Identification of IPV by Different Data Sources

Even though IPV is common and a serious threat to women's health and social situation, it only constitutes one part of all violence against women. The proportion of overall violence against women attributable to IPV differs in different data sources. For example, from a total of 4,000 police-reported cases of violence against women in Denmark in 2010, in about 500 cases (12%) this violence was committed by a person living in the same residence as the victim, hence cases of violence in close relationships. From the total of 6,000 emergency department contacts due to violence against women in 2010, about 3,000 (50%) had occurred in a residential area, and it was estimated that in two thirds of these cases, the offender was a current partner or former partner. In the national health interview survey 2010 (NHIS 2010), 4.4% of 16- to 74-year-old women reported exposure to any type of physical violence during the last 12 months, and 1.5% reported physical violence by a current or former partner. Thus, depending on the data source, IPV constituted from 12% to about 34% of all reported cases of physical violence against women.

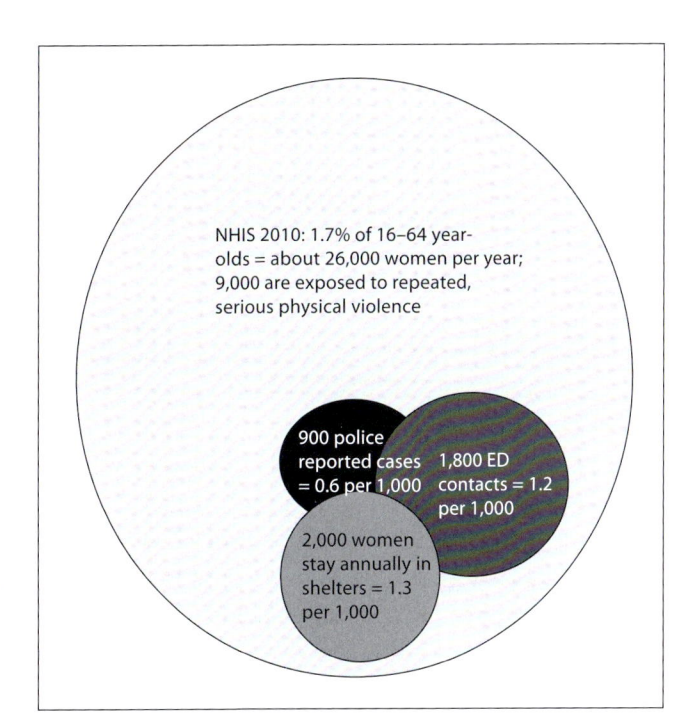

Fig. 1. The annual prevalence among women aged 16–64 years of police recorded intimate partner violence, emergency department contacts, stay in shelters and self-reported exposure to intimate partner violence in Denmark, 2010. NHIS: National Health Interview Survey, conducted in 2010 among 6,500 women.

NHIS 2010: 1.7% of 16–64 year-olds = about 26,000 women per year; 9,000 are exposed to repeated, serious physical violence

900 police reported cases = 0.6 per 1,000

1,800 ED contacts = 1.2 per 1,000

2,000 women stay annually in shelters = 1.3 per 1,000

There are important differences in the number of victims and types of violence against women depending on which data source is used as the reference. Figure 1 shows the prevalence of IPV in Denmark in 2010 based on data in Victim Statistics, the National Patient Register, shelter statistics and results in the NHIS 2010 concerning self-reported exposure to physical violence by a current or former partner. The figures demonstrate that the prevalence of self-reported exposure to IPV as reported by the health interview survey is about 30 times higher than the prevalence of IPV reported to the police and about 15 times higher than the prevalence of emergency department contacts due to IPV. About 2,000 women, 0.1% of 16- to 64-year-olds, are housed annually in a shelter for victims of violence, and in about 100 % the violence was committed by a current or ex-partner.

In a given year, the same incident of violence may both be reported to the police and result in a contact with an emergency department (ED), and the victim may also have participated in an annual national survey and answered 'Yes' to questions about violence exposure. By merging data in the three different data sources, it was shown that about 34% of women registered in the Danish Victims Statistics were also registered in the National Patient Register with an ED contact due to violence, and about 50% of ED contacts due to violence also had been reported to the police [33].

Data in the NHIS 2010 were merged with register data and revealed that only a small percentage, 4%, of women who had answered 'Yes' to exposure to violence, had also reported a case of violence to the police or contacted an emergency department due to violence. The two register sources for reporting prevalence of IPV, are, thus, – as would be expected – more consistent among themselves than are register data and self-reported data.

Prevalence of Intimate Partner Violence in Europe

The majority of European countries have conducted at least one national survey on violence against women. Most of these surveys on violence focus on IPV, defined as physical and sexual violence by a current or former partner, while other surveys relate to the definition by the WHO: Any behavior within an intimate relationship that causes physical, psychological or sexual harm to those in the relationship. It includes acts of physical aggression, psychological abuse, forced intercourse or other forms of sexual coercion and various controlling behaviors [1].

Many surveys report exposure to violence through the duration of a close relationship or they include any violence by a partner since the age of 16 or 18. Most surveys record both lifetime prevalence and occurrence during the last 12 months.

In the late 1990s and at the beginning of the 2000s, some European countries reported a 20% lifetime prevalence of threats and physical and/or sexual violence from a current or previous partner [13, 17, 31], whereas much higher figures were reported in other countries, e.g. 35% in Sweden among women, who were or had been in an intimate relationship [15].

Many factors, other than methodological differences in sampling, definition of violence and measures, influence the reported lifetime prevalence of IPV, including: recall bias, changes over the years in the interpretation of violent acts, reactions to domestic conflicts and acceptance/nonacceptance of partner violence as a private problem. These factors may partly explain that in general older women report much lower lifetime prevalence than younger women.

In the Danish NHIS, a low validity in the recording of lifetime prevalence of violence is found. In the NHIS 2000, the reported lifetime prevalence of any physical violence among women varied from 31% among 16- to 24-year-olds to 5% among 67 years and older women, thus declining strongly with age [33]. Consequently, we found it of low value to report life time prevalence, and at present only record the prevalence of exposure to violence during the last 12 months by the NHIS 2010 [34].

Table 1 presents selected figures from a number of relatively recent European victimization surveys that have recorded the prevalence of IPV during the last 12 months. In some countries, different forms of harassment, degrading treatment, stalking and other psychological maltreatment by a partner are included, whereas in other countries only physical violence by a current or former partner.

In general, surveys focused on VAW report a higher prevalence of violence exposure than general victimization surveys. For example, the reported prevalence of IPV during the last 12 months varies from 8.6% in Finland to about 1% in Denmark and Switzerland. Similarly, Sweden reported a low prevalence in the 2006–2008 victim surveys conducted by the crime prevention council [35], which greatly differ from the previous 9% annual prevalence reported by the Swedish national VAW survey in the late 1990s [15].

The age of the study population influences the reported prevalence, e.g. the Norwegian survey in 2006 included only 20- to 55-year-olds and reported a relatively high prevalence of IPV, 5.5%, compared to surveys that include 16- to 74-year-olds, e.g. in Sweden and Denmark.

The reported prevalence in the European countries is based on different samples composed of different age groups, survey methods vary from face-to-face interviews, internet-based surveys to telephone interviews, and the definition and measure of IPV differ significantly. Physical partner violence is often recorded by Straus' conflict tactics scales that include minor assaults like being pushed, shaken or hit. The recorded prevalence of IPV seldom distinguishes between one-time exposure to minor physical violence in a given year and repeated exposure to more severe violence such as being kicked, punched, strangled or attacked with weapons. In Denmark, among women aged 16–74 years, the prevalence of physical partner violence last year was 1.5%; however, if IPV is more strictly defined as repeated exposure to more than minor physical violence, the prevalence is about 0.5%.

Trends in Intimate Partner Violence

To illuminate the trends in IPV some countries, as for example Spain, annually report the number of murders committed by partners and regularly conduct population based surveys that document IPV exposure among women [19]. The British Crime Survey is also conducted regularly and has with intervals focused on IPV and published data on a declining trend in IPV [36]. In Finland, the national survey on violence against women first conducted in 1997/1998 was repeated in 2005, and it is reported that intimate partner violence declined from 8.6% in 1997 to 7.9% in 2005, while violence by an ex-partner declined from 7.0 to 6.1% [14].

Few countries combine register and survey data to monitor the trends in both cases reported to public institutions and self-reported IPV. In Denmark, the share of IPV among all police-reported cases of violence against women decreased from 16% in 2004/2005 to 11% in 2008/2009, the number of hospital contacts due to violence in a residential area was about 3,200 in 2005 and 2,800 in 2010, and the last year prevalence of self-reported exposure to IPV declined from 1.6% in 2005 to 1.4% in 2010 among women 16 years and older [34]. The same tendency is recorded by the national surveys in Spain and Sweden, where national policies and target action plans to combat IPV have been implemented since the beginning of the 2000s.

Violence and Mental Health

During the last 20–25 years, a large number of studies have analyzed correlations between exposure to IPV and physical and mental health problems. The WHO multi-country on women's health and domestic violence against women conducted between 2000 and 2003 found that for all settings combined, women who reported partner violence at least once in their life reported significantly more emotional distress, suicidal thoughts, and suicidal attempts than nonabused women [21].

Violence against women is a major public health problem, which affects all of society, and causes a significantly higher use of health care services, including mental health services, among victims of violence compared to nonvictims.

This was one of the results that came out of a study of the health care costs of violence against women in Denmark. In a well-defined population of female victims of violence, we computed the attributable costs, i.e. the excess health care costs for victims compared to an identified reference population of nonvictims. Only costs within the health care sector were included, i.e. somatic and psychiatric hospital costs, costs within the primary health care sector and costs of prescription medications. We tested whether socioeconomic status, multiple episodes of violence, and psychiatric contacts had any impact on health care costs. It was found that the health care costs were about EUR 1,800 higher for victims of violence than for nonvictims per year, driven mostly by higher psychiatric costs and multiple episodes of violence [7].

The Oslo Health Study 2000/2001 recently reported the results of analyses of the prescription of psychotropic drugs to women who had experienced IPV and found that these women compared to other women more often received prescriptions of potentially addictive drugs [36].

The reported correlation of violence and mental health is mostly based on cross-sectional studies and few have analyzed if mental health problems apart from severe mental illness are risk factors for exposure to violence. Based on the Danish NHIS in 2000 and 2005 that included re-interview of respondents, we identified women who in 2000 reported mental health problems but no exposure to violence and who in the 2005 interview reported exposure to violence during the last 12 months compared to women with no mental health complaints in 2000 [unpubl. data]. A correlation was found between mental health complaints and risk of exposure to IPV but not to other forms of violence. Similar results have been reported by other longitudinal studies [37, 38].

The associations between mental health problems and risk of exposure to IPV might very well be bidirectional. Mental problems and consequent prescription of tranquilizers and other psychotropic drugs may have an influence on intimate relationships and themselves be risk factors for inadequate reactions to marital conflicts. Furthermore, the high prevalence of mental health disorders among victims of IPV might also be correlated to their exposure to adverse childhood experiences. Associations between child abuse and/or witnessing IPV during childhood and women's health, adult IPV exposure, and health care have been reported [39].

In the implementation of effective prevention strategies, there is a need for further knowledge on adverse experiences during childhood and adolescence as predictors of problems in intimate relationships related to mental health problems and risk of IPV. There is also a need for identification of factors that increase the risk of mental health problems among victims of IPV.

References

1 Krug E, Mercy J, Dahlberg L, Zwi A: The world report on violence and health. Lancet 2002;360: 1083.
2 Sundaram V, Helweg-Larsen K, Laursen B, Bjerregaard P: Physical violence, self-rated health, and morbidity: is gender significant for victimisation? J Epidemiol Community Health 2004;58:65–70.
3 Helweg-Larsen K, Kruse M: Violence against women and consequent health problems: a register-based study. Scand J Publ Health 2003;31:51–57.
4 Heise L: Violence against women: the hidden health burden. World Health Stat Q 1993;46:78–85.
5 Walby S: The Cost of Domestic Violence. London: www.womenandequalityunit.gov.uk; 2004.
6 Waters HR, Hyder AA, Rajkotia Y, Basu S, Butchart A: The costs of interpersonal violence – an international review. Health Policy 2005;73:303–315.
7 Kruse M, Sørensen J, Brønnum-Hansen H, Helweg-Larsen K: The health care costs of violence against women. J Interpers Violence 2011;26:3494–3508.
8 WHO: European Strategies to Combat Violence against Women. Copenhagen, WHO, 1998.
9 UN's Economic Commission for Europe: Manual on Victimization Surveys. Geneva, United Nations, 2010.
10 Walby S, Allen J: Domestic Violence, Sexual Assault and Stalking: Findings from the British Crime Survey. London, Home Officer Research, Development and Statistics Department, 2004.
11 Johnson H, Ollus N, Nevala S: Violence against Women. An International Perspective. New York, Springer, 2008.
12 Olafsdottir H: Violence against Women in Iceland. Reykjavik, Ministry of Justice, 1997.
13 Heiskanen M, Piispa M: Faith, Hope and Battering. Statistics Finland. Helsinki, 1998.
14 Heiskanen M, Piispa M: Violence against women in Finland. Results from two national victimisation surveys; in Aromaa K, Heiskanen M (eds): Victimisation Surveys in Comparative Perspective. Helsinki, HEUNI, 2008, pp 136–59.
15 Lundgren E, Heimer G, Westerstrand J, Kallokoski AM: Slagen dam. Mäns våld mot kvinnor i jämställda Sverige – en omfangsundersökning. Stockholm, 2001.
16 Neroien AI, Schei B: Partner violence and health: results from the first national study on violence against women in Norway. Scand J Public Health 2008;36:161–168.
17 Jaspard M, Brown F, Condon S: Les violences envers les femmes en France. Une enquête nationale. Paris, La documentation française, 2003.
18 Watson D, Parsons S: Domestic Abuse of Women and Men in Ireland. Dublin, Government Publication Office, 2005.
19 Gobierno de Espana: Annual Report of the National Observatory on Violence against Women. Madrid, Ministerio de Trabajo y Asuntos Sociales, 2007.
20 Jaspard M: Des comparaisons européennes encore incertaines; in Jaspard M, Condon S (eds): Nommer et compter les violences envers les femmes en Europe. Enjeux scientifiques et politiques. Paris, Institut de démographie Université Paris, 2005, pp 81–91.
21 Ellsberg M, Jansen HA, Heise L, Watts CH, Garcia-Moreno C: Intimate partner violence and women's physical and mental health in the WHO multi-country study on women's health and domestic violence: an observational study. Lancet 2008;371: 1165–1172.

22 Lehrer JA, Buka S, Gortmaker S, Shrier LA: Depressive symptomatology as a predictor of exposure to intimate partner violence among US female adolescents and young adults. Arch Pediatr Adolesc Med 2006;160:270–276.
23 Collin M, De Troy C: Unveiling the Hidden Data on Domestic Violence in the EU. Bruxelles, The European Women's Lobby, 1999.
24 Hagemann-White C, Bohn S: Protecting women against violence. Analytical study on the effective implementation of Recommendation (2002)5 on the protection of women against violence in Council of Europe member states. Council of Europe, 2007.
25 Thygesen LC, Ersboll AK: Danish population-based registers for public health and health-related welfare research: introduction to the supplement. Scand J Public Health 2011;39(7 suppl):8–10.
26 Davidsen M, Kjoller M, Helweg-Larsen K: The Danish National Cohort Study (DANCOS). Scand J Publ Health 2011;39(7 suppl):131–135.
27 Albrektsen SB, Thomsen JL, Aalund O, Breiting VB, Danielsen L, Helweg-Larsen K, et al: Injuries due to deliberate violence against women. The Copenhagen Study Group. Forensic Sci Int 1989;41:181–191.
28 Helweg-Larsen K, Kruse M: Men's Violence against Women. The Extent, Characteristics and Measures to Eliminate Violence. Copenhagen, National Institute of Public Health, 2004.
29 Helweg-Larsen K, Sorensen J, Bronnum-Hansen H, Kruse M: Risk factors for violence exposure and attributable healthcare costs: results from the Danish national health interview surveys. Scand J Public Health 2011;39:10–16.
30 Kruse M, Sorensen J, Bronnum-Hansen H, Helweg-Larsen K: Identifying victims of violence using register-based data. Scand J Public Health 2010;38:611–617.
31 Gillioz L, De Puy J, Ducret V: Domination et violence envers la femme dans le couple. Lausanne, Editions Payot, 1997.
32 Straus MA, Douglas EM: A short form of the Revised Conflict Tactics Scales, and typologies for severity and mutuality. Violence Vict 2004;19:507–520.
33 Helweg-Larsen K: Vold og seksuelle overgreb. København, Statens Institut for Folkesundhed, 2002.
34 Helweg-Larsen K: Violence in intimate relationship. The extent, nature and trend in intimate partner violence against women and men in Denmark 2010. Copenhagen, National Institute of Public Health and Ministry of Gender Equality, 2012.
35 Brå brottsörebyggende rådet: Våld mot kvinnor och män i nära relationer. Våldets karakter och offrens erfarenheter av kontakter med rättsväsendet. (Violence against women in intimate relationships. The experiences of victims contact to judicials.) Stockholm, 2009.
36 Stene LE, Dyb G, Tverdal A, Jacobsen GW, Schei B: Intimate partner violence and prescription of potentially addictive drugs: prospective cohort study of women in the Oslo Health Study. BMJ Open 2012;2:e000614.
37 Finney A: Domestic Violence, Sexual Assault and Stalking: Findings from the 2004/05 British Crime Survey. London, 2006.
38 McPherson MD, Delva J, Cranford JA: A longitudinal investigation of intimate partner violence among mothers with mental illness. Psychiatr Serv 2007;58:675–680.
39 Cannon EA, Bonomi AE, Anderson ML, Rivara FP, Thompson RS: Adult health and relationships outcomes among women with abuse experiences during childhood. Violence Vict 2010;25:291–305.

Karin Helweg-Larsen
National Institute of Public Health
Oster Farimagsgade 5
DK–1399 Copenhagen (Denmark)
E-Mail khl@niph.dk

Intimate Partner Violence as a Risk Factor for Mental Health Problems in South Africa

Rachel Jewkes

Gender and Health Research Unit, Medical Research Council, Pretoria, South Africa

Abstract

Gender-based violence (GBV) is an important risk factor for ill health among adult women in South Africa, particularly mental health problems. Adult women in the general population who have experienced intimate partner violence (IPV) and rape have a much higher prevalence of depression, PTSD, binge drinking and suicidal thoughts and attempts. Longitudinal research is needed to determine the temporal sequence of GBV exposure and mental health problems. Analysis of the Stepping Stones Study cohort shows that adolescent women without mental health morbidity exposed to physical or sexual IPV were significantly more likely to develop depression, alcohol abuse or suicidal thoughts over two years of observation. Emotional abuse increased the risk of depression among all women and in those with physical or sexual IPV exposure. Cross-sectional analyses show a wider range of forms of GBV associated with mental health problems, including a cumulative effect of non-partner rape and emotional abuse as well as sexual or physical IPV. The analysis shows that mostly mental health impact of GBV occurs relatively contemporaneously and if this does not happen women will be resilient. The population-based data indicate that in the absence of mental health treatment the burden of ill health remains substantial, although much depression is self-limiting.

Copyright © 2013 S. Karger AG, Basel

Background

Gender-based violence is a risk factor for mental ill health. In South Africa, interpersonal violence is the second most important cause of loss of disability adjusted life years (DALYS), and in women 21% of depression, 14% of anxiety disorders and 36% of suicides are attributed to IPV and 8.9% of depression, 24% of PTSD and 14% of suicides to child sexual abuse [1]. IPV is also important in alcohol use, drug use, and panic disorders [1].

These estimates depend on the availability of population-based data on women's mental health and exposure to forms of gender-based violence. In research terms these are contested terrains. Gender-based violence prevalence estimates are highly sensitive to methods, and using fewer, better trained and supported interviewers and multiple questions that ask about specified violent acts results in the highest levels of reporting. Estimates of mental health prevalence depend on the screening instrument used, and decisions around use of scale cut points (if any). Generally, surveys use screening tools for symptomatology, rather than diagnostic clinical interviews, and so findings have an uncertain relationship with mental health diagnoses. Manifestations of mental ill health often intersect, and may compound each other, but it is also true that not all women develop mental health problems after experiencing gender-based violence. Understanding who is at risk is critical.

In this chapter, we review population-based findings from South Africa on associations between mental ill health and gender-based violence. We examine in more detail forms of gender-based violence as risk factors for mental ill health in a longitudinal dataset of adolescent women and we reflect on the factors that influence whether exposed women will develop mental ill health, given that they do not all do so.

Population-Based Research on Gender-Based Violence and Mental Health

The most recent South African population-based data on associations between gender-based violence and mental health was gathered in a household survey of women living in the province of Gauteng. This was conducted by the NGO Genderlinks with technical assistance from the Medical Research Council [2]. A randomly selected sample of 511 women aged 18 years and over was interviewed. The women fell fairly equally into three age groups, 18–29 years, 30–44 years and over 44 years. Most were Black African South Africans (86%) and over half were unemployed (56%). Overall 37.7% of women had experienced physical or sexual IPV in their lifetime. A third (33.1%) had experienced physical IPV and 18.8% experienced sexual IPV. In all 12.2% of women had been raped by a man who was not their husband or boyfriend. Women completed the Centre for Epidemiological Studies on Depression (CES-D) [3] to assess depressive symptomatology, they were asked about suicidal thoughts in the last 4 weeks and about whether they had ever attempted to take their lives, about binge drinking in the past year, and PTSD symptoms were assessed using the Hopkins Symptom Checklist-25 [4].

The findings are presented in table 1. High levels of depressive symptoms (a score of 21+ on the CES-D) were twice as common among women exposed to physical or sexual IPV than those who were not exposed. There was also a suggestion that they were more common among women who had been raped (p = 0.08). A lifetime history of having ever attempted suicide was reported by nearly 1 in 5 women who had experienced IPV and 1 in 4 of those raped. These proportions were significantly higher than that found among nonexposed women. A quarter of women who had experienced IPV or rape disclosed binge drinking alcohol monthly or more often, which was significantly more common than among those not exposed.

Table 1. Indicators of the health status of women who have experienced physical or sexual IPV or been raped by a nonpartner, among 511 women in Gauteng Province, South Africa

	Any sexual or physical IPV			Any nonpartner rape		
	% exposed	% nonexposed	aOR* 95% CI	% exposed	% nonexposed	aOR* 95% CI
High levels of depressive symptoms (CES-D 21+)	34.2	15.3	3.13 (1.95, 5.05)	31.3	21.6	1.66 (0.89, 3.09)
Ever attempted suicide	19.1	6.4	3.55 (1.94, 6.50)	25.0	9.2	3.09 (1.58, 6.06)
Suicidal thoughts in past 4 weeks	10.6	4.7	2.63 (1.24, 5.56)	14.3	6.5	2.44 (1.04, 5.73)
Has 5 or more drinks on one occasion weekly or monthly	24.7	7.2	4.32 (2.43, 7.69)	27.4	11.9	2.86 (1.46, 5.61)
PTSD-DSM-IV score >2.5	15.4	9.2	1.84 (0.97, 3.51)	28.1	8.8	4.53 (2.12, 9.68)

* Age and race adjusted.

More than a quarter of women who had been raped and 15% of those who had experienced IPV had symptomatology indicative of a diagnosis of post-traumatic stress disorder (PTSD). These proportions were significantly higher than those found among nonexposed women.

These findings indicate a particularly high burden of mental ill health among women who have been raped or experienced IPV, but they also show a high prevalence among all women. In South Africa, as in many developing countries, mental health services are a neglected sector of the public health system. Those services that are available focus predominantly on care for people with psychosis. Most women who experience depression and PTSD do not have access to any form of mental health care.

A national study of 2,550 women examined associations between PTSD and partner violence and non-partner rape in South Africa using a diagnostic interview. Its findings are somewhat hard to interpret as it used a rather limited measure of violence exposure ('Have you ever been badly beaten by a partner?') resulting in 13.6% prevalence, which is well below most other estimates [2, 5, 6]. The association between PTSD and IPV was strong, OR 3.2 (95% CI 1.48–7.10) [7]. Their rape measure was also a single item and resulted in a low prevalence of rape reported (3.7%), but the association with PTSD was strong, OR 5.6 (95% CI 2.87–10.78). The authors highlight the co-exposure between IPV or rape and other trauma exposure that might be important in their PTSD symptomatology.

South African Adolescent Women: Longitudinal Analyses of Mental Health and Gender-Based Violence

Cross-sectional data is generally viewed with some caution in understanding causation because of inherent uncertainty of timing of exposure and health outcome. Whilst current mental health status is often measured, uncertainty about time of onset of the mental health problem remains for conditions that are not self-limiting. The importance of this was highlighted by a finding that women who are depressed are at greater risk of IPV than other women over a period of 12 months of follow-up [8]. Thus, longitudinal research is particularly valuable.

Research in South Africa on adolescent women substantially advanced understanding of gender-based violence as a risk factor for mental ill health. The cluster randomized-controlled trial evaluation of the HIV behavioral intervention Stepping Stones generated a longitudinal dataset of interviews with what was initially 1,415 women volunteers, followed up for 2 years. This dataset has been used for a number of cross-sectional and longitudinal analyses that are unrelated to the primary goal of the study, with the longitudinal analyses adjusted for trial treatment arm allocation and study design. At each round of interviews women participants were assessed for depression using the CES-D scale (measuring symptomatology in the last week), asked about suicidal thoughts in the previous 4 weeks, and their alcohol use was assessed using the AUDIT scale (alcohol use over a year). They were also asked about exposure to emotional, physical and sexual partner violence using a slightly modified version of the instrument developed for the WHO's multi-country study. They were asked about rape by a non-partner and gang rape and at baseline about abuse in childhood (including sexual abuse). The sample was not population-based, so the prevalence estimates cannot be generalized to the South African population of that age, and it is vulnerable to healthy volunteer effects, which may underestimate the prevalence of mental health problems. However, there are generally high levels of reporting of violence, which is partly due to its collection by small numbers of very carefully supervised and supported interviewers. A full account of the study methodology can be found elsewhere [9]. The women in the study were aged 15–26 at recruitment (mean age 18.6) and almost all (98%) were in school at the start of the study. At baseline, experiences of different forms of partner violence overlapped. Twelve percent of women had experienced only emotional abuse in their lifetime, 28% had experienced emotional abuse with physical or sexual abuse and 13% experienced physical or sexual abuse without emotional abuse.

Depression
At baseline, 10.9% of women had high levels of depressive symptoms (CES-D cut point 21+) and a further 9.6% had moderately high levels (CES-D score 16–20). Using multivariable regression modeling adjusting for age, socioeconomic status and social support, depression (cut point 21+) was associated with sexual abuse in childhood:

OR 1.65 (95% CI 1.10, 2.46; p = 0.015), with experiencing more than one episode of physical or sexual IPV (OR 1.69, 95% CI 1.10, 2.60; p = 0.017), and experience of emotional abuse: OR 1.74 (95% CI 1.14, 2.66; p = 0.01). Women with more power within the relationship (compared to those with the least), measured on a modified version of the sexual relationship power scale [10], were less likely to be depressed: OR 0.40 (95% CI 0.19, 0.83; p = 0.014).

In this sample having been raped by a nonpartner was not associated with depression at baseline in the multivariable model after adjusting for other violence exposures. However, 22.4% of women who had been raped by a nonpartner were depressed, compared to 10.3% of those who had not been (p = 0.003). Part of the explanation was that two thirds of women who had been raped by a nonpartner reported emotional IPV. When the overlap between these exposures was examined, the women who had experienced both had more than three times the risk of being depressed: OR 3.29 (95% CI 1.52, 7.14; p = 0.003), a risk much higher than that found among those with emotional abuse alone: OR 1.92 (95% CI 1.17, 2.76; p = 0.008).

Over the period of follow-up 1,245 women (88.5% of the original sample) were re-interviewed, either at 12 or 24 months time points, or at both. Using a CES-D cut point of 21 and over, which is a level of symptomatology that has a high likelihood of equating to clinical depression, 211 women were assessed as 'depressed' during the follow-up period. One third of those depressed during follow-up (n = 45) were depressed at baseline, i.e. most of those who had high levels of depressive symptomatology at baseline had recovered during the period of follow up. To examine the relationship between IPV and depression we used a measure of IPV that compared reporting more than one episode or act of physical or sexual IPV with experience of just one act or of none. This measure has been shown in multiple datasets in South Africa to be a better predictor of health outcomes than 'ever' exposure. The measure was a lifetime measure at baseline and one of exposure 'since the last interview' for assessments during the follow-up period. In all, 39.5% of women had experienced physical or sexual partner violence at baseline, and 24.5% had had more than one episode or act. 24.1% experienced more than one act of physical or sexual IPV during follow up when nondepressed, i.e. before reporting symptomatology indicative of depression (if this was developed), or the last interview when nondepressed.

At follow-up, 36.5% of women with depression had had a more severe IPV exposure during follow-up and 25.5% of women with the more severe IPV exposure also had high levels of depressive symptomatology. For the longitudinal analysis, the population of interest was women who had not been depressed at baseline. Among those not depressed at baseline these proportions were very similar, 34.9 and 22.8%.

Using Poisson regression modeling of the incidence of depression, adjusted for study design, other associated factors and person years of follow-up, we found that the incidence among those exposed to physical or sexual intimate partner violence at baseline was significantly elevated (IRR 1.84, 95% CI 1.30, 2.62, p = 0.001). It was also elevated among those who had ever experienced emotional abuse at baseline: IRR

1.46 (95% CI 1.03, 2.09; p = 0.034). Calculation of the attributable fraction revealed that 16.3% of depression among these young women could have been avoided in the absence of exposure to physical or sexual partner violence and 14.9% could have been avoided without emotional abuse. We examined whether baseline exposure to physical or sexual IPV (either ever or the greater severity measure), child sexual abuse, low power in the relationship and sexual violence from a nonpartner were risk factors for depression during follow-up among the previously nondepressed and found they were not. Emotional abuse, in the absence of sexual and physical abuse, had a lingering impact on depression, but other forms of violence did not. Put differently, if women are going to become depressed after physical or sexual partner violence, child sex abuse, nonpartner rape or because of low relationship power, it will manifest itself contemporaneously.

A further question of importance, given that a high proportion of exposed young women did not develop depression, is what predicted becoming depressed among the IPV-exposed previously not depressed. A range of social and demographic variables were examined including multiple measures of social support such as nonorphanhood, being active in church, community cohesiveness score and club membership. The multivariable regression analysis showed that there is a much higher risk of depression among women with IPV exposure who had lost both parents (double orphans) (OR 7.68, 95% CI 1.60, 36.95, p = 0.011). In total, 62.5% of IPV-exposed double orphans became depressed, and they comprised 9% of all depressed women with IPV exposure. Exposure to emotional abuse before baseline also predicted the development of depression in this subgroup (OR 2.03, 95% CI 1.04, 3.94; p = 0.037). We also examined whether re-victimization was a risk factor for depression among those experiencing IPV. Neither prior rape by a nonpartner, nor child sex abuse, physical or sexual IPV predicted depression in the more severely IPV-exposed adolescents.

Thus, more severe exposure to physical and sexual IPV was a risk factor for depression in this longitudinal study, with effect relatively contemporaneous. Emotional abuse has a more lingering impact. Among the abused women, orphans who lacked parental support at home were the most vulnerable to depression. Perhaps because in the absence of parents, even more was invested on dating and this may have rendered the young women more vulnerable to disappointment when faced with lack of love expressed in the use of violence. Women who had experienced prior emotional abuse were also more vulnerable.

Suicide

Suicidal thoughts are relatively uncommon among young women, and so the power to examine associations with these and a range of potential risk and protective factors is limited in small or medium-sized studies. They are a sign of mental distress, but their relationship with suicide attempts is uncertain. Suicide was an important problem in the age group and 3 women did take their lives during the study, only 1 of these had revealed suicidal thoughts at her last interview. One of the suicides was of a young woman who had been raped and was distressed. The trigger for the suicide was her mother being diagnosed with HIV.

Among 1,408 women providing information for the Stepping Stones baseline, 37 had had suicidal thoughts in the month before the interview (2.6%; 95% CI 1.7–3.5). Multivariable logistic regression modeling showed that there was an association between reporting these and having ever experienced more than one episode of physical and/or sexual intimate partner violence (OR 3.93, 95% CI 2.02, 7.67; $p < 0.0001$). No association was found for child sex abuse, emotional abuse or relationship power.

When examined as an isolated exposure, rape by a nonpartner was not associated with suicidality at baseline, but when the exposure was examined with co-occurrence of physical or sexual IPV a strong association between nonpartner rape and suicidality was visible. The odds of suicidality among those women who were dual exposed was 9.57 (95% CI 2.86, 32.05; $p < 0.0001$), compared to nonexposed women.

During the follow-up, 1,239 women provided information on whether they had had suicidal thoughts in the previous 4 weeks. Forty-four women had had these, and among them 40.9% had exposure to more than one episode or act of physical or sexual IPV at baseline (41% of the previously nonsuicidal). In all, 6% of women with IPV exposure developed suicidal thoughts. Suicidality was much less common than having high levels of depressive symptomatology, but the two overlapped: 56.8% of those with suicidal thoughts were depressed (using the 21+ cut point) and 12.0% of those depressed had thoughts of suicide.

Exposure to severe IPV during the follow-up period was an important risk factor for suicidality. Poisson regression modeling of the incidence of suicidality, adjusted for study design, baseline suicidality, other associated factors and person years of follow-up, showed the incidence among those exposed to intimate partner violence to be significantly elevated (IRR 2.26, 95% CI 1.18, 4.32, $p = 0.014$). The population-attributable fraction was 22.9%, indicating that nearly a quarter of suicidality would have been avoided by the absence of severe IPV. The contemporaneous nature of exposure and mental health impact was again shown by the absence of impact of baseline IPV exposure, prior nonpartner rape, child abuse, emotional abuse and low relationship power on suicidality during follow-up.

Again the question was examined as to whether socioeconomic factors, social support or multiple abuse exposures are associated with the development of suicidality in IPV-exposed adolescents. This analysis showed that some aspects of social support were very important protective (or in their absence vulnerability) factors. Women active in their church membership were much less likely to have suicidal thoughts (OR 0.29, 95% CI 0.10, 0.82, $p = 0.019$) and those who were maternal orphans were at much greater risk (OR 3.18, 95% CI 1.00, 10.08, $p = 0.05$). 14.7% of all maternal orphans with IPV exposure had suicidal thoughts. This amounted to 31.3% of all IPV-exposed young women with suicidal thoughts. Other social and demographic characteristics (such as socioeconomic status or having had a pregnancy or perceived community support) were not risk or protective factors. Measures of multiple prior trauma exposure also were not risk factors for suicidality among IPV-exposed, previously not suicidal women.

Alcohol Abuse

In the female study population levels of alcohol abuse were generally low. This is not a social norm for South African women but rather reflects the fact that the women in the study were largely teenagers, still in school and not earning. Not drinking is seen as socially desirable for women in South Africa, but alcohol consumption is highly prevalent and binge drinking is very widespread among men and women.

At the baseline interviews just 47 women (3.3%) of the sample disclosed levels of problem drinking. This was strongly associated with exposure to all forms of gender-based violence examined in the study after adjusting for age, socio-economic status and study design. The adjusted OR for exposure to more than one act of child sexual abuse was 3.76 (95% CI 1.76, 8.03, p = 0.001), for more than one act of physical or sexual abuse was 2.25 (95% CI 1.08, 4.68, p = 0.030) and for emotional abuse in the past year (but not prior) was 2.80 (95% CI 1.34, 5.88, p = 0.006). The association with non-partner sexual violence was in the opposite direction, OR 0.18 (95% CI 0.04, 0.86, p = 0.031), possibly reflecting changes in behavior characterized by social withdrawal after nonpartner rape.

In all, 65 of 1,252 women were assessed as having problem drinking at 12 or 24 months using the AUDIT scale cut point of 8 [11]. Among these 56.9% had experienced more than one episode or act of sexual or physical IPV. Among those with IPV, 12.2% developed a drinking problem. IPV was the most important risk factor for problem drinking among women in this dataset. The incidence rate among those exposed to IPV was IRR 4.53 (95% CI 2.61, 7.86, p < 0.0001). The attributable fraction calculation showed that nearly half (42.6%) of problem drinking would have been prevented in the absence of IPV, if the assumption is made that the IPV preceded the drinking problems. Although the analysis was done on women without a prior alcohol problem, there remains some uncertainty about whether the violence preceded drinking because violence is known to commonly occur during fights when drunk. Once again the association with problem drinking was mostly contemporaneous, and neither prior IPV exposure, nor non-partner sexual violence, child sexual abuse, emotional abuse, or low relationship power were risk factors for alcohol abuse prospectively among women without a drinking problem.

The question of what predicts problem drinking among those exposed to IPV again arose. Exploration of social support and demographic factors, and a range of re-victimization measures failed to show any that were associated with alcohol abuse among IPV-exposed women. It is therefore likely that unmeasured specific context factors, such as peer drinking practices, and genetic factors may explain engagement in problem drinking in women experiencing IPV.

Advancing Understanding of Gender-Based Violence as a Risk Factor for Mental Health Problems in South Africa

South African research highlights the very high prevalence of gender-based violence among women in the general population and a high prevalence of mental health problems. The longitudinal analysis presented here is somewhat different in that the sample was not population-based, probably had fewer mental health problems since those with them tend to volunteer less often for research, and was from a young age group. However, we have shown that exposure to physical or sexual IPV was associated with all the mental health problems studied, when examined both cross-sectionally and in the longitudinal data. Further, we have shown that emotional abuse was particularly strongly associated with depression, even after adjusting for exposure to physical and sexual abuse. Rape by a nonpartner was also associated with depression, especially when occurring in women who also experienced emotional abuse. Child sexual abuse was associated with depression and drinking at baseline. This is important as the abuse would in all likelihood have preceded the mental health problem.

Other authors have found that mental health outcomes of abuse are cumulative over time and with additional exposures to abuse [12–14]. In this study we have found limited evidence that re-victimization influenced the development of mental health problems during the prospective analysis. It was only apparent for emotional abuse and depression. Although nonpartner rape exposure had a cumulative impact on risk of depression and suicidality cross-sectionally, this was not seen in the longitudinal analysis when co-exposure to physical and sexual IPV and, for depression, emotional abuse was examined. What we have shown is that the mental health problems examined tended to develop in the same general time frame as the abuse exposure, and if women did not develop these problems at this time, they were generally resilient. The one exception was the relationship with prior emotional abuse and subsequent development of depression about IPV exposure. This analysis is limited as only 2 years of the lives of relatively young women were examined. The proportion experiencing suicidal thoughts and alcohol abuse was low, thus the power for analysis was limited.

In the longitudinal study mental health problems consequent to rape by a nonpartner were not conspicuous. This may well be explained by the relatively low prevalence of women disclosing nonpartner rape. The prevalence was much lower than that of perpetration disclosed by men from the same study area [15], which raises the question of whether the women under-reported possibly due to rape stigma, or whether raped women were much less likely to participate in the study. We were not able to look at experience of nonpartner rape prospectively as the number of women disclosing completed rape by a nonpartner was too small (n = 21). These findings cannot exclude the impact of rape on mental health, and indeed are counter to the population-based findings among women of all ages; they are very likely to reflect limitations of the Stepping Stones study dataset.

References

1 Norman R, Schneider M, Bradshaw D, Jewkes R, Abrahams N, Matzopoulos R, Vos T: Interpersonal violence: an important risk factor for disease and injury in South Africa. Population Health Metrics 2010;8:32.
2 Machisa M, Jewkes R, Lowe-Morna C, Rama K: The War at Home. Johannesburg, GenderLinks, 2011.
3 Radloff L: The CES-D scale: A self-report depression scale for research in the general population. Appl Psychol Meas 1977;1:385–401.
4 Lipman RS, Covi L, Shapiro A: The Hopkins symptom checklist: factors derived from the HSCL-90. Psychopharmacol Bull 1977;13:43–45.
5 Dunkle KL, Jewkes RK, Brown HC, Yoshihama M, Gray GE, McIntyre JA, SD H: Prevalence and patterns of gender-based violence and revictimization among women attending antenatal clinics in Soweto, South Africa. Am J Epidemiol 2004;160:230–239.
6 Jewkes R, Sikweyiya Y, Morrell R, Dunkle K: The relationship between intimate partner violence, rape and HIV amongst South African men: a cross-sectional study. PLoS ONE 2011;6:e24256.
7 Kaminer D, Grimsrud A, Myer L, Stein DJ, Williams D: Risk for post-traumatic stress disorder associated with different forms of interpersonal violence in South Africa. Soc Sci Med 2008;67:1589–1595.
8 Nduna M, Jewkes R, Dunkle K, Jama-Shai N, Coleman I: Associations between depressive symptoms, sexual behaviour and relationship characteristics: a prospective cohort study of young women and men in the Eastern Cape, South Africa. J Int AIDS Soc 2010;13:44.
9 Jewkes R, Nduna M, Levin J, Jama N, Dunkle K, Khuzwayo N, Koss M, Puren A, Wood K, Duvvury N: A cluster randomised controlled trial to determine the effectiveness of stepping stones in preventing HIV infections and promoting safer sexual behaviour amongst youth in the rural eastern cape, South Africa: trial design, methods and baseline findings. Trop Med Int Health 2006;11:3–16.
10 Pulerwitz J, Gortmaker S, DeJong W: Measuring sexual relationship power in HIV/STD research. Sex Roles 2000;42:637–660.
11 Saunders JB, Aasland O, Babor T, de la Fuente JR, Grant M: Development of the alcohol use disorders identification test (AUDIT): WHO collaborative project on early detection of persons with harmful alcohol consumption II. Addiction 1993;88:791–804.
12 Lau Y, Keung Wong DF, Chan KS: The impact and cumulative effects of intimate partner abuse during pregnancy on health-related quality of life among Hong Kong Chinese women. Midwifery 2008;24:22–37.
13 Blasco-Ros C, Sánchez-Lorente S, Martinez M: Recovery from depressive symptoms, state anxiety and post-traumatic stress disorder in women exposed to physical and psychological, but not to psychological intimate partner violence alone: a longitudinal study. BMC Psychiatry 2010;10:98.
14 Lindhorst T, Oxford M: The long-term effects of intimate partner violence on adolescent mothers' depressive symptoms. Soc Sci Med 2008;66:1322–1333.
15 Jewkes R, Dunkle K, Koss MP, Levin JB, Nduna M, Jama N, Sikweyiya Y: Rape perpetration by young, rural South African men: prevalence, patterns and risk factors. Soc Sci Med 2006;63:2949–2961.

Prof. Rachel Jewkes
Gender and Health Research Unit, Medical Research Council
Private Bag X385
Pretoria 0001 (South Africa)
Tel. +27 12 339 8525, E-Mail rjewkes@mrc.ac.za

Special Aspects of Violence

García-Moreno C, Riecher-Rössler A (eds): Violence against Women and Mental Health.
Key Issues Ment Health. Basel, Karger, 2013, vol 178, pp 75–85 (DOI: 10.1159/000342015)

Intimate Partner Violence and Mental Health

Siân Oram · Louise M. Howard

Institute of Psychiatry, King's College London, London, UK

Abstract

Intimate partner violence is a major public health problem that is associated with a range of mental health problems. There is a high prevalence of intimate partner violence victimisation among people with mental disorders but violence is under-detected by mental health professionals. There is a limited evidence base on interventions to address the intimate partner violence experienced by people with mental disorders. However, the introduction of routine enquiry about intimate partner violence into mental health services may start to address problems of poor identification and care where healthcare professionals are trained to respond safely.

Copyright © 2013 S. Karger AG, Basel

Intimate partner violence is one of the most pervasive forms of violence against women. It is a major public health issue that has been shown to be associated with a range of mental health problems, including depression, post-traumatic stress disorder (PTSD), suicidal ideation, substance misuse, and functional symptoms, and the exacerbation of psychotic symptoms [1–3]. In this chapter, we review the literature on the prevalence of intimate partner violence among women with mental disorders and present evidence that suggests a causal relationship between intimate partner violence and mental disorder. We also discuss issues that arise in relation to responding to intimate partner violence and mental disorder, including barriers to disclosing and responding, screening, and effective interventions.

In this chapter we use the term 'intimate partner violence' to refer to acts of physical, sexual and emotional abuse, alone or in combination, and a range of controlling or coercive behaviors, perpetrated against women by a current or former partner. People may suffer adulthood abuse not only at the hands of their partners but also by family members ('domestic violence'). In practice, however, most research has been conducted in relation to violence perpetrated by current and former partners. Around half of women suffering from intimate partner violence are subjected to more than one type of abuse by their partner [4, 5]. Men can also be the victims of intimate partner violence and in the general population the prevalence of isolated incidents of partner violence is comparable between men and women [6]. However, studies do not usually make a distinction between situational mutual couple violence and the violence that occurs in the context of controlling behaviours [7, 8], and it is the latter that is referred to here, and which is more commonly experienced by women. Within relationships, women are at greater risk of serious assaults and of repeated severe physical and sexual violence [9, 10]. The British Crime Survey for England and Wales, for example, estimates that 89% of people who suffer four or more domestic assaults are women [6]. Throughout the chapter we therefore focus on the relationship between intimate partner violence and mental disorder among women.

Prevalence of Intimate Partner Violence

As discussed in detail in the chapter by Jewkes?? [this vol., pp. 65–74], research has shown that intimate partner violence is a reality for many women in both high- and low-income settings. The WHO multi-country study on women's health and intimate partner violence, conducted across fifteen sites in ten countries, found that the lifetime prevalence of physical or sexual partner violence varied between 15 and 71% [11]. Violence was reported by less than 25% of women in two sites, by between 25 and 50% in seven sites and by between 50 and 75% of women in six sites. In all but one setting women were at far greater risk of physical or sexual violence by a partner than by other people. The same study found that the past year prevalence of physical or sexual partner violence varied between 4 and 54% [11]. Research on the prevalence of intimate partner violence within same-sex relationships is limited, although evidence from the USA increasingly suggests that the prevalence of intimate partner violence is similar across same-sex and heterosexual relationships [12].

Data from a number of nationally representative psychiatric morbidity surveys suggest that there is a high prevalence of intimate partner violence among women with a variety of mental disorders. In the USA, for example, the National Epidemiologic Survey on Alcohol and Related Conditions (a nationally representative cohort study of 34,653 USA household residents) identified a high prevalence of intimate partner violence among women diagnosed with a range of disorders including bipolar disorder (26.7%), depression (15.6%), generalised anxiety disorder (22.4%), PTSD (29.4%), panic disorder (22.9%) and social or specific phobia (15.5%) [13]. In the UK, the Adult Psychiatric Morbidity Survey (a nationally representative survey of 4,047 UK household residents) similarly found a high prevalence of intimate partner violence among women with mental disorders [14]. Among women diagnosed with Common Mental Disorder (depressive episode, mixed anxiety/depression, generalised anxiety disorder, panic disorder phobic disorder, or obsessive compulsive disorder), for example, the prevalence of lifetime intimate partner violence was 48.2% and the prevalence of past year intimate partner violence was 15.2%. Among women without a mental disorder, the prevalence of lifetime and past year intimate partner violence was 22.7 and 3.9%, respectively. Smaller studies, conducted in healthcare settings or with community samples, also contribute to knowledge in this area and have focused particularly on the prevalence of violence among women with depressive, anxiety, and post-traumatic stress disorders. The majority of such studies have been conducted in the USA [15–19] and other high income settings, but a small number report on the prevalence of intimate partner violence among women with mental disorder in low income countries. A community-based survey conducted in Ethiopia, for example, found that 71.9% of women with diagnosed depression reported physical violence compared to 48.4% of women without any mental disorder [20]. In Pakistan, a study of female primary care users found that 89.2% of women with depression and 89.5% of women with PTSD reported physical and psychological violence, compared to 70.0% of women with no mental disorder [21]. Less evidence is available on the prevalence of intimate partner violence among women with schizophrenia; the prevalence among women with psychosis ranged in three studies from 41.7 to 83.3% [22–24]. Each of these study samples, however, included fewer than 25 women with psychosis.

Evidence for a high prevalence of intimate partner violence among people with mental disorder is also provided by a recent systematic review of 134 prevalence studies [25]. The review noted that when comparing the mean lifetime prevalence across various healthcare settings, studies conducted in psychiatric clinics and obstetrics and gynaecology clinics recorded the highest prevalence of physical violence (30–50%) and sexual violence (30–35%), while the highest mean lifetime prevalence of psychological violence was reported by studies conducted in psychiatry clinics and emergency departments (65–87%) [25]. Due to higher utilisation of healthcare services by victims of abuse, the prevalence of intimate partner violence may be higher in clinical settings than in the general population [1]. Our review of the prevalence of domestic violence (i.e. violence perpetrated by an intimate partner or by a family member in adulthood) among mental health service users found that, excluding one study with a very highly selected sample, the reported lifetime prevalence among female psychiatric inpatients ranged from 34 to 92% and that past-year prevalence varied between 22 and 76% [26]. The wide variation in prevalence estimates may be partly explained by the different instruments and methods used by researchers to measure violence, in addition to different definitions of partner violence. Among female psychiatric outpatients the lifetime prevalence of domestic violence ranged from 15 to 90% and past-year prevalence from 19 to 86% [26]. Most of the studies were, however, conducted with small numbers of service users who were recruited through convenience sampling. The most comprehensive assessment of the prevalence of intimate partner violence among mental health service users was a Swedish study that attempted to survey, over the course of 1 week, all adult female users of psychiatric inpatient and outpatient services about their experiences of violence [27]. Self-administered questionnaires were completed by 1,382 women, 25.6% of whom reported violence from a current partner and 23.1% by a previous partner [27]. None of the studies identified in the review included a direct comparison with a general population or other clinical group, however, making it difficult to draw conclusions on the extent to which mental health service users are at greater risk of intimate partner violence.

Relationship between Intimate Partner Violence and Mental Disorder

As described above, multiple studies, conducted across a variety of countries and in a range of settings, suggest that there a high prevalence of intimate partner violence among women with mental disorder. This does not appear to be specific to certain disorders: studies have found intimate partner violence to be associated with depression, anxiety disorders, eating disorders, psychotic disorders [2, 14, 28], antenatal and postnatal mental disorders [29–31] and alcohol and substance misuse [2, 32, 33]. Although most of the available evidence is drawn from cross-sectional studies and cannot infer causation, there is some research to suggest that there may be a causal association between intimate partner violence and mental disorder. A systematic review found, for example, that the severity and duration of physical intimate partner violence is associated with the prevalence and severity of depression, and that rates of depression decrease as time since the cessation of violence increases [2]. A review which examined PTSD among victims of intimate partner violence similarly reported that the extent, severity and type of abuse were associated with the intensity of post-traumatic stress symptoms [34]. While women's experiences of physical, psychological and sexual abuse often overlap [35, 36], studies suggest that women who experience more than one form of abuse, or who are re-victimised, are at increased risk of mental disorder and co-morbidity [34, 37–41]. Although there are few prospective studies, the Dunedin Multidisciplinary Health and Development Study in New Zealand, a representative birth cohort study, found that psychiatric disorder increased vulnerability to intimate partner violence (women who experienced abuse between the ages of 24 and 26 had reported significantly higher rates of major depression and substance misuse at age 18) and that intimate partner violence was associated with an increased risk of psychiatric disorder among women at age 26 even after controlling for a previous history of mental disorder [42]. Data from the National Survey of Families and Households, a nationally representative US cohort, similarly suggest that women who experience intimate partner violence are more likely to report depressive symptoms after 5 years of follow-up [43]. A recent pregnancy cohort study also reported that antenatal violence was associated with postnatal depression, but did not adjust for antenatal depression [30].

Evidence therefore suggests that the causal relationship between intimate partner violence and mental disorder operates in both directions: mental disorder can increase women's vulnerability to intimate partner violence and intimate partner violence can damage mental health [26]. Evidence that the relationship between intimate partner violence and mental disorder may be causal further underlines the importance of intimate partner violence as a public health issue. The calculation of population attributable fractions (PAFs) is one way of quantifying the public health implications of violence. PAFs represent the proportion of mental disorders that can be attributed to exposure to intimate partner violence, based on an assumption of causality. The intimate partner violence-related PAF for postnatal depression, for example, was recently estimated to be 10% in a Brazilian population [30]. A study using data from the Adult Psychiatric Morbidity Survey 2007 reported that the intimate partner violence-related PAF for women was 29% for Common Mental Disorder, 52% for PTSD symptoms, 51% for eating disorder symptoms and 32% for psychosis [14]. Such estimates suggest that reducing prevalence of intimate partner violence could contribute to a substantial reduction in the burden of mental disorder and reduce health service costs; in England and Wales alone it is estimated that around 10 years ago intimate partner violence cost the health service GBP 176 million per annum in treatments for associated mental disorders [6].

Women with pre-existing mental disorders may experience an exacerbation of symptoms if they experience intimate partner violence [3]. It has been suggested that mental disorder may increase vulnerability to intimate partner violence by increasing the likelihood that women will be in unsafe relationships and environments [44] and increase women's vulnerability to violent victimisation [45, 46].

Responding to Intimate Partner Violence and Mental Disorder

Routine Enquiry in Healthcare Settings
Despite evidence to suggest both that vulnerability to intimate partner violence is increased among people with mental disorders and that intimate partner violence may worsen mental health, surveys of mental health service users have found that most are not asked about their experiences of abuse [47–49]. Our review of identification in mental health services found that, internationally, mental health services detect only about 10–30% of recent intimate partner violence victimisation [26], which is comparable to detection rates within primary care [50]. More recently, a study of women in contact with community mental health teams in South London similarly found that although 60% had experienced violence from partners (27% during pregnancy), only 24% had been questioned about abuse [51].

Qualitative studies have identified a range of barriers to disclosing intimate partner violence and suggest that mental health service users may not disclose unless they are asked about abuse [52, 53]. A UK study found that barriers to disclosure among psychiatric patients include fear that they would not be believed; fear that disclosure could lead to further violence; fear that disclosure could result in social services involvement, the commencement of child protection proceedings, and the disruption of family life; feelings of shame, self-blame and embarrassment; the failure of professionals to respond to signs of abuse; and actions taken by the perpetrator to isolate the victim from family and friends and to interrupt appointments [52, 53]. The same study found that the key barriers to enquiry by mental health professionals include a lack of confidence, knowledge and expertise about how to raise the issue of intimate partner violence and respond appropriately; non-prioritisation of violence issues, and beliefs that enquiring about intimate partner violence is not part of their role as health professionals [52, 53].

Routine enquiry (the practice of asking all people within certain parameters about the experience of intimate violence, regardless of whether or not there are signs of abuse, or whether violence is suspected) [54] has now been introduced into a number of psychiatric settings, including in the UK and in parts of the USA and New Zealand [55–58]. A recent systematic review of intimate partner violence screening in a range of healthcare settings found there is insufficient evidence to suggest that routine enquiry about violence improves mortality or morbidity [50]. Indeed, routine enquiry can have adverse consequences if professionals are not trained to enquire safely about intimate partner violence [59]. In particular, victims of violence may be placed at risk by enquiry if the perpetrator finds out about a disclosure. Good clinical practice includes making accurate notes, conducting a risk assessment (particularly with regards to immediate safety, the need for emergency action and/or child protection procedures), prioritising safety planning, discussing potential options, and avoiding blaming the victim [60].

In mental health services, there is evidence to suggest that detection rates are improved by the introduction of routine enquiry about intimate partner violence, but the effectiveness of routine enquiry depends on health professionals being able to respond appropriately to disclosures of abuse. Our review found, however, that management plans rarely include violence issues and thus do not include safety planning or trauma-focused therapy [26].

Interventions

Several recent systematic reviews have examined evidence for the effectiveness of interventions in improving outcomes for victims/survivors of partner violence identified in community and healthcare settings [61–64]. A range of interventions have been identified, including individual and group psychological therapies, psychosocial support, and advocacy, but overall little is known about the efficacy of interventions that might reduce the psychological impact of partner violence. Furthermore, although mainstream services may encounter difficulties in supporting the needs of victims with mental disorders, there is very little evidence regarding how to support mental health service users who are experiencing violence.

A recent review conducted by Feder et al. [50] found that a wide range of individual psychological interventions benefit abused women with depression and PTSD. In particular, two trials of cognitive behavioural therapy (CBT) for women with PTSD who were no longer experiencing violence found that receiving the intervention (8–11 individual sessions of psycho-education on PTSD and feminist modules on empowerment strategies and self-advocacy) was associated with a reduction in PTSD and depressive symptoms and an improvement in self-esteem [65, 66]. A number of group psychological interventions have also been studied in trials and show improved psychological outcomes among participants, but the studies have major methodological limitations [50]. Furthermore, findings from these trials of individual and group psychological interventions cannot be extrapolated to women who are still in abusive relationships or to women with severe psychiatric illnesses who are in contact with mental health services. A review of interventions for mental health service users who are experiencing domestic violence (i.e. violence perpetrated by an intimate partner or family member in adulthood) [53] identified one small randomised controlled trial (RCT) of trauma-focussed CBT for patients with severe mental illness [67]. This study found that the intervention was effective in reducing co-morbid PTSD in patients with a primary diagnosis of major mood disorders and schizophrenia [67]. The trial did not, however, focus on trauma specifically within the context of partner or family violence.

Recent reviews concluded that there is insufficient evidence on the effectiveness of psychosocial support in improving outcomes for victims of intimate partner violence, particularly in respect of victims who are currently experiencing abuse [50, 68]. Since then, an RCT to evaluate the efficacy of an intervention to address multiple risks (cigarette smoking, depression and intimate partner violence) among pregnant women has been published [69]. Women who received a combination of CBT for depression and smoking cessation and individualised counselling for intimate partner violence (which was based on feminist empowerment theory, provided information about the types of abuse and the cycle of violence, and included a danger assessment component and the development of a safety plan) reported a greater resolution of risks compared to controls. In particular, for women who had reported at baseline that they had experienced intimate partner violence in the year preceding pregnancy, the recurrence of violence was significantly lower among women in the intervention group than among women in the usual care group (7.9 vs. 21.6%, $p = 0.004$). The effectiveness of a psychotherapy intervention in reducing PTSD and depression among pregnant women experiencing intimate partner violence has also recently been evaluated in a pilot randomised trial. Receiving the intervention was associated with a moderate reduction in depressive and post-traumatic stress symptoms during pregnancy, but the reduction in symptom level was not sustained at three months postpartum [70].

There is more robust evidence for the effectiveness of advocacy/support in reducing intimate partner violence among women who have actively sought help or who are in refuge accommodation [50, 63]. Advocates provide practical as well as emotional support to victims of violence, including through conducting risk assessments, providing advice and information on welfare rights, legal issues, and housing options, and making referrals to other agencies. To date, there are no randomised trials that examine advocacy/support for women who are in contact with secondary mental health services [26, 50]. However, a cluster RCT in primary care, which involved the provision of training for general practice staff and a linked advocate for intervention practices, showed a significant improvement in identification and referral to advocacy/support services [71], though the mental health of women identified as victims of partner violence was not measured. A recent small pilot study of 27 women, however, assessed the effectiveness of providing advocacy/support to community mental health service users who disclosed past year violence [72]. The intervention, which was delivered by violence advocacy workers who had received mental health training as part of the intervention, was found to be associated with a significant decrease in the frequency and severity of abuse and an improvement in victims' overall quality of life. There is therefore some early, though weak, evidence to suggest that the provision of emotional and practical support by advocates may be useful for women with mental disorders.

Conclusions

There is a strong association between intimate partner violence and mental disorder, with evidence of bidirectional causality. Mental health services, both primary and secondary care, should therefore ensure this violence is identified in order to reduce the risk of further violence, improve safety and potentially improve mental health. There is a limited evidence base on interventions but the introduction of routine enquiry about intimate partner violence into psychiatric settings may start to address problems of poor identification among mental health service users where healthcare professionals are trained to respond safely. Further research is needed to identify specific interventions for this group of at-risk women.

References

1 Campbell JC: Health consequences of intimate partner violence. Lancet 2002;359:1331–1336.
2 Golding MJ: Intimate partner violence as a risk factor for mental disorders: a meta-analysis. J Fam Violence 1999;14:99–132.
3 Neria Y, Bromet EJ, Carlson GA, Naz B: Assaultive trauma and illness course in psychotic bipolar disorder: findings from the Suffolk county mental health project. Acta Psychiatr Scand 2005;111:380–383.
4 Coleman K, Jansson K, Kaiza P, Reed E: Homicides, firearm offences and intimate violence 2005/6: Supplementary volume I to crime in England and Wales 2005–6. Home Office Statistical Bulletin 02/07, Office for National Statistics, 2007.
5 Donaldson A, Marshall LA: Domestic Abuse Prevalence: Argyll and Clyde DAP Study. Glasgow, West Dunbartonshire Domestic Abuse Partnership, 2005.
6 Walby S, Allen J: Domestic Violence, Sexual Assault And Stalking: Findings from the British Crime Survey. London, Home Office, 2004, Home Office Research Study No. 276.
7 Johnson MP: Patriarchal terrorism and common couple violence: Two forms of violence against women. J Marriage Family 1995;57:283–294.
8 Stark E: Commentary on Johnson's 'conflict and control: gender symmetry and asymmetry in domestic violence'. Violence Against Women 2006; 12:1019–1025.
9 Walby S, Myhill A: Assessing and managing the risk of domestic violence; in Taylor-Browne J (ed): Reducing Domestic Violence. London, Home Office, 2000.
10 Tjaden P, Thoennes N: Extent, Nature, and Consequences of Intimate Partner Violence. Washington, US Department of Justice, 2000.

11 Garcia-Moreno C, Jansen H AFM, Ellsberg M, Heise L, Watts CH: Prevalence of intimate partner violence: findings from the WHO multi-country study on women's health and domestic violence. Lancet 2006;368:1260–1269.

12 McClennen JC: Domestic violence between same-gender partners: recent findings and future research. J Interpers Violence 2005;20:149–154.

13 Grant BF, Goldstein RB: Unpublished data (wave 2 of the national epidemiologic survey on alcohol and related conditions). Supplements Pietrzak RH, et al 'prevalence and axis I comorbidity of full and partial posttraumatic stress disorder in the United States: results from wave 2 of the national epidemiologic survey on alcohol and related conditions'. J Anxiety Disord 2011;25:456–465.

14 Jonas S, Khalifeh H, Bebbington PE, McManus S, Brugha T, Meltzer H, Howard LM: Intimate partner violence and psychiatric disorder in England: results from the 2007 adult psychiatric morbidity survey. In preparation.

15 Cascardi M, O'Leary K, Lawrence EE, Schlee KA: Characteristics of women physically abused by their spouses and who seek treatment regarding marital conflict. J Consult Clin Psychol 1995;63:616–623.

16 Cerulli C, Talbot NL, Tang W, Chaudron LH: Co-occurring intimate partner violence and mental health diagnoses in perinatal women. J Women's Health 2011;20:1793–1803.

17 Chang DF, Shen BJ, Takeuchi DT: Prevalence and demographic correlates of intimate partner violence in Asian Americans. Int J Law Psychiatry 2009;32: 167–175.

18 Tolman RM, Rosen D: Domestic violence in the lives of women receiving welfare – mental health, substance dependence, and economic well-being. Violence Against Women 2001;7:141–158.

19 Tuten M, Jones HE, Tran G, et al: Partner violence impacts the psychosocial and psychiatric status of pregnant, drug-dependent women. Addict Behav 2004;29:1029–1034.

20 Deyessa N, Berhane Y, Alem A, Mary E, Emmelin M, Hogberg U, Kullgren G: Intimate partner violence and depression among women in rural Ethiopia: a cross-sectional study. Clin Pract Epidemiol Mental Health 2009;5:1–10.

21 Ayub M, Irfan M, Nasr T, Lutufullah M, Kingdon D, Naeem F: Psychiatric morbidity and domestic violence: a survey of married women in lahore. Soc Psychiatry Psychiatr Epidemiol 2009;44:953–960.

22 Danielson KK, Moffitt TE, Caspi A, Silva PA: Comorbidity between abuse of an adult and DSM-III-R mental disorders: evidence from an epidemiological study. Am J Psychiatry 1998;155:131–133.

23 Weizmann-Henelius G, Viemero V, Eronen M: Psychological risk markers in violent female behavior. Int J Forens Mental Health 2004;3:185–196.

24 Wong SPY, Phillips MR: Nonfatal suicidal behavior among Chinese women who have been physically abused by their male intimate partners. Suicide Life Threatening Behav 2009;39:648–658.

25 Alhabib S, Nur U, Jones R: Domestic violence against women: systematic review of prevalence studies. J Fam Violence 2010;25:369–382.

26 Howard LM, Trevillion K, Khalifeh H, Woodall A, Agnew-Davies R, Feder G: Domestic violence and severe psychiatric disorders: Prevalence and interventions. Psychological Medicine 2010;6:1–13.

27 Bengtsson-Tops A, Markstrom U, Lewin B: The prevalence of abuse in Swedish female psychiatric users, the perpetrators and places where abuse occurred. Nordic J Psychiatry 2005;59:504–510.

28 Trevillion K, Oram S, Feder G, Howard LM: Systematic review of the prevalence and risk of domestic violence victimisation in people with mental disorders. In Preparation.

29 Flach C, Leese M, Heron J, Evans J, Feder G, Sharp D, Howard LM: Antenatal domestic violence, maternal mental health and subsequent child behaviour: a cohort study. BJOG 2011;118:1383–1391.

30 Ludermir A, Lewis G, Valongueiro S: Violence against women by their intimate partner during pregnancy and postnatal depression: a prospective cohort study. Lancet 2010;376:903–910.

31 Howard LM, Oram S, Galley H, Trevillion K, Feder G: Systematic review of the prevalence and risk of domestic violence victimisation in women with perinatal mental disorder. In preparation.

32 Golinelli D, Longshore D, Wenzel SL: Substance use and intimate partner violence: clarifying the relevance of women's use and partners' use. J Behavl Health Serv Res 2009;36:199–211.

33 Testa M, Livingston JA, Leonard KE: Women's substance use and experiences of intimate partner violence: a longitudinal investigation among a community sample. Addict Behav 2003;28:1649–1664.

34 Jones L, Hughes M, Unterstaller U: Post traumatic stress disorder (PTSD) in victims of domestic violence. A review of the research. Trauma Violence Abuse 2001;2:99–119.

35 Krug E, Mercy J, Dahlberg L, Ziwi A: The world report on violence and health. Lancet 2002;360: 1083–1088.

36 Watts C, Zimmerman C: Violence against women: global scope and magnitude. Lancet 2002;359: 1232–1237.

37 Echeburua E, Corral P, Amor PJ: Evaluation of psychological harm in the victims of violent crime. Psychol Spain 2003;7:10–18.

38 Kilpatrick D, Ruggiero KJ, Acierno R, Saunders BE, Resnick H, Best CL: Violence and risk of ptsd, major depression, substance abuse/dependence, and comorbidity: Results from the national survey of adolescents. J Consult Clin Psychol 2003;71:692–700.

39 Owens GP, Chard KM: Comorbidity and psychiatric diagnoses among women reporting child sexual abuse. Child Abuse Neglect 2003;27:1075–1082.

40 Roberts GL, Lawrence JM, Williams GM, Raphael B: The impact of domestic violence on women's mental health. Austr NZ J Publ Health 1998;22:796–801.

41 Romito P, Turan JM, Marchi MD: The impact of current and past interpersonal violence on women's mental health. Soc Sci Med 2005;60:1717–1728.

42 Ehrensaft MK, E MT, Caspi A: Is domestic violence followed by an increased risk of psychiatric disorders among women but not among men? A longitudinal cohort study. Am J Psychiatry 2006;163:885–892.

43 Zlotnick C, Johnson DM, Kohn R: Women intimate partner violence and long-term psychosocial functioning in a national sample of Americans. J Interpers Violence 2006;21:262–275.

44 McHugo GJ, Kammerer N, Jackson EW, Markoff LS, Gatz M, Larson MJ, Mazelis R, Hennigan K: Women, co-occurring disorders, and violence study: evaluation design and study population. J Subst Abuse Treat 2005;28:91–107.

45 Briere J, Jordan CE: Violence against women: outcome complexity and implications for assessment and treatment. J Interpers Violence 2004;19:1252–1276.

46 Khalifeh H, Dean K: Gender and violence against people with severe mental illness. Int Rev Psychiatry 2010;22:535–546.

47 Cusack K, Grubaugh A, Knapp R, Frueh B: Unrecognized trauma and PTSD among public mental health consumers with chronic and severe mental illness. Commun Ment Health J 2006;42:487–500.

48 Frueh BC, Knapp GR, Cusack JK, Grubaugh LA, Sauvageot AJ, Cousins CV, Yim E, Robins SC, Monnier J, Hiers GT: Patients' reports of traumatic or harmful experiences within the psychiatric setting. Psychiatr Serv 2005;56:1123–1133.

49 Lothian J, Read J: Asking about abuse during mental health assessments: Client views and experience. NZ J Psychol 2002;31:98–103.

50 Feder G, Ramsay J, Dunne D, Rose M, Arsene C, Norman R, Kuntze S, Spencer A, Bacchus L, Hague G, Warburton A, Taket A: How far does screening women for domestic (partner) violence in different health-care settings meet criteria for a screening programme? Systematic reviews of nine UK national screening committee criteria. Health Technol Assess 2009;13:111––113.

51 Morgan JF, Zolese G, McNulty J, Gebhardt S: Domestic violence among female psychiatric patients: cross-sectional survey. Psychiatrist 2010;34:461–464.

52 Feder G, Hutson M, Ramsay J, Taket AR: Women exposed to intimate partner violence. Expectations and experiences when they encounter health-care professionals: a meta-analysis of qualitative studies. Annals of Internal Medicine 2006;166:22–37.

53 Rose D, Trevillion K, Woodall A, Morgan C, Feder G, Howard L: Barriers and facilitators of disclosures of domestic violence by mental health service users: qualitative study. Br J Psychiatry 2011;1983:189–194.

54 Department of Health, Home Office: No Secrets: Guidance on Developing and Implementing Multi-Agency Policies and Procedures to Protect Vulnerable Adults from Abuse. London, Department of Health, 2000, pp 1–42.

55 Department of Health: Refocusing the Care Programme Approach: Policy and Positive Practice Guidance. London, Department of Health, 2008.

56 Read J, Fraser A: Abuse histories of psychiatric inpatients: to ask or not to ask? Psychiatr Serv 1998;49:355–359.

57 US Department of Health HSNIoH: NIH Policy and Guidelines on the Inclusion of Women and Minorities as Subjects in Clinical Research, 2001.

58 Department of Health: Report from the Sexual Violence against Women Sub-Group: Responding to Violence against Women and Children – the role of the NHS. London, Department of Health, 2010.

59 Bacchus L, Bewley S, Torres Vitolas C, Aston G, Jordan P, Murray SF: Evaluation of a domestic violence intervention in the maternity and sexual health services of a UK hospital. Reproduct Health Matters 2010;18:147–157.

60 Hegarty K, Taft A, Feder G: Violence between intimate partners: Working with the whole family. Br Med J 2008;337:346–351.

61 Ramsay J, Carter Y, Davidson L, Dunne D, Eldridge S, Feder G, Hegarty K, Rivas C, Taft A, Warburton A: Advocacy interventions to reduce or eliminate violence and promote the physical and psychosocial well-being of women who experience intimate partner abuse. Cochrane Database of Systematic Reviews 2009:Art No.: CD005043. DOI: 005010. 001002/14651858.CD14005043.pub14651852.

62 Ramsay J, Richardson J, Carter YH, Davidson LL, Feder G: Should health professionals screen for domestic violence? Systematic review. Br Med J 2002;325:1–13.

63 World Health Organisation: Clinical Interventions for Women Survivors of Intimate Partner Violence. Geneva, World Health Organisation, in preparation.

64 World Health Organisation, London School of Hygiene and Tropical Medicine: Preventing Intimate Partner and Sexual Violence against Women: Taking Action and Generating Evidence. Geneva, World Health Organization, 2010,

65 Kubany ES, Hill EE, Owens JA: Cognitive trauma therapy for battered women with PTSD: preliminary findings. J Trauma Stress 2003;16:81–91.

66 Kubany ES, Hill EE, Owens JA, Iannce-Spencer C, McCaig MA, Tremayne KJ, et al: Cognitive trauma therapy for battered women with PTSD (CTT-BW). J Consult Clin Psychol 2004;72:3–18.

67 Mueser KT, Rosenberg SD, Xie H, Jankowski MK, Bolton EE, Lu W, Hamblen JL, Rosenberg HJ, McHugo GJ, Wolfe R: A randomized controlled trial of cognitive-behavioral treatment for posttraumatic stress disorder in severe mental illness. J Consult Clin Psychol 2008;76:259–271.

68 Sadowski L, Casteel L: Intimate partner violence towards women. Clin Evidence (Online) 2010;02: 1013.

69 El-Mohandes AAE, Kiely M, Joseph JG, Subramanian S, Johnson AA, Blake SM, Gantz MG, El-Khorazaty MN: An intervention to improve postpartum outcomes in African-American mothers: a randomized controlled trial. Obstet Gynecol 2008;112:611–620.

70 Zlotnick C, Capezza NM, Parker D: An interpersonally based intervention for low-income pregnant women with intimate partner violence: a pilot study. Arch Womens Ment Health 2011;14:55–65.

71 Feder G, Agnew-Davies R, Baird K, Dunne D, Eldridge S, Griffiths C, Gregory A, Howell A, Johnson M, Ramsay J, Rutterford C, Sharp C: Identification and referral to improve safety (IRIS) of women experiencing domestic violence with a primary care training and support programme: a cluster randomised controlled trial. Lancet 2011; 11:1–8.

72 Trevillion K, Byford S, Cary M, Rose D, Oram S, Feder G, Agnew-Davies R, Howard L: A pilot study of domestic violence advocacy integrated within community mental health services. Submitted.

Louise M. Howard
Section for Women's Mental Health, Institute of Psychiatry at King's College London
PO31, David Goldberg Centre, De Crespigny Park
Denmark Hill, London SE5 8AF (UK)
E-Mail Louise.Howard@iop.kcl.ac.uk

Sexual Assault and Women's Mental Health

Sandra L. Martin · Angela M. Parcesepe

Department of Maternal and Child Health, Gillings School of Global Public Health, University of North Carolina at Chapel Hill, Chapel Hill, N.C., USA

Abstract

Sexual assault of women is a common worldwide problem, with such violence being perpetrated by women's intimate partners as well as other types of persons (acquaintances, friends, family members other than partners, strangers). Not only does sexual assault pose physical health risks to women, but it also has been associated with many types of mental health problems, including substance use disorders, post-traumatic stress disorder and other anxiety disorders, depression, and suicidal ideation and attempts. While most female sexual assault survivors experience negative mental health sequelae immediately following the assault, there is significant variability in the severity and duration of these symptoms. Factors influencing this variability include the survivor's prior history of violence, the severity of the assault, and whether the survivor receives negative social reactions to her disclosure concerning the assault. Several brief cognitive behavior therapies (including Cognitive Processing Therapy, Prolonged Exposure, and Stress Inoculation Training) and Eye Movement Desensitization and Reprocessing have been shown to improve the mental health of many adult female sexual assault survivors.

Copyright © 2013 S. Karger AG, Basel

Sexual violence has been defined in many ways, with one of the most commonly used definitions being that of the World Health Organization (WHO). WHO defines sexual violence to include coerced sexual acts or attempts to obtain sexual acts, unwanted sexual comments or advances, and sex trafficking [1]. Coercion may take the form of using physical force, psychological intimidation, or threats/blackmail, as well as taking action against persons who are unable to provide consent due to alcohol/drug intoxication, being asleep, or cognitive limitations.

This chapter presents a brief overview of sexual assault of women and its impact on women's mental health. Although all forms of sexual violence may adversely affect women's well-being, this chapter focuses primarily on a particular type of sexual violence, namely, sexual assault or rape. While intimate partners are one of the most common types of perpetrators of sexual assault, this chapter addresses sexual violence committed by all types of perpetrators, both intimate partners and others. Moreover, while females of all ages may be sexually assaulted, the research presented here concentrates on sexual assault of adult females (typically defined to include those aged 18 years or older, however, some studies also include adolescent women in their samples). This chapter is not a comprehensive review of the literature, but rather a general synopsis illustrated with select research findings. Information is presented concerning the prevalence of sexual assault of women, associations between sexual assault and women's mental health, variables influencing women's mental health responses to sexual assault, and interventions for women who present with sexual assault-related mental health problems.

Sexual Assault Prevalence

Although sexual assault of women is a worldwide problem, estimates of the prevalence of such violence vary between studies. Some variation is due to true differences in the extent of sexual assault within diverse study populations, while other variation is due to methodological differences between studies (e.g. differences in assessment procedures, definitions, samples).

Since intimate partners are one of the most common perpetrators of sexual assault of women [2], several studies have estimated the annual prevalence of intimate partner sexual assault. For example, the WHO Multi-Country Study on Women's Health and Domestic Violence, a study of more than 24,000 women (aged 15–49), in 15 sites in 10 countries, found annual estimates of intimate partner sexual assault ranging from 1% to 44% among ever-partnered women (1% in Yokohama, Japan and Belgrade, Serbia; 3% in Sao Paolo, Brazil; 7% in Lima, Peru; 9% in Windhoek, Namibia; 12% in Samoa; 13% in Dar-es-Salaam, Tanzania; 17% in Bangkok, Thailand; 20% in Dhaka, Bangladesh; and 44% in Butajira province, Ethiopia) [3]. The 2010 National Intimate Partner and Sexual Violence Survey (NIPSVS), a nationally representative survey of women (aged 18 and older) in the United States, found that 0.6% of women reported having been raped by an intimate partner during the past 12 months [4]. Other geographically-based studies of the annual prevalence of intimate partner sexual assault also have found such violence to be common [5, 6].

Research also has estimated the annual overall prevalence of sexual assault of women, with this overall prevalence including sexual assaults perpetrated by persons with any type of relationship to the victim (e.g. intimate partners, acquaintances, family members, strangers). For example, the U.S. NIPSVS study found that 1% of women reported having been raped by someone in the previous 12 months [4]. A representative survey of women (aged 18–49) in three provinces of South Africa found that 2% of women reported experiencing attempted or completed rape during the previous 12 months [7]. A study of women aged 18–49 in five districts of Botswana and in four districts of Swaziland found that 5% of women in each country reported experiencing forced sex by someone during the past 12 months [8].

Although some annual prevalence estimates of sexual assault (by intimate partners as well as by anyone) may seem rather small, one must recall that this translates into much greater percentages of women being sexually assaulted at some point during their lifetimes. For example, the WHO Multi-Country study [3] found site-specific lifetime intimate partner sexual assault prevalence estimates among women 15–49 years of age ranging from 6% through 59%. The US NIPSVS study found lifetime intimate partner sexual assault prevalence estimates of 9%, and lifetime overall sexual assault prevalence estimates (including any type of perpetrator) of 18% [4].

Sexual Assault and Mental Health

It is well documented that women sexually assaulted during adulthood have poorer mental health than nonassaulted women [9, 10], including having multiple types of mental health symptoms and disorders [11]. Among the more commonly studied of these problems are substance use disorders, post-traumatic stress disorder (PTSD), depression, and suicidal ideation and attempts.

Substance Use and Substance Use Disorders
Many studies have found high levels of substance use and substance use disorders among women who have been sexually assaulted during adulthood. However, few of these studies are longitudinal in nature. Therefore, in most studies, it is impossible to determine the timing of the sexual assault relative to the onset of the substance problems.

Alcohol. Many studies have found high levels of alcohol use and alcohol-related disorders among female sexual assault survivors. For example, a recent review of the literature found that studies reported that 13–49% of the female sexual assault survivors in their samples evidenced alcohol dependence [12].

Other research has shown that heavy alcohol use and alcohol disorders are more common among women sexual assault survivors than other women. For example, research with a representative sample of 1,157 women from central North Carolina found that those who had experienced sexual assault were more likely than other women to have a lifetime diagnosis of alcohol abuse or dependence based on the Diagnostic and Statistical Manual of Mental Disorders, ed. 3 (DSM-III) diagnostic criteria [13]. A study of a representative sample of 3,632 female US military veterans found that those sexually assaulted while in the military were twice as likely to screen positive for alcohol abuse and to report that substance use interfered with their readjustment to civilian life [14, 15]. Other research found that pregnant women had four times the odds of using alcohol during pregnancy if they also experienced intimate partner sexual violence during pregnancy [16].

Illicit Drugs. Studies focused exclusively on women sexual assault survivors show that they also have high levels of illicit drug use. Various studies report that between 28 and 61% of the female sexual assault survivors in their samples use illicit drugs [12].

Moreover, women sexual assault survivors are more likely than other women to use illicit drugs and to have psychiatric diagnoses related to their illicit drug use. For example, research with a representative sample of women from central North Carolina found that female sexual assault survivors were more likely than other women to meet DSM-III criteria for drug abuse and dependence [13]. Similarly, a survey of female US military veterans found that those who were raped after their military service ended were significantly more likely than those who had never been raped to meet criteria for a DSM-IV diagnosis of lifetime drug dependence or abuse [17].

Prescription Drugs. Prescription drug use and abuse are more common among women sexual assault survivors than other women. The US National Violence against Women Survey found that prescription drug use was greater among women who experienced sexual assault during adulthood than other women [18]. Moreover, a study of two representative samples of women in the US (one a sample of 2,000 college women and the other a sample of 3,000 women in the community) found that those with a history of rape were significantly more likely than those never raped to have misused prescription drugs on at least four occasions during the past year [19].

Timing. A few studies have compared the timing of women's sexual assault experiences and their substance use/abuse to determine the direction of this association (i.e. to examine whether sexual assault is a risk factor for substance use/abuse, or whether substance use/abuse is a risk factor for sexual assault). A small-scale study using a cross-sectional retrospective recall approach found that female sexual assault survivors reported increasing their alcohol use after the assault [20]. Another similar recall study found that female sexual assault survivors reported increasing their use of anabolic steroids after the assault in an attempt to enhance their capacity to defend themselves from potential subsequent sexual assault [21]. A prospective longitudinal study of a select group of women (those who consumed at least 3–4 drinks per occasion once a week, had more than one male sex partner in the past year, and had sexual intercourse within the past month) found that high levels of alcohol use increased women's vulnerability to subsequent sexual aggression (defined as any unwanted sexual contact or sexual coercion); however, experiencing sexual aggression (since the age of 14) did not appear to lead to subsequently higher levels of alcohol use [22]. A large-scale longitudinal study of 3,006 US women found evidence of an iterative bidirectional effect; more specifically, violent assault (including rape and/or physical violence) led to women's increased use of both alcohol and illicit drugs, while this increased drug use (but not increased alcohol use) led to further increases in women's probability of violent assault [23].

Post-Traumatic Stress Disorder

It is well documented that many sexual assault survivors have PTSD symptoms or a diagnosis of PTSD. For example, studies have found that between 17 and 65% of the women sexual assault survivors in their samples evidence PTSD, with the majority of these studies reporting rates between 33 and 45% [12].

Not only do many sexual assault survivors have PTSD symptoms/diagnoses, but they are significantly more likely than non-assaulted women to have these types of problems [1, 24]. For example, a nationally representative study of women in South Africa found that those with a history of rape had approximately six times the odds of meeting the WHO Composite International Diagnostic Interview (CIDI) criteria for a lifetime diagnosis of PTSD compared to those with no exposure to violence [25]. A study of representative samples of women in four cities in Mexico found that those who had been sexually assaulted were significantly more likely than other women to meet the CIDI diagnostic criteria for PTSD [26]. In addition, a nationally representative survey of more than 10,000 persons (including women and men) in six European countries found that being raped was significantly associated with a diagnosis of PTSD based on the CIDI criteria [27].

Women's symptoms of PTSD may present soon after sexual assault, and, for some women, may continue for a long period of time. For instance, a study of 67 women at a referral center for sexual assault survivors in Sao Paolo, Brazil found that 64% of the women endorsed PTSD symptoms during the first month following the assault and 37% met diagnostic criteria for PTSD using the Clinician-Administered Posttraumatic Stress Disorder Scale (CAPS) 6 months after the incident [28].

Depression

Depressive symptoms, as well as diagnoses of depression, are common among women sexual assault survivors. Various research studies report that between 13 and 51% of the female sexual assault survivors in their samples meet diagnostic criteria for depression [12].

Given these high levels of depressive symptoms among female sexual assault survivors, it is not surprising that research has found that symptoms of depression and a diagnosis of depression are more common among female sexual assault survivors than other women. For example, a representative sample of 3,001 English- or Spanish-speaking women (aged 18–86 years) in the US found that 23% of those who were raped experienced a major depressive episode in the past year based on DSM-IV criteria, compared to 6% of those who were not raped [19]. A survey of 16,000 college students in 22 sites in 21 countries, found that severe intimate partner sexual violence was significantly correlated with women's depression, as assessed by the depression scale of the Personal and Relationship Profile [29]. A case-control study of 304 women (aged 15–48 years) in Karachi, Pakistan, found that women who reported a history of marital rape had three times the odds of depression as determined by the Self Report Questionnaire (SRQ 20), compared to women without a history of marital rape [30]. Study of a random sample of pregnant women from a rural district in Bangladesh found that those who reported experiencing forced sex had twice the odds of experiencing antepartum depressive symptoms on the Edinburgh Postnatal Depression Scale compared to women without a history of forced sex [31].

As with PTSD, depression may begin soon after sexual assault, and for some women, it will continue long after the assault. For example, a study of women at a referral center for survivors of sexual violence in Sao Paolo, Brazil, found that 52% endorsed symptoms of moderate-to-severe depression on the Beck Depression Inventory during the first month following the assault, with this depression persisting for at least 6 months after the assault in 20% of the women [28].

Suicidal Ideation and Attempts

Not only do female sexual assault survivors have high levels of depressive symptoms and diagnoses, but they also have elevated rates of suicidal ideation and attempts. For example, research with 16,000 college students in 22 sites in 21 countries found that severe sexual assault by an intimate partner was positively correlated with women's suicidal ideation and self-harm [29]. Similarly, a survey of 1,152 women from family practice clinics in the US found that women who reported sexual assault by an intimate partner were four times more likely than nonassaulted women to have attempted suicide [32].

Variables Influencing Women's Mental Health Responses to Sexual Assault

Women have differential mental health responses to sexual assault. Most sexually assaulted women experience mental health symptoms immediately after the assault, even though the severity of these symptoms may vary. Although most sexual assault survivors show considerable recovery within a year's time, some continue to evidence such symptoms years after the event [33–35].

Several variables have been identified that influence the severity of sexual assault mental health sequela [36]. Variables consistently associated with survivors' mental health sequela include whether or not the survivor had a previous sexual assault experience (i.e. revictimization), the severity of the assault, and whether or not the survivor experienced negative social reactions from those to whom she disclosed information about the assault. Another variable, the relationship of survivor and perpetrator, has been less consistently associated with the duration and severity of sexual assault-related mental health problems, as will be discussed.

Prior Experiences of Sexual Assault

Severe mental health symptoms are more likely among women sexually assaulted multiple times during their lifetimes than among women sexually assaulted one time [36]. For example, a general population survey of 1,325 female residents of Washington State found that experiencing greater numbers of sexual assaults was associated with women's increased number of PTSD and depression symptoms [37]. A Chicago-based study of 600 women sexually assaulted as adults found that those with a prior history of childhood sexual abuse reported more severe PTSD symptoms [38].

Somewhat similarly, a California survey of more than 13,000 women (aged 18 years or older) found that clinically relevant levels of anxiety, depression and PTSD symptoms were more often reported by women sexually and/or physically assaulted both during childhood and adulthood than by women sexually and/or physically assaulted only during childhood or only during adulthood [39]. Although there is no definitive explanation as to why past victimization influences mental health responses to a new violent incident, it is likely that the earlier violence affects women's stress reactions (e.g. cortisol responses) which may in turn affect women's mental health responses to the recent violent event [40, 41].

Severity of Sexual Assault
Women's mental health responses to sexual assault vary by assault severity, with women who have experienced more severe assaults having more severe mental health problems [35]. For example, within a Chicago-based sample of 323 media-recruited women sexually assaulted at age 14 years or older, those who felt that their life was threatened during the assault evidenced more severe PTSD symptoms [42]. Similarly, research conducted with 1,084 adult female sexual assault survivors in a Midwestern metropolitan area of the US found that those who experienced more severe and life-threatening sexual assaults reported a greater number of PTSD symptoms [43].

Social Reactions
Research also has examined whether the manner in which persons (family, friends and others) react to survivors' disclosure about their experiences of sexual victimization is related to survivors' mental health responses to sexual assault [12, 32]. Negative social reactions have been associated with survivors' increased levels of PTSD, depression and anxiety symptoms; however, research findings are inconsistent regarding whether positive social reactions to sexual assault disclosure are related to survivors' mental health [12, 38, 44].

Relationship between Perpetrator and Survivor
There is inconsistent evidence regarding whether the nature of the relationship between the survivor and the perpetrator influences adult survivor's mental health sequela. A study of 700 women who experienced sexual assault at age 14 or older found that those who were victimized by a relative reported the highest level of PTSD symptoms, while those who were victimized by an acquaintance reported the lowest level [43]; however, a similar pattern was not found for depressive symptoms. Having been raped by a stranger has also been associated with increased PTSD and depressive symptoms [43, 45]; however, this finding may be attributed, at least in part, to the fact that assault by strangers is often more violent than assault by nonstrangers. Other studies have not found that rape by strangers, compared to rape by others, results in greater PTSD and depressive symptom severity [42, 46].

Mental Health Interventions for Sexual Assault Survivors

Given that many sexual assault survivors have mental health problems, research has begun to examine the effectiveness of relatively brief (typically between 5 and 18 h of treatment) mental health interventions designed to address these needs. A recent literature review examined 17 studies investigating the efficacy of mental health interventions for female adolescent and adult sexual assault survivors with PTSD, depression and/or anxiety [47]. The interventions included cognitive behavior therapies (e.g. Cognitive Processing Therapy, Prolonged Exposure Therapy, Stress Inoculation Training, other forms of Cognitive Behavioral Treatment) as well as Eye Movement Desensitization and Reprocessing, Supportive Counseling, and Pharmacotherapy. Beneficial effects were found for four interventions: Cognitive Processing Therapy, Eye Movement Desensitization and Reprocessing, Prolonged Exposure Therapy, and Stress Inoculation Training. Although each of these four treatments was more helpful than no treatment, there was little difference in the effectiveness of these four treatments. In addition, approximately a third of women provided with these generally effective interventions either dropped out of treatment early or maintained a diagnosis of PTSD at the end of treatment.

Conclusions

Research has clearly documented that sexual assault of women is a common problem across the globe that inflicts a high burden of suffering. Women who have been sexually assaulted are more likely than nonassaulted women to experience many types of mental health problems, including substance disorder, post-traumatic stress disorder and other anxiety disorders, depression, and suicidal ideation and attempts. Several factors influence women's mental health responses to sexual assault, with more severe and long-lasting mental health problems being experienced by those with a prior history of violence, those experiencing the most severe assaults, and those who receive negative social reactions when they disclose information about their sexual assault experience. Several brief mental health interventions, including particular types of cognitive behavior therapies (Cognitive Processing Therapy, Prolonged Exposure Therapy, and Stress Inoculation Training) and Eye Movement Desensitization and Reprocessing have been shown to be fairly similarly effective in treating the mental health symptoms associated with sexual assault.

In recent years, we have made great strides toward understanding women's mental health responses to sexual assault, and how these mental health sequelae may be successfully treated. Continued collaboration among researchers, funders, advocates, and others is needed to help refine this understanding to better inform the design and implementation of effective sexual assault prevention and intervention strategies.

References

1 World Health Organization: Mental Health Aspects of Women's Reproductive Health: A Global Review of the Literature. Geneva, World Health Organization, 2009.
2 Krug EG, Dhalberg LL, Mercy JA, Zwi A, Lozono R (eds): World Report on Violence and Health. Geneva, World Health Organization, 2002.
3 Garcia-Moreno C, Jansen H, Ellsberg M, Heise L, Watts C: Prevalence of intimate partner violence: findings from the WHO multi-country study on women's health and domestic violence. Lancet (North American edition) 2006;368:1260–1269.
4 Black MC, Basile KC, Breiding MJ, Smith SG, Walters ML, Merrick MT, Chen J, Stevens MR: The National Intimate Partner and Sexual Violence Survey (NISVS): 2010 Summary Report. Atlanta, Centers for Disease Control and Prevention. 2011.
5 Yanqiu G, Yan W, Lin A: Suicidal ideation and the prevalence of intimate partner violence against women in rural Western China. Violence Against Women 2011;17:1299–312.
6 Lamichhane P, Puri M, Tamang J, Dulal B: Women's status and violence against young married women in rural Nepal. BMC Womens Health 2011;11:19.
7 Jewkes R, Abrahams N: The epidemiology of rape and sexual coercion in South Africa: an overview. Soc Sci Med 2002;55:1231–1244.
8 Tsai AC, Leiter K, Heisler M, Iacopino V, Wolfe W, Shannon K, Phaladze N, Hlanze Z, Weiser SD: Prevalence and correlates of forced sex perpetration and victimization in Botswana and Swaziland. AJPH 2011;101:1068–1074.
9 Cloutier S, Martin SL, Poole C: Sexual assault among North Carolina women: Prevalence and health risk factors. J Epidemiol Community Health 2002;56: 265–271.
10 Martin SL, Rentz ED, Chan RL, Givens J, Sanford CP, Kupper LL, Garrettson M, Macy RJ: Physical and sexual violence among North Carolina women: Associations with physical health, mental health, and functional impairment. Women's Health Issues 2008;18:130–140.
11 Zinzow HM, Resnick HS, McCauley JL, Amstadter AB, Ruggiero KJ, Kilpatrick DJ: Prevalence and risk of psychiatric disorders as a function of variant rape histories: results from a national survey of women. Soc Psychiatry Psychiatr Epidemiol 2012;47:893–902.
12 Campbell R, Dworkin E, Cabral G: An ecological model of the impact of sexual assault on women's mental health. Trauma Violence Abuse 2009;10: 225–246.
13 Winfield I, George LK, Swartz M, Blazer DG: Sexual assault and psychiatric disorders among a community sample of women. Am J Psychiatry 1990;147: 335–341.
14 Hankin CS, Skinner KM, Sullivan LM, Miller DR, Frayne S, Tripp TJ: Prevalence of depressive and alcohol abuse symptoms among women VA outpatients who report experiencing sexual assault while in the military. J Trauma Stress 1999;12:601–612.
15 Skinner KM, Kressin N, Frayne S, Tripp TJ, Hankin CS, Miller DR, Sullivan LM: The prevalence of military sexual assault among female Veterans' Administration outpatients. J Interpers Violence 2000;15: 291–310.
16 Martin SL, Beaumont JL, Kupper LL: Substance use before and during pregnancy: Links to intimate partner violence. Am J Drug Alcohol Abuse 2003;29: 599–617.
17 Booth BM, Mengeling M, Torner J, Sadler A: Rape, sex partnership, and substance use consequences in women veterans. J Trauma Stress 2011;24:287–294.
18 Kaukinen C, Demaris A: Age at first sexual assault and current substance use and depression. J Interpers Violence 2005;20:1244–1270.
19 Kilpatrick DJ, Resnick H, Ruggiero K, Conoscenti L, McCauley J: Drug Facilitated, Incapacitated, and Forcible Rape: A National Study. Charleston, Medical University of South Carolina, 2007.
20 McFarlane J, Malecha A, Gist J, Watson K, Batten E, Hall I, Smith S: Intimate partner sexual assault against women and associated victim substance use, suicidality, and risk factors for femicide. Issues Ment Health Nurs 2005;26:953–967.
21 Gruber AJ, Pope HG Jr: Compulsive weight lifting and anabolic drug abuse among women rape victims. Compr Psychiatry 1999;40:273–277.
22 Testa M, Livingston JA, Collins RL: The role of women's alcohol consumption in evaluation of vulnerability to sexual aggression. Exp Clin Psychopharmacol 2000;8:185–191.
23 Kilpatrick DG, Acierno R, Resnick HS, Saunders BE, Best CL: A 2-year longitudinal analysis of the relationships between violent assault and substance use in women. J Consult Clin Psychol 1997;65:834–847.
24 Jordan CE, Campbell R, Follingstad D: Violence and women's mental health: the impact of physical, sexual, and psychological aggression. Annu Rev Clin Psychol 2010;6:607–628.
25 Kaminer D, Grimsrud A, Myer L, Stein DJ, Williams DR: Risk for post-traumatic stress disorder associated with different forms of interpersonal violence in South Africa. Soc Sci Med 2008;67:1589–1595.

26 Baker CK, Norris FH, Diaz DM, Perilla JL, Murphy AD, Hill EG: Violence and PTSD in Mexico: gender and regional differences. Soc Psychiatry Psychiatr Epidemiol 2005;40:519–528.
27 Darves-Bornoz J, Alonzo J: Main traumatic events in Europe: PTSD in the European study of the epidemiology of mental disorders survey. J Trauma Stress 2008;21:455–462.
28 Machado CL, de Azevedo RC, Facuri CO, Vieira MJ, Fernandes AS: Posttraumatic stress disorder, depression, and hopelessness in women who are victims of sexual violence. Int J Gynaecol Obstet 2011;113:58–62.
29 Chan KL, Staruss MA, Brownridge DA, Tiwari A, Leung WC: Prevalence of dating partner violence and suicidal ideation among male and female university students worldwide. J Midwifery Women's Health 2008;53:529–537.
30 Ali FA, Israr SM, Ali BS, Janjua NZ: Association of various reproductive rights, domestic violence and marital rape with depression among Pakistani women. BMC Psychiatry 2009;9:77.
31 Nasreen HE, Kabir AN, Forsell Y, Edhborg M: Prevalence and associated factors of depressive and anxiety symptoms during pregnancy: a population based study in rural Bangladesh. BMC Women's Health 2011;11:22.
32 Coker AL, Smith PH, Thompson MP, McKeown RE, Bethea L, Davis KE: Social support protects against the negative effects of partner violence on mental health. J Women's Health Gend Based Med 2002;11:465–476.
33 Dancu CV, Riggs DS, Hearst-Ikeda D, Shoyer BG, Foa EB: Dissociative experiences and posttraumatic stress disorder among female victims of criminal assault and rape. J Trauma Stress 1996;9:253–267.
34 Kimerling R, Calhoun KS: Somatic symptoms, social support, and treatment seeking among sexual assault victims. J Consult Clin Psychol 1994;62:333–340.
35 Rothbaum BO, Foa EB, Riggs D, Murdock T, Walsh W: A prospective examination of post-traumatic stress disorder in rape victims. J Trauma Stress 1992;5:455–475.
36 Martin SL, Macy RJ, Young SK: Health and economic consequences of sexual violence; in White JW, Koss MP, Kazdin AE (eds): Violence against Women and Children: Mapping the Terrain. Washington, American Psychological Association. 2010, vol 1, pp 173–195.
37 Casey EA: Trauma exposure and sexual revictimization risk: comparisons across single, multiple incident, and multiple perpetrator victimizations. Violence Against Women 2005;11:505–530.
38 Ullman SE, Filipas HH, Townsend SM, Starzynski SS: Psychosocial correlates of PTSD symptom severity in sexual assault survivors. J Trauma Stress 2007;20:821–831.
39 Kimerling R, Alvarez J, Pavao J, Kaminski A, Baumrind N: Epidemiology and consequences of women's revictimization. Women's Health Issues 2007;17:101–106.
40 Resnick HS, Yehuda R, Acierno R: Acute post-rape plasma cortisol, alcohol use, and PTSD symptom profile among recent rape victims. An NY Acad Sci 1997;821:433–436.
41 Resnick HS, Yehuda R, Pitman RK, Foy DW: Effect of previous trauma on acute plasma cortisol level following rape. Am J Psychiatry 1995;152:1675–1677.
42 Ullman SE, Filipas HH: Predictors of PTSD symptom severity and social reactions in sexual assault victims. J Trauma Stress 2001;14:369–389.
43 Ullman SE, Filipas HH, Townsend SM, Starzynski LL: The role of victim-offender relationship in women's sexual assault experiences. J Interpers Violence 2006;21:798–819.
44 Borja SE, Callahan JL, Long PJ: Positive and negative adjustment and social support of sexual assault survivors. J Trauma Stress 2006;19:905–914.
45 Ellis EM, Atkeson BM, Calhoun KS: An assessment of long-term reaction to rape. J Abnorm Psychol 1981;90:263–266.
46 Mackey T, Sereika SM, Weissfeld LA, Hacker SS, Zender JF, Heard SL: Factors associated with long-term depressive symptoms of sexual assault victims. Arch Psychiatr Nurs 1992;6:10–25.
47 Vickerman KA, Margolin G: Rape treatment outcome research: empirical findings and state of the literature. Clin Psychol Rev 2009;29:431–448.

Sandra L. Martin
Department of Maternal and Child Health, CB #7445
Gillings School of Global Public Health, University of North Carolina
Chapel Hill, NC 27599-7445 (USA)
Tel. +1 919 966 5973, E-Mail sandra_martin@unc.edu

Child Sexual Abuse of Girls

Harriet L. MacMillan[a] · C. Nadine Wathen[b]

[a]Offord Centre for Child Studies, McMaster University, Hamilton, Ont., and [b]Faculty of Information and Media Studies, Western University, London, Ont., Canada

Abstract

Child sexual abuse is a common and devastating problem affecting as many as 15 to 30% of girls. Perpetrators of child sexual abuse are more likely to be male; most often someone known to the child. It is now well established that child sexual abuse is a non-specific risk factor for both internalizing and externalizing disorders in girls and adult women, and is associated with neurobiological dysregulation in both childhood and adulthood. Children's exposure to sexual abuse continues to be underrecognized and underdetected. Generally, sexual abuse of a child is detected when a child discloses to another person. A comprehensive assessment is the first step in determining the treatment needs for a child who has been sexually abused and should include evaluation of risk for recurrence, as well as the child's behavioral, emotional and cognitive functioning and the family environment, including level of support. Cognitive-behavioral therapy for sexually abused children with symptoms of posttraumatic stress disorder (PTSD) shows the best evidence for reducing subsequent impairment; however, it is important to consider the child's context and risk of recurrence when determining treatment needs. Although the main focus of sexual abuse prevention has been on education programs aimed at children, and offender management, it remains unknown whether such programs actually prevent child sexual abuse. Most information about sexual abuse of girls is based on studies from high-income countries; further research is needed to improve our understanding of child sexual abuse experienced by children in low and middle-income countries and global strategies for prevention.

Copyright © 2013 S. Karger AG, Basel

Child sexual abuse (CSA) is a prevalent and devastating problem with immediate and long-term consequences on the health and well-being of children, youth and adults. As the epidemiological evidence-base in the area of child maltreatment (CM) has grown, there is increasing clarity regarding the prevalence, risks, causes and consequences of maltreatment, generally, and CSA in particular. For example, we know that girls and boys experience different types of child maltreatment at different rates, and with varying consequences. Similarly, as research efforts are increasingly dedicated to evaluating interventions for CSA, our understanding of how and when to intervene in different contexts has evolved.

This chapter will describe the extent of the problem of CSA with a particular emphasis on the role of sex and gender, and present a summary of existing evidence regarding interventions for how to prevent both initial and repeat exposures to CSA, and, especially, the negative mental health impairment, across the lifespan, associated with CSA. While the focus of this chapter is on the sexual abuse of girls, some information about boys is included for comparison purposes. Most of the studies evaluating the effectiveness of interventions for preventing CSA or associated impairment include samples with both female and male children. Where it is possible to examine specific effects for girls, these findings are highlighted.

Definitions of Child Sexual Abuse
For this chapter, we adopt the broad definitions of CSA proposed by the World Health Organization and the International Society for the Prevention of Child Abuse and Neglect (ISPCAN) [1]:

'Sexual abuse is defined as the involvement of a child in sexual activity that he or she does not fully comprehend, is unable to give informed consent to, or for which the child is not developmentally prepared, or else that violates the laws or social taboos of society. Children can be sexually abused by both adults and other children who are – by virtue of their age or stage of development – in a position of responsibility, trust or power over the victim.'

And by the US Department of Health and Human Services [2]:

'A type of maltreatment that refers to the involvement of the child in sexual activity to provide sexual gratification or financial benefit to the perpetrator, including contacts for sexual purposes, molestation, statutory rape, prostitution, pornography, exposure, incest, or other sexually exploitative activities.'

Additionally, the uniform definitions suggested by the US Centers for Disease Control and Prevention add clarification regarding specific acts (abusive, nonabusive, with and without contact, including prostitution and pornography) and perpetrators, including primary and substitute/temporary caregivers, such as teachers coaches, clergy, and relatives [3].

Epidemiology of CSA

Incidence and Prevalence
Assessing the prevalence of child maltreatment must take into account both the purpose and timing of assessment (e.g. research survey versus clinical assessment; retrospective versus contemporaneous), as well as the type of report (self-, informant or official/agency reports) and child age ranges. The impact of these factors on estimations of prevalence and incidence of maltreatment and its subforms, including CSA, is thoroughly reviewed elsewhere [4, 5]; however, it is important to note that these, as well as variations in context (clinical versus community setting, geography, culture, etc.) contribute to the wide ranges in prevalence reported in the literature.

Several recent comprehensive analyses of CSA were reviewed and are summarized here. Gilbert et al. [4, p. 68] summarize their review of existing data as follows '[d]uring childhood, between 5 and 10% of girls and up to 5% of boys are exposed to penetrative sexual abuse, and up to three times this number are exposed to any type of sexual abuse'. However, they provide the following clarifications. When examining only population-based studies conducted in developed countries, the cumulative prevalence of any sexual abuse (including noncontact, contact, or penetrative abuse) is estimated at 15–30% for girls and 5–15% for boys, with penetrative sexual abuse ranging from 5 to 10% for girls and 1 to 5% for boys. A more comprehensive analysis for the World Health Organization by Andrews et al. [6] found similar results when including studies worldwide, citing estimated prevalence of noncontact sexual abuse at 3.1% for boys and 6.8% for girls; contact sexual abuse at 3.7% for boys and 13.2% for girls; penetrative sexual abuse at 1.9% for boys and 5.3% for girls, and any sexual abuse at 8.7% for boys, and 25.3% for girls. Of the 22 studies that presented data on age at onset of abuse, onset was more prevalent in the 5 to 14-year age group among both girls and boys. Results of two studies indicated that approximately 6.5% of CSA begins in the 0- to 4-year-old age group. The prevalence estimates reported by Andrews et al. [6] are consistent with the very recent meta-analysis of global studies conducted by Stoltenborgh et al. [5, p. 79], which examined estimates by type of report, and concluded that 'overall estimated CSA prevalence was 127/1,000 in self-report studies and 4/1,000 in informant studies. Self-reported CSA was more common among female (180/1,000) than among male participants (76/1,000). Lowest rates for both girls (113/1,000) and boys (41/1,000) were found in Asia, and highest rates were found for girls in Australia (215/1,000) and for boys in Africa (193/1,000)'.

In terms of trends in the incidence of CSA, the evidence is mixed; some studies have noted that rates of CSA, along with crime rates generally, are declining, particularly in the US [7]; however, more comprehensive analyses point to differences in trajectories according to type of report, type of abuse and geographic setting [8].

Determinants

Children in all socioeconomic and ethnic groups experience sexual abuse; risk increases with age [9]. Despite variations according to reporting type and other factors, a consistent trend is that girls experience CSA at a rate on average 2–3 times more frequently than do boys. In terms of risk factors for CSA other than female sex, these include living in a family without a natural parent, poor relationship between parents, presence of a stepfather, poor child-parent relations, young maternal age and parental death [7].

The picture regarding who perpetrates CSA is also complex. As reported in the review by Gilbert et al. [4], a US Department of Health and Human Services report on substantiated cases in the USA in 2006 [2] indicated that 26% of CSA perpetrators were parents, while 29% were a relative other than a parent; however, in other analyses of self-reported CSA, parents represent a much smaller proportion (3–5%) of perpetrators of self-reported sexual abuse [10]. Perpetrators of CSA are more likely to be male, and perpetration onset has been found to peak during adolescence, along with other delinquent behavior, and again in the 30s, when access to children increases [7, 11].

Impairment

It is now well established that exposure to CSA is associated with impairment in a broad range of domains, including mental health, physical health, education, criminal behavior and interpersonal functioning [4, 12]. Although the focus of this volume is on mental health, it is important to recognize the overlap that exists across these domains. For example, a girl who has suffered sexual abuse and is experiencing one or more mental health problems is also at risk for low educational achievement and involvement with the law, among other negative outcomes.

The methods used to examine the relationship between CSA exposure and mental health problems in childhood, adolescence and adulthood have involved predominantly cross-sectional surveys [13], which then limits what is known about CSA as a causal risk factor for psychiatric conditions. Given the ethical and measurement challenges in assessing CSA exposure and impairment, community-based studies that assess contemporaneous mental health consequences generally only include adolescent girls and/or adult women, while studies of mental health problems among sexually abused girls younger than adolescence have typically involved only clinical or court samples. Findings from adult twin cohort studies provide support for a causal relationship because of their ability to control for genetic and common family environmental risk factors for psychiatric disorders [6]. Longitudinal cohort studies that included prospective ascertainment of CSA exposure and subsequent follow-up have improved our ability to understand the temporal relationship between CSA and subsequent outcomes [4, 13]. However, studies that determine exposure using only official reports of CSA are limited in generalizability since children who come to the attention of child protection agencies may differ in important ways, including outcomes, from other sexually abused children [4]. Despite their common reliance on retrospective self-reports of CSA, cross-sectional community-based surveys can provide important information about representativeness and generalizability, thereby adding to what is known about consequences of CSA from cohort studies.

Sexual abuse of girls is associated with both short- and long-term negative effects on mental health, depending on the severity, persistence and presence of risk, and protective factors, both genetic and environmental [9]. Of particular note, children who have experienced CSA are at increased risk of exposure to other types of maltreatment, including physical abuse and neglect and for sexual revictimization in subsequent years [14]. Factors associated with more negative outcomes among those exposed to CSA include increased severity (contact or intercourse compared with noncontact sexual abuse), frequency and duration, and the occurrence of other types of maltreatment [6]. Surprisingly, there is no clear evidence about the role of age at onset of CSA and a meta-analysis found that the relationship between the child and offender did not increase the risk of negative outcome [15]. Much less is known about protective factors; there is some evidence that a supportive relationship with a nonoffending parent and less stress in other areas may reduce the likelihood of negative outcomes [16].

CSA is a nonspecific risk factor for both internalizing and externalizing disorders in girls and adult women; it is associated with neurobiological dysregulation in both child- and adulthood including alterations in the hypothalamic-pituitary-adrenal (HPA) axis [17], the sympathetic nervous system and, as identified more recently, the immune system [18]. Regardless of whether individuals exposed to CSA develop a specific psychiatric disorder, they are at risk for difficulties with affect regulation, impulse control, somatization, cognitive distortions, altered self-perceptions and socialization problems [9]. The following sections provide further details about mental health problems based on age and developmental stage.

Children and Youth

Girls who have been sexually abused may present with a wide range of symptom patterns, including no symptoms [19, 20]. In a comprehensive review of studies that involved predominantly samples from sexual abuse assessment or treatment programs [19], between 21 and 49% were asymptomatic at the time of initial assessment. Sexually abused children were more symptomatic than their nonabused, nonclinical control group counterparts in a broad range of domains that included depression, PTSD, somatic complaints, aggression, behavior problems and sexualized behavior. For two other outcomes – suicidal behavior and poor self-esteem – minimal differences were found. When the comparison group involved a nonabused (reportedly) clinical group of children, sexually abused children were less symptomatic than their nonabused counterparts for many of the symptoms in most of the studies, with the exception of PTSD (one study) and sexualized behavior (six of eight studies). Most of the studies to date and all of those in the meta-analysis by Kendall-Tackett et al. [19] have been conducted in high-income settings. One of the few surveys to examine impairment among sexually abused girls and youth in a low-income country involved a nationally representative sample living in Swaziland [21]. Exposure to CSA was associated with feelings of depression, suicidal ideation and alcohol consumption.

Adults

Among adult women, there is strong evidence of significant associations between CSA and depression, PTSD, panic disorder, drug and alcohol dependence and suicide attempts; relative risks did not differ significantly by disorder [6, 22, 23]. Other mental health conditions for which there is evidence of a relationship include somatization, eating disorders, personality disorders and, more recently, psychotic symptomatology [24]. Certain family variables such as conflict or dysfunction are confounded with CSA and these factors have often not been adequately controlled for when examining associated impairment. Such factors may independently increase the risk for both CSA and psychiatric illness in adulthood or the risk of psychological impairment in sexually abused children [24]. Most studies have found that although the effect of CSA on mental health problems is reduced when family environment is controlled for, CSA still has a significant association with a broad range of adult mental health outcomes [6]. As is the case for children, within nonclinical samples, adults exposed to CSA may experience fewer mental health problems when compared to those from clinical but non-CSA samples.

Some literature suggests that exposure to CSA is linked with higher risk of impairment among adult women compared with men, while others have concluded there is no significant difference, or that males have higher rates of impairment for some outcomes. It is clear, however, given the higher prevalence of CSA among girls, that CSA is associated with a higher percentage of disability-adjusted life years for females compared with males [6].

Identification

Children's exposure to sexual abuse continues to be under-recognized and under-detected. Most commonly, the issue arises when a child discloses to another person; presenting symptoms are often nonspecific and may be associated with a range of additional stressors that make identification of CSA difficult in the absence of a disclosure. In high-income countries, in addition to involvement with child protection services, a health care provider such as a pediatrician or other professionals with a hospital or advocacy-center protection program typically become involved. Key issues to consider when CSA is identified include the child's immediate safety, mental health assessment, the need for a physical examination, including forensic evidence collection, and follow-up with the child and family to reduce the impairment associated with CSA (see 'Treatment', below).

Treatment

A comprehensive assessment is the cornerstone to determining the treatment needs for a child who has experienced sexual abuse. CSA is an exposure, not a disorder, and as outlined above, not all children are symptomatic following sexual abuse. In addition to the above issues to be considered when CSA is identified, an assessment should include evaluation of risk for recurrence, as well as the child's behavioral, emotional and cognitive functioning and the family environment, including level of support. At least eight meta-analyses have reviewed the effectiveness of psychological treatments aimed at reducing impairment in children following exposure to sexual abuse or trauma that includes CSA. Some treatments have included parents or involved family or multilevel treatment, in addition to the child. Children participating in the studies have ranged from 2 to 17 years of age and outcomes have included a broad range of internalizing and externalizing symptoms or disorders, as well as sexualized behaviors. Some meta-analyses have been very broad in their inclusion of uncontrolled studies [25–28], whereas others have included only controlled trials focusing on cognitive-behavioural therapy [29]. Across meta-analyses and other systematic reviews [30, 31] that exclude studies with weaker designs, there is general agreement that cognitive-behavioral therapy is considered the most effective approach to treatment for sexually abused children; however, results vary with regard to magnitude of treatment effect and intervention characteristics. Those reviews that restrict their included studies to controlled trials and apply rigorous criteria in assessing study quality generally conclude that CBT can improve specific mental health outcomes for sexually abused children who present for treatment with posttraumatic stress symptoms, including PTSD, but there is conflicting evidence for reduction of behavioral problems, such as sexualized behaviors [31]. Involvement of a nonoffending parent in treatment appears to improve outcomes for the child [30]. While the interventions vary in program content and frequency, common themes for the child sessions include: safety education, coping skills, identification of inappropriate behaviors, processing of the abusive experience, relaxation strategies, graduated exposure in decreasing avoidance behavior and assistance in dealing with problems related to the victimization [29]. Sessions conducted with the parent or parent and child jointly, should focus on communication, cognitive reframing, psycho-education and parent-management training [29]. In trauma-focused CBT [32], the model of CBT for which there is the best evidence of effectiveness in treating sexually abused children, treatment as provided in a multisite trial involved 12-weekly individual 45-min sessions for parents and children delivered by one therapist and three sessions that included a joint parent-child session. Effect sizes based on results from those reviews that applied more rigorous inclusion criteria were generally in the moderate range for PTSD symptoms [29].

While it is encouraging that randomized trials have shown CBT to be beneficial for sexually abused children, studies have been limited in power and length of follow-up. Furthermore, Ramchandani and Jones [30, p. 488] emphasize that treatment of children exposed to sexual abuse must occur 'within the context of the child's circumstances, often including other coexisting difficulties'. In regions where resources are limited, provision of CBT, which requires a trained therapist and regular attendance by the child and nonoffending parent in a program that typically extends over 3 months, can be challenging. Ramchandani and Jones [30] highlight the need for 'a multi-modal therapeutic approach' that takes into account such issues as outreach, provision of support and treatment services for the nonoffending parent and consideration of obstacles such as transport issues and stigma. These issues become magnified in regions with more limited services.

Although a detailed discussion of interventions for women sexually abused as children is beyond the scope of this chapter, a recent meta-analysis of treatment outcome studies of psychotherapeutic approaches for adults exposed to CSA is available [33]. The authors did not restrict their sample to high-quality studies, because these are very few; however, they did consider variation in methodological quality as a factor in the meta-analysis. While the authors concluded that psychotherapeutic treatment overall showed moderate benefits for adults who had been sexually abused in childhood, when one considers the methodologic limitations of the individual studies, there does not appear to be good evidence for a specific type of intervention, nor is it possible at this time to say 'what works for whom' [33, p. 763].

Prevention

Sexual abuse prevention has focused on two main strategies: school-based education programs for children and offender management, including registering sex offenders and efforts to increase their incarceration [7]. With regard to education programs, several systematic reviews including the most recent [34, 35] have concluded that while there is evidence that such programs can improve children's knowledge and awareness about sexual abuse, it remains unknown whether these approaches actually prevent sexual abuse or lead to disclosures. A minority of programs have reported negative effects such as increased anxiety among children. Many of the studies have major methodological weaknesses, including lack of blinding and limited follow-up. Overall and consistent with previous systematic reviews, it remains unclear whether increased knowledge and abuse prevention skills actually translate into reduction in CSA. It is also unknown whether offender management reduces sexual abuse of children as outlined in a review by Finkelhor [7]. Most adults who abuse children are likely not caught, arrested or convicted. More recent efforts have focused on community-based primary prevention strategies – for example, aimed at increasing awareness of situations that increase risk of CSA and enhancing protection of children. The effectiveness of such strategies is unknown.

Conclusions

This chapter presented a summary of current best evidence for the identification, prevention and treatment of CSA, with a specific focus on the epidemiology and impact of CSA on girls and women. Several issues regarding sex and gender are interesting to note. As discussed in the comprehensive review by Stoltenborgh et al. [5], some important factors related to gender roles may be at play when considering differential prevalence and incidence rates of CSA among boys and girls. First, it may simply be the case that girls are more likely to experience all forms of CSA. However, it may also be the case that males are more reluctant to disclose abuse, or to even view their experiences as abusive. As stated by Stoltenborgh, this can be for several reasons, including feelings of weakness or failure in being a victim when males are normed as aggressors, fear that in fact they will be assumed to be the instigator rather than the victim, or seen to be homosexual for having been subjected to acts by male perpetrators. Extending this concept of social norms, males may not even view experiences of sexual acts with older women as being abusive. Overall, male victims tend to disclose CSA experiences, on average, 10 years later than female victims [36], which led Stoltenborgh et al. [5] to conclude that in their findings the prevalence of CSA in adult samples, compared to child samples, was higher for boys, but not for girls.

Full examination of the role of gender in the perpetration and experience of CSA is beyond the scope of this chapter, however, as stated by Nelson and Oliver [37, p. 554]: '[n]either legalistic gender-neutral categories nor prior feminist theories adequately capture all of the gender dynamics of child sexual abuse.' Consideration of these factors may assist researchers and clinicians in framing approaches to prevention, identification, and treatment of CSA among girls, and boys.

Finally, most information about sexual abuse of girls is based on studies from high-income countries; further research is needed to improve our understanding of CSA experienced by children in low and middle-income countries. Although there is evidence about therapeutic approaches to reducing impairment in both girls and women exposed to CSA, the generalizability of such programs beyond high-income countries is unclear. Investigation of what works in preventing CSA at both an individual and a policy level is needed globally.

References

1 Butchart A, Kahane T, Phinney Harvey A, Mian M, Fürniss T: Preventing Child Maltreatment: a Guide to Taking Action and Generating Evidence. Geneva, WHO and International Society for the Prevention of Child Abuse and Neglect, 2006.

2 US Department of Health and Human Services, Administration for Children and Families, Administration on Children, Youth and Families, Children's Bureau: Child Maltreatment 2006. Available at: http://www.acf.hhs.gov/programs/cb/stats_research/index.htm#can. 20.

3 Leeb RT, Paulozzi L, Melanson C, Simon T, Arias I: Child Maltreatment Surveillance: Uniform Definitions for Public Health and Recommended Data Elements, V. 1.0. Atlanta (GA): Centers for Disease Control & Prevention, National Center for Injury Prevention & Control; 2008. Available: http://www.cdc.gov/ViolencePrevention/pub/CMP-Surveillance.html.

4 Gilbert R, Widom CS, Browne K, Fergusson D, Webb E, Janson S: Burden and consequences of child maltreatment in high-income countries. Lancet 2009;373:68–81.

5 Stoltenborgh M, van Ijzendoorn MH, Euser EM, Bakermans-Kranenburg MJ: A global perspective on child sexual abuse: meta-analysis of prevalence around the world. Child Maltreat 2011;16:79–101.

6 Andrews G, Corry J, Slade T, Issakidis C, Swanston H: Child sexual abuse; in Ezzati M, Lopez AD, Rodgers A, Murray CJL (eds): Comparative Quantification of Health Risks: Global and Regional Burden of Disease Attributable to Selected Major Risk Factors. Geneva, WHO, 2004, vol. 2, pp 1851–1940.

7 Finkelhor D: The prevention of childhood sexual abuse. Future Child 2009;19:169–194.

8 Gilbert R, Fluke J, O'Donnell M, Gonzalez-Izquierdo A, Brownell M, Gulliver P, Janson S, Sidebotham P: Child maltreatment: variation in trends and policies in six developed countries. Lancet 2012;379:758–772.

9 Putnam FW: Ten-year research update review: child sexual abuse. J Am Acad Child Adolesc Psychiatry 2003;42:269–278.

10 Fergusson DM, Mullen PE: Childhood sexual abuse-an evidence-based perspective. Thousand Oaks, Sage, 1999.

11 Smallbone S, Wortley R: Onset, persistence, and versatility of offending among adult males convicted of sexual offenses against children. Sex Abuse 2004;16:285–298.

12 Friesen MD, Woodward LJ, Horwood LJ, Fergusson DM: Childhood exposure to sexual abuse and partnership outcomes at age 30. Psychol Med 2010;40:679–688.

13 Cutajar MC, Mullen PE, Ogloff JR, Thomas SD, Wells DL, Spataro J: Psychopathology in a large cohort of sexually abused children followed up to 43 years. Child Abuse Negl 2010;34:813–822.

14 Roodman ACA, Clum GA: Revictimization rates and method variance: a meta-analysis. Clin Psychol Rev 2001;21:183–204.

15 Paolucci EO, Genuis ML, Violato C: A meta-analysis of the published research on the effects of child sexual abuse. J Psychol 2001;135:17–36.

16 Spaccarelli S, Kim S: Resilience criteria and factors associated with resilience in sexually abused girls. Child Abuse Negl 1995;19:1171–1182.

17 Heim C, Shugart M, Craighead WE, Nemeroff CB: Neurobiological and psychiatric consequences of child abuse and neglect. Dev Psychobiol 2010;52:671–690.

18 Nunes SOV, Watanabe MAE, Morimoto HK, Moriya R, Reiche EMV: The impact of childhood sexual abuse on activation of immunological and neuroendocrine response. Aggress Violent Behav 2010;15:440–445.

19 Kendall-Tackett KA, Williams LM, Finkelhor D: Impact of sexual abuse on children: a review and synthesis of recent empirical studies. Psychol Bull 1993;113:164–180.

20 Deblinger E, Mannarino AP, Cohen JA, Steer RA: A follow-up study of a multisite, randomized, controlled trial for children with sexual abuse-related PTSD symptoms. J Am Acad Child Adolesc Psychiatry 2006;45:1474–1484.

21 Reza A, Breiding MJ, Gulaid J, Mercy JA, Blanton C, Mthethwa Z, Bamrah S, Dahlberg LL, Anderson M: Sexual violence and its health consequences for female children in Swaziland: a cluster survey study. Lancet 2009;373:1966–1972.

22 Scott KM, Smith DR, Ellis PM: Prospectively ascertained child maltreatment and its association with DSM-IV mental disorders in young adults. Arch Gen Psychiatry 2010;67:712–719.

23 Hillberg T, Hamilton-Giachritsis C, Dixon L: Review of meta-analyses on the association between child sexual abuse and adult mental health difficulties: a systematic approach. Trauma Violence Abuse 2011;12:38–49.

24 Maniglio R: The impact of child sexual abuse on health: a systematic review of reviews. Clin Psychol Rev 2009;29:647–657.

25 Hetzel-Riggin MD, Brausch AM, Montgomery BS: A meta-analytic investigation of therapy modality outcomes for sexually abused children and adolescents: an exploratory study. Child Abuse Neg 2007;31:125–141.

26 Harvey ST, Taylor JE: A meta-analysis of the effects of psychotherapy with sexually abused children and adolescents. Clin Psychol Rev 2010;30:517–535.

27 Sánchez-Meca J, Rosa-Alcázar AI, López-Soler C: The psychological treatment of sexual abuse in children and adolescents: a meta-analysis. Int J Clin Health Psychol 2011;11:67–93.

28 Trask EV, Walsh K, DiLillo D: Treatment effects for common outcomes of child sexual abuse: a current meta-analysis. Aggress Violent Behav 2011;16:6–19.

29 Macdonald GM, Higgins JP, Ramchandani P: Cognitive-behavioural interventions for children who have been sexually abused. Cochrane Database Syst Rev 2006;4:CD001930.

30 Ramchandani P, Jones DP: Treating psychological symptoms in sexually abused children: from research findings to service provision. Br J Psychiatry 2003;183:484–490.

31 MacMillan HL, Wathen CN, Barlow J, Fergusson DM, Leventhal JM, Taussig HN: Interventions to prevent child maltreatment and associated impairment. Lancet 2009;373:250–266.

32 Cohen JA, Deblinger E, Mannarino AP, Steer RA: A multisite, randomized controlled trial for children with sexual abuse-related PTSD symptoms. J Am Acad Child Adolesc Psychiatry 2004;43:393–402.
33 Taylor JE, Harvey ST: A meta-analysis of the effects of psychotherapy with adults sexually abused in childhood. Clin Psychol Rev 2010;30:749–767.
34 Zwi KJ, Woolfenden SR, Wheeler DM, O'Brien TA, Tait P, Williams KW: School-based education programmes for the prevention of child sexual abuse. Cochrane Database Syst Rev 2007;3:CD004380.
35 Topping KJ, Barron IG: School-based child sexual abuse prevention programs: a review of effectiveness. Rev Educ Res 2009;79:431–463.
36 O'Leary PJ, Barber J: Gender differences in silencing following childhood sexual abuse. J Child Sex Abus 2008;17:133–143.
37 Nelson A, Oliver P: Gender and the construction of consent in child-adult sexual contact: beyond gender neutrality and male monopoly. Gender Soc 1998;12:554–577.

Harriet L. MacMillan, MD
Departments of Psychiatry and Behavioural Neurosciences and Pediatrics
Offord Centre for Child Studies, McMaster University
Patterson Building, 1280 Main Street West
Hamilton, ON L8S 4K1 (Canada)
E-Mail macmilnh@mcmaster.ca

Special Aspects of Violence

Sexual Violence and Armed Conflict: A Systematic Review of Psychosocial Support Interventions

Vivi Stavrou

Independent Social Development Consultant, Columbia Group for Children in Adversity and REPSSI Associate, Bethesda, Md., USA

Abstract

High rates of psychological distress and mental disorders have been documented in survivors of sexual violence in areas of armed conflict. The history of conflict-related sexual violence is a long one, but it was not until the 1990s that gender-based violence and in particular sexual violence, was viewed as a widespread international public health and human rights issue. Mental health and psychosocial support is recognized as a core public health, social welfare and protection area in complex emergencies, including armed conflicts. Despite the acknowledged scale of the problem, little is known about effective interventions for survivors of sexual violence in areas of armed conflict in low- and medium income countries. This systematic review found only five documented outcome studies which met the inclusion criteria. Although evidence is extremely limited and methodological limitations make it difficult to make firm conclusions as to what extent the intervention's outcomes contributed to achieving their stated goals, the reviewed studies reinforce what is considered 'best practice' for psychosocial interventions with survivors of sexual violence in settings of armed conflict. Further rigorous research is needed.

Copyright © 2013 S. Karger AG, Basel

Armed conflicts often do not only aim to achieve a military victory, but are also an attempt to destroy the opponent's culture and society. A key feature of armed conflicts can be acts of sexual violence that are neither random opportunistic acts nor methods of warfare, but can be understood as a sexual expression of aggression conditioned by historical grievances that can include ethnic, religious, economic, and social conflicts that give rise to violent hatred [1]. The occurrence of conflict-related sexual violence is neither confined to the present day nor to particular groups, it has taken place throughout history and across continents, and varies in extent and form across different war settings [2]. While acts of conflict related gender-based violence, which includes sexual violence, are perpetrated against males and females, in global terms it has a significantly greater impact on women and girls than on men and boys.

Sexual violence in conflict is not restricted to rape, nor does conflict-related sexual violence end with the war. As in many other contexts of socio-political and economic transition, volatile postconflict environments with fragile and often malfunctioning state and social structures, means that the population continues to experience extreme hardship and exposure to ongoing violence [3]. Such social dynamics can result in the forced displacement of masses of people, the breakup of established communities, family separation and the inability to create an adequate livelihood [4, 5]. A review of prevalence studies of sexual violence in settings of armed conflict observed that rates of intimate partner violence were high across all included studies, often higher than rates of wartime rape and sexual violence perpetrated by individuals outside of the home [6].

A high prevalence of psychological distress and mental disorders has been documented in survivors of sexual violence in areas of armed conflict, and these findings are to a large extent similar to those conducted with survivors of sexual abuse in nonconflict-affected settings [7–14]. Systematic reviews of the published literature indicate that survivors have higher rates of anxiety disorders (including posttraumatic stress disorder), major depressive disorder, somatic complaints, suicidal thoughts and attempts, sexually transmitted infections, eating disorders and substance abuse [15–17]. Associations between sexual abuse and depression, eating disorders, and PTSD are strengthened by a history of rape [17]. Health consequences not only include sexually transmitted infections, but also unwanted pregnancies, gynecological problems, physical injuries, and higher maternal mortality [18, 19].

Cultural and traditional norms dictate the support received by the survivor and/or the perpetrator [20]. Survivors of sexual violence, including children born of rape, are often blamed for the assault and are shunned by family and the community as they are considered to bring dishonor to all with whom they associate [21]. The social impacts for survivors, their families and communities are profound and long-lasting, and gender-based violence (GBV) poses significant costs for the economies of developing countries, including lower worker productivity and incomes and lower rates of accumulation of human and social capital [22].

The history of conflict-related sexual violence is a long one, but it was not until the 1990s that GBV, and in particular sexual violence, was viewed as a widespread international public health and human rights issue. This spurred the recognition that policies and interventions addressing GBV needed to be accepted as a basic part of any humanitarian response [23–27].

Despite the acknowledged scale of the problem, little is known about effective mental health and psychosocial (MHPSS) interventions for survivors of sexual violence in areas of armed conflict in low and medium income countries. Most evaluations of MHPSS interventions with survivors of sexual violence have taken place in high income countries and outside of conflict-affected areas, and those within conflict-affected areas focus on the general population of adults and children. These outcome studies tend to focus largely on mental health interventions that center on counseling approaches and clinical mental health categories such as major depression or PTSD. Much can be learnt from such MHPSS interventions; however, these intervention strategies cannot be unconditionally extrapolated and applied to survivors of sexual violence in conflict-affected areas. The dynamics of the perpetration, violation experiences, the social and cultural impact of sexual violence, the influence of sociocultural norms on help-seeking behavior, social support and exclusion and service provision, are very different for gender-based violence. For example, there is evidence that sexual assault victims may have higher initial levels of mental health symptoms and psychosocial distress than the general population and other people who have experienced armed conflict [6, 28]; that rape as part of war is strongly related to mental health status and is not so strongly mediated by 'daily stressors' experienced postconflict [29], and that survivors of sexual violence may have a slower pattern of recovery than other conflict-affected people in the population [30].

The aim of this review is to summarize existing evidence on the effectiveness of interventions to address the psychosocial well-being of women and girls who have suffered sexual violence in areas of armed conflict.

Review Methodology

Four themes structured the review's inclusion criteria: armed conflict, sexual violence, psychosocial intervention and evaluation. An article or programme evaluation had to address all four of these thematic areas to be accepted. Intervention evaluations were included if they:

1. Described an evaluation or outcome study of an intervention aimed at the prevention of psychosocial distress and the strengthening of psychosocial well-being associated with sexual violence in conflict affected settings. Using the Uppsala Conflict Data Program, countries were identified in which armed conflict was recorded between 2001 and 2009. Data was obtained from 53 territories and countries in Africa, the Middle East, the Americas, and Europe [31].
2. This review's definition of sexual violence is based on the WHO World Report on Violence and Health definition [2] as, 'any sexual act, attempt to obtain a sexual act, unwanted sexual comments or advances, or acts to traffic, or otherwise directed, against a person's sexuality using coercion, by any person regardless of their relationship to the victim, in any setting, including but not limited to home and work. . . .Sexual violence includes rape, coerced undressing, and nonpenetrating sexual assault such as sexual mutilation.'
3. The evaluations had to include evidence that positive psychosocial outcomes at the level of the survivors were enhanced or negative outcomes were reduced, or that both occurred. With regard to psychosocial well-being and distress, the review refers to psychosocial interventions outlined in The Inter-Agency

Standing Committee Guidelines on Mental Health and Psychosocial Support in Emergencies [25]. Interventions had to address at least one quantifiable measure of psychosocial well-being or distress out of the three core psychosocial well-being domains referred to by the Inter-Agency Guide to the Evaluation of Psychosocial Programming in Emergencies [32]: emotional and social well-being, acquisition of skills and knowledge. Interventions were included if they demonstrated behavioral outcomes at any point, even if these results decayed over time.

4   Finally, the evaluation had to show adequate study design and outcome measures indicating a measure of internal validity and to allow conclusions to be drawn regarding programme effectiveness.

The search strategy looked for outcomes-based programme evaluations reported in the grey and academic literature. Contacts in the field were requested to forward relevant references, studies and reports to the researchers. The review does not focus on children. Separate systematic reviews of interventions for children in post-conflict settings have recently been published [8, 14]. The search was conducted between 20 July and 30 August 2011, and was limited to English language documents written in the past 10 years (January 2000 to July 2011).

Results

In total, 5 studies were identified with levels of evidence that best met the inclusion criteria – 52,693 reports and articles were screened, 189 were selected for full review, 184 were excluded as not meeting the review criteria, leaving 5 for inclusion. Four further studies are discussed that describe psychosocial interventions for survivors of sexual violence in armed conflict settings, but that did not meet the selection criteria as they do not include a formal evaluation strategy of changes in psychosocial well-being or distress [1, 37, 38, 21].

Hustache et al. [33] report postintervention improvement in functioning among 70 women survivors of 'sexual violence by unknown perpetrator wearing military clothes' in the Republic of the Congo. The intervention consisted of between one and four individual consultations as part of medical service delivery. Psychological support, delivered by a psychologist, included offering a safe environment for sharing of experiences and expression of distress, active listening, normalizing reactions, work on coping strategies and development of future plans. Leskes et al. [34] report PTSD scores decreased for a trauma counseling intervention (eight sessions of individual trauma counseling over 3 months) in Liberia, but increased for an intervention aimed at income generation and waitlist controls among 66 women (68% survivors of sexual violence). The skills training and income generating intervention was only effective in reducing PTSD symptoms with regard to women with higher PTSD scores, and the evaluation recommends a combination package of psychosocial counseling and income generating activities. In an uncontrolled study, Plester [35] shows improvement in PTSD symptoms, depression, anxiety, somatic concerns and empowerment among 39 women in Albania (most of whom were sexual violence survivors) who received group counseling (9 sessions over 12 weeks) of a combination of cognitive behavioral therapy (CBT), psychodrama, imagination exercises and relaxation techniques; those with highest PTSD scores improved the most.

Two evaluations examined the impact of multi-modal community-based approaches. A study by Ager et al. [36] conducted among women who were formerly abducted and held by an armed group in Sierra Leone, found that girls and young women in both intervention and comparison communities made progress towards integration. Psychological support, delivered by a psychologist, included offering a safe environment for sharing of experiences and expression of distress, active listening, normalizing reactions, work on coping strategies and development of future plans. The intervention combined traditional healing, economic strengthening, outreach and education, medical care, and micro-credit (n = 142). Bolton [3] demonstrates post-intervention improvement in functioning and indices of psychological distress among 65 women sexual violence survivors in the Democratic Republic of the Congo. The intervention programme mixed support to service providers (health, psychosocial and legal) and grassroots women's projects with interagency mechanisms for service delivery and referral.

Discussion

The State of the Evidence Base
Despite the limited number of evaluations included in this review, consistent findings emerged across the evaluations and the different countries and offer useful lessons for policy and practice.

An Integrated Approach to Psychosocial Interventions for Survivors of Conflict Related Sexual Violence
The type of intervention most strongly emerging from the evidence base is the location of psychosocial interventions for survivors of sexual violence in conflict affected settings within broader, community-based, multidisciplinary support programmes. In terms of programming, a multidisciplinary and multisectoral approach remains, to date, the 'best practice' for the prevention of and response to GBV within the humanitarian field. All of the included outcome studies adopted an integrated approach to psychosocial programming with survivors of conflict-related sexual violence – including different combinations of medicolegal services and/or referral to such services; support groups and economic strengthening activities (skills training in vocational and income generating skills, access to microcredit); community outreach (advocacy and psychoeducation); interagency collaboration and capacity

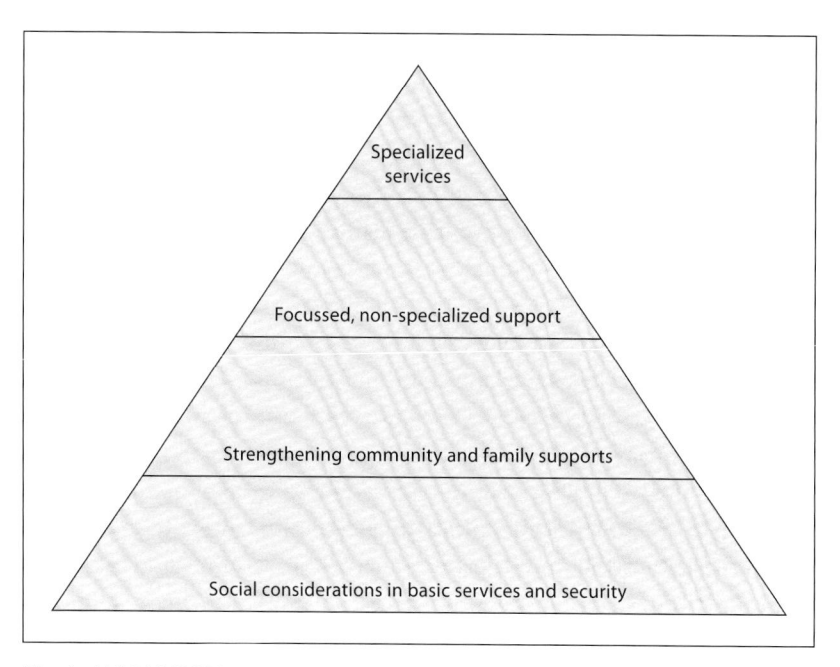

Fig. 1. IASC MHPSS intervention pyramid.

building (service delivery development and referral systems). None described stand-alone psychosocial interventions. There is a deliberate and explicit bringing together of psychological factors and social inclusion and not focusing only on either medical, legal, material, psychological, spiritual or welfare support.

Counseling and strengthening community-based supports are among the most popular interventions in humanitarian settings. The interventions included in the review largely slotted into the two middle layers of the IASC MHPSS pyramid – 'focused nonspecialized supports' and on 'strengthening community and family supports,' and not on the population-based approaches of the bottom layer – social considerations in basic services and security (fig. 1) [25].

Linking Psychosocial Support with Access to Education, Medical Care and Economic Strengthening Activities
Two programming linkages in particular were a feature of the psychosocial interventions included in the review: medical care for sexually transmitted infections and gynecological treatment, and the establishment of linkages between psychosocial counseling support and economic strengthening activities. All the women in the MSF intervention in the Republic of Congo received psychosocial support and medical care as part of integrated sexual violence, hospital-based, medical services [33]. The Liberian evaluation of two types of community-based support interventions recommends a combination package of psychosocial counseling and income generating

activities [34]. The SEFAFU programme in Sierra Leone combined access to traditional healing ceremonies with vocational skills training and access to microcredit [36]. A key lesson from an innovative participatory action research programme with war affected and vulnerable young mothers in three sub-Saharan countries was that when the young mothers participating in the programme had sustainable livelihoods, sex work was much less likely to be used as a survival strategy [21].

Access to formal and informal education is a strong feature of the included evaluation studies. The literature examining interventions with young children and adolescents exposed to armed conflict that are participating in school-based psychosocial interventions, demonstrate positive psychosocial outcomes, in particular for improving social behavioral and resilience indicators [39, 40].

While MHPSS interventions for survivors of sexual violence are often addressed at an individual level, two of the evaluations [3, 36] and the description of the intervention for refugees in Canada [1] directed interventions at the community level through advocacy, community-based education, consultations and community ceremonies, and strengthening inter-agency service delivery and referral systems that respond to the security and protection needs of women and girls.

Short-Term, Context and Culturally Adapted Individual and Group Counseling
There is inadequate evidence to comment on the specificity of the counselling techniques and treatment settings, and very little was written about the nature and duration of the improvements of psychosocial well-being. That said, the evaluations suggest that while the majority of female survivors of sexual violence who participated in short-term individual and group counseling in conflict affected settings are likely to gain some benefit and to maintain this benefit over time, the magnitude may not be very large. Women who participated in individual and group counseling and in traditional healing ceremonies showed greater improvements than women in the wait-list comparison groups.

The types of individual and group counseling approaches described in three of the five evaluations used supportive counseling techniques that are broadly based on cognitive behavioral approaches (without exposure procedures). The brief descriptions provided of the counseling process are in line with good practice in this field which recommends the provision of short term psychological counseling services including a focus on the social reintegration and empowerment of the survivor of sexual violence [13, 24, 28, 30, 41].

The SEFAFU evaluation showed a statistically significant association between inclusion in the programme and improved reintegration outcomes and underscores that community and family acceptance are powerful mediating factors and can improve reintegration outcomes for victims of sexual violence. These mechanisms for acceptance and reintegration already exist in communities around the world, and it is important that psychosocial interventions identify and strengthen positive community-originated processes without putting additional stigma on survivors already dealing with a host of problems [36]. Similarly, assessment of the possibility to collaborate with traditional healers is part of current consensus on best practices [12]. The SEFAFU study [36] represents one of the few quantitative studies that measures its effectiveness on locally derived indicators of wellbeing. Such efforts are crucial to strengthen evidence and provide accountability to stakeholders in real-world settings.

Ongoing Community Engagement
All the interventions included an outreach component, such as advocacy and community engagement with local leadership and family members; information/education on sexual violence, the availability and type of service provision, and encouraging community mechanisms for psychosocial support. Sexual violence creates a significant risk for social, especially familial, exclusion; however, to date there has been limited research as to the impact of psycho-education and targeted advocacy campaigns in reducing the incidence of sexual assault, and, if so, what strategies are the most effective.

Community-Based, Primary Care, Low Cost Approaches
Cost-effectiveness was not explicitly explored, but the trend was for community-based, primary care, low cost approaches. All of the interventions assessed used local staff to conduct the psychosocial interventions – most were trained counselors, with some psychologists, social workers and nurses. The interventions reviewed support research which indicates that a system of primary care providers, traditional healers, and community workers, if properly trained and supported, can provide cost-effective, good quality MHPSS services in low resource, conflict affected settings [3, 4, 8].

However, a cautionary note is that a discussion of the quality of the counseling interventions by the evaluators reveals that the counselors struggled to provide psychosocial counseling and group facilitation to an adequate enough standard and found it very difficult to deal with gender issues and understanding and dealing with sex and sexuality [1, 34]. Some counselors reported severe symptoms of stress [34]. The evaluations reported that agencies struggled financially to access adequate funding for sufficient resourcing for the interventions (ongoing training, supervision and support of staff), as well as material support for community-based interventions.

Conclusion

In terms of the very small number of evaluation studies identified, it is evident that the number of studies conducted does not match the significance of the problem. The limited evidence base restricts the ability to compare the limitations and successes of different type of interventions, preventing firm recommendations for scaling up interventions. This situation is due in part to the high levels of complexity associated with gender-based violence, the challenges of developing culturally appropriate measures of psychosocial well-being, and the difficulties in data collection in settings of armed conflict and with regard to sexual violence issues which are a source of shame and stigma. While controlled studies are difficult to conduct in insecure and unstable environments like those in which the selected evaluations took place, this review indicates that evaluations of these interventions can be feasibly conducted through partnerships with implementing organizations. The challenge for psychosocial work in humanitarian emergencies is that it is exactly in these types of environments that such studies are most needed [3]. There is a strong need to direct resources towards systematizing the field and strengthening the quality and impact of supports for survivors of conflict related sexual violence.

The five evaluations included in this review are too few to allow for any definitive conclusions as to the effectiveness of the psychosocial interventions. What is clear however is that the evaluated interventions, despite their limitations, reinforce what is considered 'best practice' for psychosocial interventions with survivors of sexual violence in settings of armed conflict, namely:

- An integrated approach to psychosocial interventions for survivors of conflict related sexual violence.
- Community-based, primary care, low-cost approaches.
- Linking psychosocial support with access to medical care and economic strengthening activities.
- Short-term, context and culturally adapted individual and group counselling.
- Ongoing community engagement.

References

1 Yohani S, Hagen KT: Refugee women survivors of war related sexualised violence: a multicultural framework for service provision in resettlement countries. Intervention: Int J Mental Health Psychosocial Work Counselling Areas Armed Conflict 2010;8:207–222.

2 Wood EJ: Sexual Violence during War: Explaining Variation. Paper presented at the Order, Conflict and Violence Conference, New Haven, 2004.

3 Bolton P: Assessing the Impact of the IRC Program for Survivors of Gender Based Violence in Eastern Democratic Republic of Congo. Final Report. Conducted with support from VTF/USAID by International Rescue Committee Democratic Republic of Congo and The Applied Mental Health Research Group Johns Hopkins and Boston Universities. October 2009.

4 Mollica R, Lopes Cardozo B, Osofsky H, Raphael B, Ager A, Salama P: Mental health in complex emergencies. Lancet 2004;364:2058–2067.

5 Stark L, Ager A: A systematic review of prevalence studies of gender-based violence in complex emergencies. Trauma Violence Abuse 2011;12:127–134.

6 Johnson K, Asher J, Rosborough S, Raja A, Panjabi R, Beadling C, Lawry, L: Association of combatant status and sexual violence with health and mental health outcomes in postconflict Liberia. JAMA 2008;300:676–690.

7 Amone-P'Olak K: Psychological impact of war and sexual abuse on adolescent girls in Northern Uganda. Intervention 2005;3:33–45.

8 Betancourt TS, Williams T: Building an evidence base on mental health interventions for children affected by armed conflict. Intervention 2008;6:39–56.

9 Tol WA, Barbui C, Galappatti A, Silove D, Betancourt TS, Souza R, Golaz A, van Ommeren M: Mental health and psychosocial support in humanitarian settings: linking practice and research. Lancet 2011;in press.

10 Bolton P, Bass J, Betancourt T, Speelman L, Onyango G, Clougherty KF, Neugebauer R, Murray L, Verdeli H: Interventions for depression symptoms among adolescent survivors of war and displacement in Northern Uganda. J Am Med Assoc 2007;298: 519–527.

11 Kalsma-Van Lith B: Psychosocial interventions for children in war-affected countries: the state of the art. Intervention 2007;5:3–17.

12 Miller K, Rasmussen A: War exposure, daily stressors, and mental health in conflict and post-conflict settings: bridging the divide between trauma-focused and psychosocial frameworks. Soc Sci Med 2010;70:7–16.

13 Nickerson A, Bryant R, Silove D, Steel Z: A critical review of psychological treatments of posttraumatic stress disorder in refugees. Clin Psychol Rev 2011; 31:399–417.

14 Jordans M, Tol W, Komproe I, de Jong J: Systematic review of evidence and treatment approaches: psychosocial and mental health care for children in war. Child Adolesc Ment Health 2009;14:2–14.

15 Ellsberg M, Jansen H, Heise L, Watts CH, Garcia-Moreno C: Intimate partner violence and women's physical and mental health in the WHO multi-country study on women's health and domestic violence: an observational study. Lancet 2008;371: 1165–1172.

16 Koss M, Heslet L: Somatic consequences of violence against women. Arch Family Med 1992;1:53–59.

17 Chen LP, Murad MH, Paras ML, Colbenson K, Sattler AL, Goranson EN, Zirakzadeh A: Sexual abuse and lifetime diagnosis of psychiatric disorders: systematic review and meta-analysis. Mayo Clin Proc 2010;85:618–629.

18 Cottingham J, García-Moreno C, Reis C: Sexual and reproductive health in conflict areas: the imperative to address violence against women. BJOG 2008;115: 301–303.

19 Kinyanda E, Musisi S, Biryabarema C, Ezati I, Oboke H, Ojiambo-Ochieng R, Were-Oguttu J, Levin J, Grosskurth H, Walugembe J: War related sexual violence and its medical and psychological consequences as seen in Kitgum, Northern Uganda: a cross-sectional study. BMC Int Health Hum Rights 2010;10:28.

20 Horn R: Responses to intimate partner violence in Kakuma refugee camp: refugee interactions with agency systems. Soc Sci Med 2010;70:160–168.

21 McKay S, Veale A, Worthen M, Wessells M: Building meaningful participation in reintegration among war-affected young mothers in Liberia, Sierra Leone and northern Uganda. Intervention 2011;9:108–124.

22 Bott S, Morrison A, Ellsberg M: Preventing and responding to gender-based violence in middle and low-income countries: a global review and analysis. World Bank Policy Research Working Paper 3618, 2005.

23 Marsh M, Purdin S, Navani S: Addressing sexual violence in humanitarian emergencies. Global Publ Health 2006;1:2:133–146.

24 Inter-Agency Standing Committee: Guidelines for Gender-Based Violence Interventions in Humanitarian Settings: Focusing on Prevention of and Response to Sexual Violence in Emergencies (Field Test Version). Geneva, Inter-Agency Standing Committee, 2005.

25 Inter-Agency Standing Committee: IASC Guidelines on Mental Health and Psychosocial Support in Emergency Settings. Geneva, IASC, 2007.

26 Convention on the Elimination of All Forms of Discrimination against Women (CEDAW). September 3, 198, 19 ILM 33.

27 Convention on the Rights of the Child (CRC): September 2, 1990;1577 UNTS 3.

28 Vickerman KA, Margolin G: Rape treatment outcome research: empirical findings and state of the literature. Clin Psychol Rev 2009;29:431–448.

29 Betancourt T, Khan KT: The mental health of children affected by armed conflict: Protective processes and pathways to resilience. Int Rev Psychiatry 2008;20:317–328.

30 Foa E, Meadows E: Psychosocial treatments for posttraumatic stress disorder: a critical review. Ann Rev Psychol 1997;48:449–480.

31 Harbom L, Wallensteen P: Armed conflicts, 1946–2009. J Peace Res 2010;47:501–509.

32 Ager A, Ager W, Stavrou V, Boothby N: Inter-Agency Guide to the Evaluation of Psychosocial Programming in Emergencies. New York, UNICEF, 2011.

33 Hustache S, Moro M, Roptin J, Souza R, Gansou GM, Mbemba A, Roederer T, Grais R, Gaboulaud V, Baubet T: Evaluation of psychological support for victims of sexual violence in a conflict setting: results from Brazzaville, Congo. Int J Mental Health Systems 2009;3:7.

34 Lekskes J, van Hooren S, de Beus J: Appraisal of psychosocial interventions in Liberia. Intervention: Int J Mental Health Psychosocial Work Counselling Areas Armed Conflict 2007;5:18–26.

35 Plester G: Evaluation of a group counselling for traumatized women in Albania. Medica Mondiale Evaluation Report, 2007.
36 Ager A, Stark L, Olsen J, Wessells M, Boothby N: Sealing the past, facing the future. an evaluation of a program to support the reintegration of girls and young women formerly associated with armed groups and forces in Sierra Leone. Girlhood Studies 2010;3:70–93.
37 Manneschmidt S, Griese K: Evaluating psychosocial group counseling with Afghan women: is this a useful intervention? Torture 2009;19:41–50.
38 Steiner B, Benner M, Sondorp E, Schmitz KP, Mesmer S, Rosenberger S: Sexual violence in the protracted conflict of DRC programming for rape survivors in South Kivu. Conflict Health 2009;3:3.
39 Ager A, Akesson B, Stark L, Flouri E, Okot B, McCollister F: The impact of the school-based Psychosocial Structured Activities (PSSA) program on conflict-affected children in northern Uganda. 2011;submitted.
40 Jordan, M, Komproe I, Wietse T, Kohrt B, Luitel N, Macy R, de Jong J: Evaluation of a classroom-based psychosocial intervention in conflict-affected Nepal: a cluster randomized controlled trial. J Child Psychol Psychiatry 2010;51:818–826.
41 Roberts N, Kitchiner N, Kenardy J, Bisson J: Systematic review and meta-analysis of multiple-session early interventions following traumatic events. Am J Psychiatry 2009;166:293–301.

Vivi Stavrou
Columbia Group for Children in Adversity
9211 East Parkhill Drive
Bethesda, MD 20814 (USA)
Tel. +1 301 915 2025, E-Mail stavrou_baskin@yahoo.com

Special Aspects of Violence

García-Moreno C, Riecher-Rössler A (eds): Violence against Women and Mental Health.
Key Issues Ment Health. Basel, Karger, 2013, vol 178, pp 118–128 (DOI: 10.1159/000342017)

Abuse and Trafficking among Female Migrants and Refugees

Marianne Kastrup

Centre for Transcultural Psychiatry, Mental Health Services Copenhagen, Copenhagen, Denmark

Abstract

The chapter provides a brief overview of the size of the female refugee and migrant population and describes the various reasons lying behind the decisions to leave the country of origin in relation to gender. The premigratory factors that may contribute to mental and physical health problems are discussed as well as postmigratory factors that further add to psychological and physical distress and contribute to social problems. The vast – and increasing – public health problem of physical and mental abuse of refugee and migrant women and in particular the problem of trafficking are analyzed in relation to the causative factors but also to possible therapeutic interventions. Strategies are outlined focusing on how to empower these populations to be better able to cope with their lives. Further, it is discussed what actions should be taken by governments and NGOs to reduce this global problem.
Copyright © 2013 S. Karger AG, Basel

Size of the Problem

An increasing proportion of the global population is migrating from their countries of origin. OECD countries are among the most frequent receivers of migrants with 4.3 million in 2009, although with a reduction of about 7% in 2009 as compared to 2008 [1]. With the current financial crisis relatively more migrant women have joined the labour force. Many reasons are given for migrating: to escape poverty, to be united with family members, to study, to look for new opportunities or jobs – to mention only a few. Seen from a gender perspective, we experience different trends in reasons for migrating, and family unification is one major cause of migration.

Another large group of female migrants is the increasing number of unskilled women from less developed/deprived parts of the world, who migrate to richer countries where they are looking for work in domestic areas or for other unskilled forms of employment. This group deserves particular attention as it is often among these women that we find women who are forced into trafficking or other kinds of abuse.

Among the migrant population, refugees constitute a particular group that from a public health perspective differs from the overall migrant group by having a higher likelihood of traumatic experiences or of being subjected to sexual abuse prior to migration [2]. By the end of 2010, 43.7 million people worldwide were forcibly displaced including 15.4 million refugees [3]. Of the refugees 47% were women and girls.

The refugee population includes a heterogeneous group of persons such as asylum seekers, returnees, internally displaced persons and war victims. It is constantly fluctuating considerably, reflecting the political situation in the world. But gender remains an important aspect that deserves continuous attention, not least from a public health perspective as a large proportion of these women have been subjected to various kinds of violations.

As pointed out by, e.g., Ekblad and Jaranson [4], migrant women often carry a triple burden linked to their sex, their class and their ethnic background, and prejudices and discrimination may be part and parcel of their daily life. As a consequence, we are faced with a public health problem of significant dimensions when dealing with the mental health challenges of female migrants and refugees per se and in particular in relation to trafficking and abuse.

This chapter will focus upon the mental health consequences of such traumatic experiences, the health needs of these women, their access to care, and strategies for how to overcome these health problems. Attention will also be paid to the role of governments, international organizations as well as NGOs in addressing these problems.

Definition and Delineation of Trafficking

Human trafficking may be described as the illegal trade of human beings for the purpose of reproductive slavery, commercial sexual exploitation, forced labor, or a modern-day form of slavery [5]. In 2000, the 'Protocol to Prevent, Suppress and Punish Trafficking in Persons, especially Women and Children', was adopted by the United Nations as the first global, legally binding instrument on trafficking [6]. The protocol aims to facilitate international cooperation in investigating and prosecuting trafficking in persons as well as assisting victims of trafficking to obtain their human rights.

According to the UN, it has been estimated in 2008 that almost 2.5 million people from 127 countries have been trafficked around the world [7], and each year hundreds of thousands of women and girls are sold into sexual slavery and prostitution [8].

Trafficking has been claimed to be the fastest growing criminal industry in the world and is only surpassed by drug trafficking as the most profitable illegal industry in the world [9]. But there is some controversy as to the reliability of such statistics, not least due to the highly political nature of the findings.

In different countries, the legislation defines trafficking differently. To illustrate the complexity of the issue and the diversity in legislation, in Sweden, for example, it is illegal to buy sex, contrary to most other countries. In the US, any sexual commercialization of minors is considered as trafficking – whether or not a movement is involved. And in a few countries like Saudi Arabia it is not prohibited by law [5].

In the present context, trafficking is concentrated on acts related to sexual exploitation of women. For a large proportion of these women, the motive behind accepting an offer to migrate – often offered by a trafficker – is the financial incentive for the women, and frequently also their family, with opportunities that may be unachievable in their home countries. Women may be lured to accompany traffickers tempted by such opportunities and promises, but most frequently the promises are false, and when arriving in the host country, the women soon recognize that they have been deceived. Once in the new country they find themselves coerced under abusive circumstances, often placed in brothels or locked up, and deprived of their passports and legal documents, thereby making them very vulnerable and escape risky.

In many cases, traffickers initially offer legitimate work. The main types of work offered are, as described, unskilled domestic or au pair work, in hotels, or in bars. Traffickers may use a variety of means to obtain power over these women including offers of marriage, direct threats, or intimidation. In a majority of cases, however, the women end up in prostitution. Some women may understand at an early point that they are facing a life as prostitutes, but they may have no knowledge about the nature of the actual life and work conditions as prostitutes that they will encounter in the country of destination.

Women from Africa – in particular Sub-Saharan Africa – and Asia are most commonly trafficked across international borders for commercial sex work in Europe [10]. But there are also an increasing number of women coming from Eastern European countries who move to Western Europe and end as victims of trafficking.

Abuse among Migrant and Refugee Women

Brundtland [11] stated in the WHO World report on violence and health that to stay out of harm's way, some may lock their doors, others have no possibility to escape as the threat lurks behind the closed doors. These others are typically women who are exposed to different kinds of violence often based upon gender inequality. This is the destiny of many women who as migrants or refugees may experience sexual assaults, and the economic dependency upon their perpetrators/traffickers has serious implications on the dynamics of the abuse and how to deal with it [8].

Rape and sexual assault are not only experiences of trafficked women but are also often used as a tactic in warfare and thus experienced by migrant and refugee women. In war zones and in refugee camps, women seek shelter from the conflicts but may end up experiencing further harassments [12]. Such abusive sexual behavior by authorities may be used to show superiority, to humiliate, or as a strategy in ethnic cleansing towards another ethnic group [12]. Furthermore, it is known that women may be forced to render sexual services to survive, to get access to daily necessities, or to protect their children. They may be in a less fortunate position when it comes to leaving refugee camps, getting access to health services or becoming part of development and integration programs. Abuse of women in times of war is nothing new and has extensively been recognized, but it is only recently that rape during war times is defined as a war crime [13].

Premigratory Stress Factors

When reviewing the size of the most common forms of violence against and abuse of women, Watts and Zimmerman [14] concluded that on a global level millions of women are faced with a life pervaded by violence and its consequences. Globalization also facilitates a tendency of making human life itself a commodity [15], thereby expediting human trafficking. A substantial proportion of refugee and trafficked women have been subjected to persecution and violence prior to their arrival in the new host country. The violent acts may be linked to war and strife in their home countries or it may relate to general poverty and exploitation, and in the world report on violence and health, the WHO [8] emphasized the particular problems of women vis-à-vis consequences of violence.

Women living in abusive relations may be the targets of multiple acts of violence over time, and the abuse they are subjected to could be seen as a reflection of their general role in society as second-class citizens who are per se neither entitled to protection from abuse by the authorities nor to access to services. So it may be hypothesized that trafficking and abusive sexual assaults towards migrant women could be seen as one end of a continuum including also sex selective abortion, the deliberate neglect of girls, and intimate partner violence to general discrimination of women or deprivation of their rights.

Consequences of Abuse or Trafficking

In recent years, international organizations have paid increasing attention to the particular problems of trafficked and refugee women. Such women are typically less likely to get access to developmental or integrative initiatives. Many refugee women are faced with life as single providers, and new and often unexpected responsibilities are placed upon them. Women subjected to trafficking may also experience that they – contrary to what they anticipated – end up having little possibility to provide for their family members back in their countries of origin.

For both groups, life in the host country may not provide the personal security they had looked for, and the women are left unprotected and at the mercy of their abusers [16, 17]. Many women may face the threat of becoming ostracized by their own families if any sexual assault is being revealed, which leaves them in a vulnerable and fragile position. To make matters worse, they may experience little understanding and empathy when contacting authorities, e.g. police, in the host country. This may be related to traditional views of a man's right to punish his wife, and victimization is just another aspect of the daily burden women are subjected to [2].

In the case of refugee women, immigration laws may not take into consideration gender-specific situations such as abusive partners and link the residence permit of the woman to that of the head of the household defined as the husband. In the case of trafficked women they may experience a feeling of staying in a legal limbo where no authority seriously takes any action to ensure their rights. In the assessment of the health situation of both groups of women it is important that health professionals are aware of and pay attention to such aspects, and adequate documentation of the abuse is essential if the needs of these women are to be fulfilled. These are issues that both from a public health as well as from a judiciary point of view require further attention.

Health Consequences

Abuse and trafficking may have negative consequences on women's physical and mental health, their ability to work, family situation, status in society, and when living in exile, their language competence and cultural environment. It is documented that a large proportion are frequently subjected to both physical and sexual violent acts, and rape is a frequent risk as well [18]. They are also endangered by their pimps and abuse from those passing by [19]. As a consequence their symptomatology will not only be due to a single, but several traumatic experiences acting cumulatively. Despite that there is a reluctance by the victims to report to the police authorities out of fear that no one will take them seriously or even that further abuse may take place.

Physical Consequences

Abused and trafficked women frequently report various physical complaints and may initially describe physical rather than psychological symptoms [20, 21]. Chronic pains in the head, back, abdomen or chest are among the major complaints. Sexual abuse may leave traces in the musculoskeletal system, and these women often have low lumbar pain and may complain of pains in genitalia, menstrual disturbances and sexual problems.

Psychological Consequences

The psychological consequences of abuse are frequently persistent and invalidating as demonstrated in an increasing body of research produced in many, mainly Western, countries over the last decades [20–25]. Diagnostically, women who have been abused demonstrate a high prevalence of PTSD, depression, anxiety, and substance abuse as well as a risk of suicide attempts. The prevailing symptom manifestations include anxiety, hopelessness, apathy, depression, irritability, emotional instability, cognitive memory and attention problems, personality changes, behavioral disturbances, neurovegetative symptoms such as lack of energy, insomnia, nightmares, and sexual dysfunction [26]. Being subject to abuse may also result in disabling feelings of shame and guilt.

Many of the psychological symptoms of, for example, irritability, sleep disturbances or loss of concentration may represent pathologies attached to the traumatic experiences themselves or may be responses to current stresses of social alienation, racial discrimination or lack of personal control in the refugee or host settings [27]. The experiences of sexual humiliation and shame are closely linked to the abuse that women are exposed to and have been shown to be of importance for the health consequences [28], and victims of sexual violence have significantly more psychiatric disturbances than nonvictims [29].

In fact, experiencing injuries and sexual violence during trafficking will result in higher levels of PTSD, depression and anxiety. The longer the period working in the sex industry, the higher the levels of depression and anxiety reported, but with the level of depression and anxiety decreasing the longer the time out of prostitution, PTSD in contrast has been reported to remain [30]. The symptoms may frequently be long lasting, and it has been demonstrated [31] that trafficked women returning to their countries of origin are likely to suffer from serious psychological distress that may continue after their return.

There is a risk that mental health professionals tend to focus on the pathological aspects of trauma and less on resilience factors such as the resources these women possess, their choice of coping styles, social involvement, or the cognitive styles they use to adapt to a new environment. When taking care of these women, awareness is needed regarding how to encourage the proliferation of protective factors, e.g. spiritual or political involvement or flexibility in coping strategies as well as encouraging self-reliance and inner locus of control [32].

Social Consequences

Due to the long-lasting traumatizing experiences extending over the years, the social and individual levels of traumatization become heavily interrelated. As pointed out societal factors may be among the decisive motives to migrate or flee from a disorganized society affecting negatively the social network. The family relations of the women may become dysfunctional or nonexistent which again leave the women with less support and may result in social exclusion in the new environment.

Cultural Aspects

Cultural and religious traditions have been used to justify discriminatory and abusive behavior towards women, and in many cultures women are under control of their fathers, brothers or husbands [33]. Irrespective of culture, women have a key role as nurturers and providers of emotional support, and they have usually the main responsibility for caregiving in the family. In situations of e.g. forced migration this may overload women's capacity to cope, as prioritizing the needs of the family may result in neglect of their own needs. On the other hand, the caregiving role may have a protective function in exile as women, contrary to their partners, have a natural role and identity in the new environment [12]. It should be kept in mind that women of migrant and refugee background are heterogeneous groups who do not share a common cultural background or similar problems, but what they may share is common influences of interpersonal violence within a sociopolitical context.

Treatment

Access to Care
Refugee women may be particularly vulnerable, as they remain in the refugee camps to a greater extent than men, have less access to health services and may also have another tradition than men in actively seeking help and counseling from strangers [34]. But also women subject to trafficking may have limited access to health services, not least due to the fact that many of them may not have adequate residency permits. Such factors partly explain the apparent higher occurrence of chronic health problems among women exposed to collective violence [35].

It should also be kept in mind that refugee and migrant women might expect a hierarchical directed relationship with the health care providers, and faced with the prevailing Western, more egalitarian, consumer-oriented approach, frustration may appear and result in lack of compliance [2].

Barriers to Help Seeking
The stigmatization related to mental health, common in many cultures, remains an important barrier that requires careful handling and adequate information. Barriers are often associated with the cultural context and may include social isolation, language fluency, shame related to the abuse, lack of resources and lack of access to them [2]. Women may express a general distrust of governmental agencies frequently based on previous experiences and the fear of being expelled from the country. Furthermore, reporting their abuser to the police may only augment the risk of further violence, or police authorities may disbelieve the woman's story, and women may be unwilling to disclose their experiences to health professionals with the result that they feel trapped in their abusive relationships [36].

Therapeutic Aspects

Working in a setting with abused and trafficked women is a challenge that demands cognitive flexibility, warmth, and empathy. The professional may further be faced with language difficulties, negative stereotypes, and different expectations of treatment.

Therapeutic programmes directed towards these groups typically base their work on a multidisciplinary approach combining physical, psychological, and social care [22]. Cognitive behavioral therapy is the best-documented therapy individually or in groups, and psychoeducation is receiving increased recognition as a useful strategy. Psychopharmacological treatment plays an important role, not least due to the high levels of comorbidity [37].

But the supportive element may be essential in certain parts of the therapy as the mere managing in the new environment is crucial and needs to be taken care of before further therapeutic interventions take place [38].

Empowerment

Many women may feel dis-empowered when arriving in a new and frequently hostile environment. It is often stressed that therapeutic interventions towards abused women should have empowerment as a defined goal thereby helping such women to become aware of power dynamics and aim to gain control over their own lives without infringing on 'others' rights [39]. But assisting this empowerment process may be a delicate task for therapists balancing between their wish to respect the values of the woman's culture and their objective to empower the woman by supporting her more assertive sides.

In order to succeed in this, professionals have to listen and discuss the solutions proposed by women in a therapeutic manner and try to build a bridge over cultural incongruence [12]. Therapists working in the West should remember that they are trained in an individualistic society emphasizing autonomy and individual privacy, but that many abused women come from more sociocentric societies where a woman's role to a larger extent is defined by others and where addressing the needs of others play a more important role.

Conclusion

The WHO [8] has emphasized the importance of international treaties setting standards for national legislation and campaigning for legal reforms. Conventions like the 'Convention against Transnational Organized Crime' [40] and the 'Convention on the Elimination of All Forms of Discrimination against Women' [41] outline norms for behavior and take a stand against gender-specific crimes. But the recognition of certain types of sexual crimes as comparable to crimes against humanity is a huge step in the development of international law.

Other steps may be taken to abolish abuse and trafficking. Awareness rising is emphasized by the WHO as a means to prevent women from entering trafficking. Immigration authorities and NGOs further need to take action to inform unskilled women entering the labor market about their rights and how to avoid exploitation.

Many tasks lie ahead, and among them:

- Research is needed on the health implications – short term as well as long term – of having been subjected to abuse and trafficking.
- In order to measure the extent and types of sexual violence in refugee and trafficked women, there is a need for an agreement on what are the appropriate data to collect and inventories to use [42].
- If we are to succeed in alleviating the public health problems among these women, there is a need for closer collaboration between involved agencies [2].
- But most of all we need a commitment from governments and civil societies to work on changing societal norms towards sexual abuse and seeing women as commodities. With increasing migration new directions for global action are needed [43].

References

1 http://www.oecd.org/document/40/0,3746,en_2649_37415_48303528_1_1_1_37415,00.html. Retrieved 08.01.2012.
2 Ekblad S, Kastrup M, Eisenman D, Arcel L: Interpersonal violence towards women: an overview and clinical directions; in Walker P, Barnett E (eds): Immigrant Medicine. Philadelphia, Saunders, Elsevier, 2007, pp 665–671.
3 UNHCR Global trends 2010. http://www.unhcr.org/4dfa11499.html. Retrieved 08.01.2012.
4 Ekblad S, Jaranson J: Psychosocial Rehabilitation; in Wilson JP, Drozdek B (eds): Broken Spirits. The Treatment of Traumatized Asylum Seekers, Refugees, War and Torture Victims. New York, Brenner-Routledge Press, 2004, pp 609–636.
5 WIKIPEDIA http://en.wikipedia.org/wiki/Human_trafficking. Retrieved 02.02.2012.
6 http://en.wikipedia.org/wiki/Protocol_to_Prevent,_Suppress_and_Punish_Trafficking_in_Persons,_especially_Women_and_Children, retrieved 02.02.2012.
7 'UN-backed container exhibit spotlights plight of sex trafficking victims'. Un.org. 2008-02-06. http://www.un.org/apps/news/story.asp?NewsID=25524&Cr=trafficking&Cr1l. Retrieved 25.06.2011.
8 Krug EG, Dahlberg LL, Mercy JA, Zwi AB, Lozano R (eds): World Report on Violence and Health. Geneva, WHO, 2002.
9 Haken, J: 'Transnational Crime in the Developing World'. Global Financial Integrity. http://www.gfintegrity.org/storage/gfip/documents/reports/transcrime/gfi_transnational_crime_web.pdf. Retrieved 25.06.2011.
10 Niaz U: Globalisation and women's mental health: cutting edge information; in Chandra P, et al (eds): Contemporary Topics in Women's Mental Health. Chichester, Wiley, 2009, pp 443–461.
11 Brundtland GH: Preface; in Krug EG, et al (eds): World Report on Violence and Health. Geneva, WHO, 2002, p xi.

12 Kastrup M, Arcel L: Gender specific treatment of refugees with PTSD; in Wilson J, Drozdek B (eds): Broken Spirits: The Treatment of Traumatized Asylum Seekers, Refugees of War and Torture Victims. New York, Brunner & Routledge, 2004, pp 547–571.

13 International Criminal Tribunal for Former Yugoslavia. http://www.icty.org/sid/10312. Retrieved 02.02.2012.

14 Watts C, Zimmerman C: Violence against women: global scope and magnitude. Lancet 2002;359: 1232–1237.

15 Niaz U, Kastrup M: Impact of violence, disasters, migration, and work; in Chandra P, et al (eds): Contemporary Topics in Women's Mental Health. Chichester, Wiley, 2009, pp 359–368.

16 Arcel L (ed): War Victims, Trauma and the Coping Process. Armed Conflict in Europe and Survivor Responses. Copenhagen, International Rehabilitation Council for Torture Victims (IRCT), 1998.

17 Arcel L: Sexual torture: still a hidden problem. Torture 2002;12:3–4.

18 Church S, Henderson M, Hart G: Violence by clients towards female prostitutes in different work settings: questionnaire survey. Br Med J 2001;322: 524–525.

19 Boynton P: Listening to working women (editorial). Br Med J 2001;322:electronic rapid response 14.03.2001.

20 Kastrup M, Jaranson J: Management of victims of torture; in Tasman A, et al (eds): Psychiatry, ed 3. Chichester, Wiley, 2008.

21 Arcel L, Kastrup M: War, women and health. NORA 2004;12:40–47.

22 Arcel L, Kastrup M, Genefke I, Wenzel T: Torture and its consequences to mental health; in Christodoulou G (ed): Advances in Psychiatry. Athens, Beta Press, 2002, pp 161–174.

23 Wenzel T, Kastrup M, Eisenman D: Survivors of torture. A hidden population; in Walker P, Barnett E (eds): Immigrant Medicine. Philadelphia, Saunders Elsevier, 2007, pp 653—663.

24 Arcel L, Genefke I, Kastrup M: The psychological consequences of torture and persecution; in Henn F, et al (eds): Contemporary Psychiatry. Berlin, Springer, 2000.

25 Niaz U: Wars and women's mental health; in Chandra P, et al (eds): Contemporary Topics in Women's Mental Health. Chichester, Wiley, 2009, pp 369–386.

26 Holtz TH: Refugee trauma versus torture trauma: a retrospective controlled cohort study of Tibetan refugees. J Nerv Ment Dis 1998;186:24–34.

27 Arcel L, Folnegovic-Smalc V, Kozaric-Kovacic D, Marusic A (eds): Psycho-Social Help to Victims of War: Women Refugees from Bosnia and Herzegovina and Their Families. Zagreb, Nakladnistvo Lumin, 1995.

28 Sundaram V, Helweg-Larsen K, Laursen B, Bjerregaard P: Physical violence, self-rated health, and morbidity: is gender significant for victimisation? J Epidemiol Commun Hlth 2004;58: 65–70.

29 Atkeson BM, Calhoun KS, Resick PA: Victims of rape: repeated assessment of depressive symptoms. J Consult Clin Psychol 1982;50:96–102.

30 Hossain M, Zimmerman C, Abas M, Light M, Watts C: The relationship of trauma to mental disorders among trafficked and sexually exploited girls and women. Am J Publ Hlth 2010;100:2442–2449.

31 Ostrovschi NV, Prince MJ, Zimmerman C, Hotineau MA, Gorceag LT, Gorceag VI, Flach C, Abas MA: Women in post-trafficking services in Moldova: diagnostic interviews over two time periods to assess returning women's mental health. BMC Publ Hlth 2011;11:232.

32 Arcel L, Folnegovic-Smalc V, Tocilj-Simunkovic G, Kozaric-Kovacic D, Ljubotina D: Ethnic cleansing and posttraumatic coping – war violence, PTSD, depression, anxiety and coping in Bosnian and Croatian refugees. A transactional approach; in Arcel L (ed): War Victims, Trauma and the Coping Process. Armed Conflict in Europe and Survivor Responses. Copenhagen, International Rehabilitation Council for Torture Victims (IRCT), 1998.

33 Kastrup M, Niaz U: The impact of culture on women's mental health; in Chandra P, et al (eds): Women's Mental Health. Chichester, Wiley, 2009, pp 463–483.

34 Helweg-Larsen K, Kastrup M: Consequences of collective violence with particular focus on the gender perspective. Secondary publication. Dan Med Bull 2007;54:155–156.

35 Ashford MW, Huet Vaugn Y: The impact of war on women; in Levy BS, Sidel VW (eds): War and Public Health. Oxford, Oxford University Press, 1997, pp 186–196.

36 Bauer HM, Rodriguez MA, Quiroga SS, Flores-Ortiz YG: Barriers to health care for abused Latina and Asian immigrant women. J Hlth Care Poor Underserved 2000;11:33–44.

37 Quiroga J, Jaranson JM: Politically-motivated torture and its survivors: a desk study review of the literature. Torture 2005;15:No 2–3.

38 Jaranson J, Kinzie D, Friedman M, Ortiz D, Friedman M, Southwick S, Kastrup M, Mollica R: Assessment, diagnosis, and intervention; in Gerrity E, et al (eds): Mental Health Consequences of Torture. New York, Kluwer Academic/Plenum Publishers, 2001, pp 249–275.
39 McWhirter EH: Counseling for Empowerment. Alexandria, American Counseling Association, 1994.
40 http://www.unodc.org/unodc/en/treaties/CTOC/. Retrieved 03.02.2012.
41 http://www.un.org/womenwatch/daw/cedaw/. Retrieved 03.02.2012.
42 Hollifield M, Eckert V, Warner TD, Jenkins J, Krakow B, Ruiz J, Westermeyer J: Development of an inventory for measuring war-related events in refugees. Compreh Psychiatr 2005;46:67–80.
43 Global Commission on International Migration. Migration in an interconnected world: New directions for action. Report of the Global Commission on International Migration. Geneve, 2005. http://www.gcim.org/.

Marianne Kastrup, MD, PhD
Centre for Transcultural Psychiatry, Mental Health Services Copenhagen
Blegdamsvej 9
DK–2100 Copenhagen (Denmark)
Tel. +45 2720 0093, E-Mail marianne.kastrup@regionh.dk

Special Aspects of Violence

Abuse in Doctor-Patient Relationships

Werner Tschan

Psychiatrist in Private Practice, Basel, Switzerland

Abstract

This chapter aims to provide orientation about professional boundaries, the resulting consequences of their transgression and how to treat affected victims. Sexual involvement of professionals with clients is a sexual crime, and not a love affair. The author sets out the definition of professional sexual misconduct (PSM). Health care institutions (doctors' surgery, clinics, hospitals, in- and out-patient departments, care and nursing homes, etc.) must be considered as high risk places for sexual offenses due to the numerous opportunities provided by the professionals' access to clients. On a structural level, this is comparable to intrafamilial sexual exploitation. Myths and facts related to professional sexual misconduct are discussed. Psychotraumatology and attachment theory are essential for the understanding of victim's reaction in the aftermath. Sexual misconduct by heath care professionals is in all cases a relational offense in addition to sometimes being a criminal offense. The historical background of the subject is compared with other medical developments. Offender strategies are outlined in order to provide an understanding of how effective preventive strategies must be implemented. The author puts emphasis on the need of integrating the topic in health professional curricula. And finally this chapter provides answers to the question: What should be done with professionals accused of sexual misconduct? A rehabilitation concept based on sexual offender treatment approaches and retraining of impaired professionals is outlined.

Copyright © 2013 S. Karger AG, Basel

Abuse in the doctor-patient relationship has a disturbing impact on the health condition of affected patients. This contribution outlines the issue and its magnitude, presents the modus operandi of offender-professionals and discusses how to handle the problem. The author also discusses gender issues related to this topic and highlights the need to overcome any form of gender polarization in relation to the issue.

Myths and Facts

Any form of sexualized involvement within the doctor-patient relationship is considered as abuse due to the fiduciary relationship and the power imbalance inherent in any such professional relationship; there can be no consensual intimate relationship between a physician and their patient. This behavior fits into what is known as disruptive behavior which was defined by the American Medical Association as 'personal conduct, whether verbal or physical, that negatively affects or that potentially may negatively affect patient care' [1]. It was clarified in the same paper that disruptive behavior by a physician does not include 'criticism that is offered in good faith with the aim of improving patient care'. The understanding of physicians' difficulties within their professional role evolved over the last forty years, starting with the publication of 'the sick physician' by the American Medical Association in 1971 [2]. In this paper the difficulties are described as related to (1) substance abuse, (2) aging, and (3) somatic and psychiatric illnesses. Patient's safety was considered as being undermined by professional incapacity, an issue at the time addressed as the 'impaired' physician. The problem of sexual abuse only came into consideration later on.

The fact that members of the helping profession abuse their role by committing sexual offenses against patients, taints the professional community overall. The immediate reaction is usually a defensive strategy through denying the facts and blaming the victims. 'A medical doctor does not commit such things.' 'Patients are exaggerating if not blatantly lying when reporting such stories.' Quite a lot of physicians assume that when sexual intimacy occurs between them and their patients, it is both legally and ethically correct. They believe that as long as it is 'consensual' it is ok; however, legal decisions have made it clear that there can be no consensual sexual relations between health care professionals and their patients. This is also reiterated by the WPA (World Psychiatric Association) in their code of conduct [3]. Article 12 of this declaration states that taking advantage of the position of power and the knowledge gained through the therapeutic approach by manipulating the patient in order to obtain sexual access is a breach of trust, regardless of consent. 'Under no circumstances, therefore, should a psychiatrist get involved with a patient in any form of sexual behavior, irrespective of whether this behavior is initiated by the patient or the therapist' (WPA Madrid Declaration 1996 and Amendments) [3]. The medical community in general, clarified the physician's role with the Physician's Charter on Medical Professionalism [4]. In this publication a set of professional commitments are stipulated: 'Commitment to maintaining appropriate relations with patients. Given the inherent vulnerability and dependency of patients, certain relationships between physicians and patients must be avoided. In particular, physicians should never exploit patients for any sexual advantage, personal financial gain, or other private purpose.'

When two centuries ago the famous physician Semmelweis (1818–1865) realized that the death of many women through childbirth was somehow caused by their doctors, an analogous defensive strategy came into play. The statement by Charles Meigs 'A doctor's hands are clean' [5] was considered the outcry of the professional community, and following basic rules of hygiene was considered a waste of time by physicians at that time. Semmelweis did not accuse his fellows – he only presented facts such as the number of women dying. In the wards where midwives were responsible for deliveries 1–2 out of a hundred women died. In the wards, where physicians were responsible up to 30% of all women died. He realized that the problem was neglecting hygiene and presented his conclusions with the sole aim of solving the tragic issue. He simply recommended the use of disinfectants. He did not accuse – however, his fellow colleagues felt accused. For reasons Pasteur found out 25 years later, several thousand women and babies died due to puerperal fever caused by the ignorance of physicians at the time.

We have a similar issue with sexual boundary violations by medical doctors and other health care professionals. Despite the well-known Hippocratic oath formulated over 2,400 years ago, the medical community still tries to downplay the problem affecting the health of both women and men. The subject of boundary violations by health care professionals and how to deal with this risk and its consequences has so far not been integrated into medical curricula. There are still considerable hurdles to a clear awareness of the issue. Just over 30 years ago, the book by Florence Rush [6]: 'The best kept secret' was published. Her book was a shock at the time. People tended to view reality through rose-tinted glasses, misguided by professionals' statements. For example the leading *Comprehensive Textbook of Psychiatry* by Freedman and Kaplan (1974) claimed: 'incest is extremely rare, and does not occur in more than 1 out of 1.1 million people' [quoted in 7]. Today, we have a better understanding about incest; however, this is still not the case for the awareness of sexual offenses committed by professionals against their clients. The WHO World Report on Violence and Health [8] does not mention the fact that around a quarter of all sexual violence incidents against children are committed by professionals having these children under their duty or care. The fact of disruptive behavior by professionals related to sexual violence is not discussed in this report – the taboo is still very powerful. As Taleb [9] has described: 'things that shouldn't happen simply don't happen'.

Definition and Prevalence

The following definition for Professional Sexual Misconduct (PSM) provides an understanding from the viewpoint of the professional role [10]. This definition does not follow legal definitions as outlined by national penal codes. The term PSM enables a better handling of boundaries in the daily practice than the legal definitions.

Definition of Professional Sexual Misconduct

PSM includes any form of sexual behavior committed within a professional role; examples are amongst others:
- (attempted) penetration (vaginal, anal, oral), genital stimulation, whether with or without ejaculation or orgasm, frotteurism

- sexual impropriety, such as kissing, fondling, taking pictures of intimate body parts, voyeuristic or exhibitionistic behavior, and presenting pornographic material
- sexual remarks and insults, (attempted) dating.

Health care institutions are high risk places for sexual boundary violations due to several factors. Among the first is the defensive strategy by decision makers to minimize the problem or even to deny its existence entirely. When there is no problem there is no need to take action and the issue is easy to dismiss as improbable hearsay. Due to the fiduciary role and the position of power, offender-professionals have unlimited opportunities to access patients in an unacceptable way. Of course it is a minority of health professionals who misuse their professional position for committing these violent acts, but their wrong-doing is defended by the majority which feels tainted by such accusations, analogous to what happened when Semmelweis identified physicians as the source of deaths of women in hospitals.

What is known about the magnitude of the problem comes from four different research avenues that have been pursued since the early 1970s [10]:
- Self-administered questionnaires
- Follow-up therapists (professionals providing care for patients in the aftermath of PSM)
- Victim reports
- Consumer reports

Self-reported questionnaires are sent to members of various professional bodies. These studies are not very reliable, but they help to at least provide some estimate of what the dimensions of the problem we face could be. One of these studies was conducted in the Netherlands comparing gynecologists and ear, nose and throat specialists. The general practitioners refused to participate – stating that this subject was not in their interest. Contrary to the general assumption both groups revealed the same number of intimate contacts. In both groups of physicians, 4% of the participants admitted to having had sexual contact with their patients [11]. Another report, for example from general practitioners from New Zealand found that 6% of GPs admitted to intimate encounters with their patients [12].

Studies among therapists who had patients in their treatment who had disclosed sexual abuse by professionals revealed that many patients are affected. These studies are of course not representative. Neither are victim reports, which again help to provide some estimate of what the dimensions of the problem could be. For example, in Switzerland ads were placed in two women's journals (Meyer's Modeblatt, Brueckenbauer) in order to collate data from affected victims. The study was performed by a research project at Fribourg University, Switzerland [13].

Consumer reports deliver representative figures. One was conducted in Canada, Ontario, as part of the Health Monitor, in 1999 [10]. One percent (110,000) of the participants indicated that they had been sexually abused by health care professionals within the last 5 years, and another 2% (220,000) indicated that they had encountered

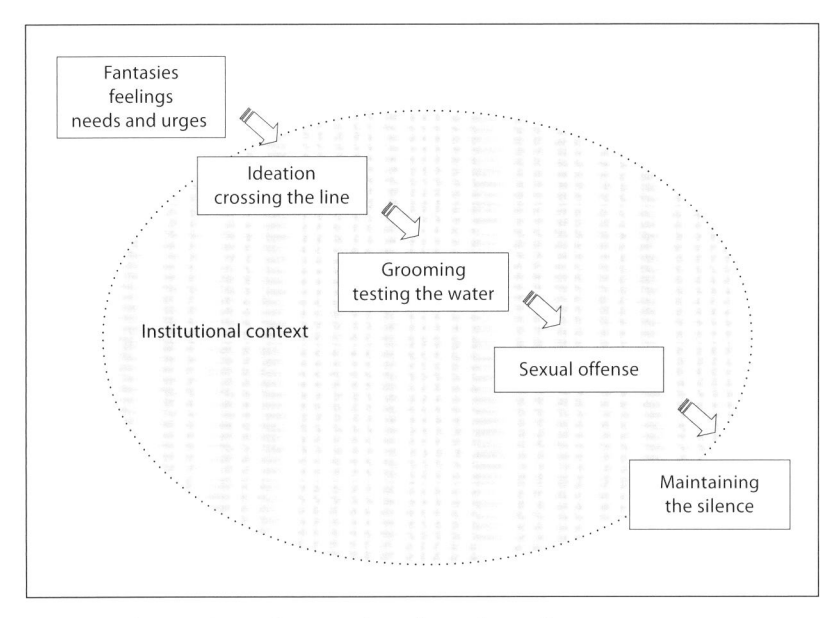

Fig. 1. Professional sexual misconduct: the path to offense.

inappropriate behavior such as undressing without a screen, sexually insulting remarks, dating attempts, etc. This report gives an idea about the magnitude of the problem; however, it must be taken into account that not all victims see themselves as being abused, and others may deny the abuse for personal reasons. Therefore, the real number is likely to be even higher. So far, to my knowledge, Canada is the only country that has conducted such a study.

Modus Operandi

Without understanding the victim-offender-institution-dynamic, no sustainable preventive strategy is possible. The institutional context always has to be considered as well; by simply focusing on the individual offender pathology, we would overlook the institutional preconditions which enable the sexual offences to take place. Creating opportunities in Finkelhor's hurdle model [14] is related to the institutional context, but also to education and training. In figure 1 the path to offense is outlined in a linear fashion embedded into the systemic conditions.

Using this model each of the steps has to be seen in the context of the institution. If someone is admitted to a hospital one assumes it to be in a safe place – it is within the responsibility of the institution to take the necessary steps to guarantee this. Two examples illustrate how the institutional context intersects with offender strategies.

A female patient was attending a consultation with an ear, nose and throat specialist, a leading academic fellow. The physician locked the door of the examination room pretending that he had to perform a delicate examination and must not be disturbed. He then sexually abused the patient on the examining chair. He was later sentenced for sexual misconduct and fired from the hospital. He has since gone on to establish his own practice where he continues to commit sexual offenses against female patients. This is in accordance with the literature on sexual reoffending of offender professionals; without any specific remedial training program around 80% relapse [10]. The tragic aspect with such cases is that regulating authorities often do not implement a monitoring of such professionals thus creating new victims due to their disruptive behavior.

A 9-year-old boy disclosed to his parents that a male nurse had 'played' with his genitals while he was in intensive care. His parents informed the police who arrested the suspect and performed a search on his properties, discovering two video clips showing him abusing a 5- and a 9-year-old boy, using sedatives. He was arrested and a further three offenses were disclosed later. Professionals often wonder how such a thing can happen in an intensive care unit, when there is always staff around. However, offender professionals set up the crime scene, as illustrated in figure 1 and in the aforementioned example, and the institutions enable the offenses to take place through their inability to imagine that these things can and do happen. Therefore, our intervention strategy should not be based on misguided assumptions but on evidence based facts.

Consequences for Victims

The psychological problems resulting from PSM are described by psychotraumatology and attachment theory. Most survivors are unable to talk about their experiences due to alexithymia and also because it triggers their fear pathways mediated through memories. The salient symptom is the loss of trust in oneself and in treating professionals, creating a knock-on effect such as leaving health problems untreated. At the core of the symptoms we see anxiety problems, phobic avoidance behavior, hyperarousal and neglect. Because of the polytraumatic nature of PSM victims suffer from complex traumatic disorders including comorbid diagnoses such as substance abuse, self-harming behavior, sucidality and various somatic symptoms. Associated survivors such as relatives may also suffer in the same way.

Healing is only possible within a societal context where the suffering of victims/survivors is acknowledged and both offender-professionals and institutions are held responsible. Trauma-sensitive therapeutic interventions are based on a dialectic behavioral treatment approach and need to proactively address the dilemma created through the offense. Patients must first learn to trust again in professionals, especially when the offense has been committed by a member of the same profession (e.g. a physician).

Handling Difficulties

Following preventive strategies, there is a need to react on various levels in order to adequately handle the arising difficulties. The following list outlines the necessary steps:
- Curriculum
- Reporting
- Support
- Institutional responses
- Help for victims and their relatives
- Help for teams and co-workers
- Dealing with disruptive professionals

Curriculum

Firstly there is an urgent need to integrate the topic of professional sexual misdunct into training curricula for physicians and other health care providers. Professionals have to be informed about the risk inherent in professional-client relationships and how to react to any resulting difficulties. They should also know how to react when colleagues are showing 'problems related to disruptive behavior'. Of equal importance is an understanding of victims' reactions and how to treat survivors. Interventions should be based on trauma-sensitive approaches.

Reporting

Laws should be put in place to make mandatory reporting of disruptive behavior/professional sexual misconduct a legal requirement. From the perspective of patient safety, the current situation is completely unacceptable. In many places cases are not reported, even where cases are clear frequently no action follows, and there is no protection for either whistleblowers or for patients reporting such incidents. Furthermore, there is no mandatory rehabilitation or retraining for those committing offenses.

Support and Institutional Response

A support network must be available for those professionals who are having behaviour problems. These facilities have to be established by professional bodies and institutions, including academia. They should be staffed by appropriately trained professionals.

Institutions have to develop and implement a code of conduct and a standardized protocol on how to react to accusations. A guideline has to be established detailing the resulting consequences for misconduct. Currently, in many countries there is no coherent answer on how to react, and each case is dealt with on an individual basis. Responsible agencies are often not aware about the literature available on this subject [15].

Support for Victims and Their Families

Supporting facilities should be available for victims and their relatives, including proper medical and therapeutic treatment for those affected. These interventions should be free of charge. Any status of limitation related to sexual offenses should be abolished, otherwise we will continue to protect offenders. In the majority of all cases it takes years for the survivors to disclose what happened to them, even in clear-cut cases.

Support for Co-Workers and Teams

Professional sexual misconduct affects not only victims, but also entire teams thus creating a negative working environment. It blocks resources and takes up both energy and finances. Similar to affected victims, affected teams also need support.

Rehabilitation of Impaired Professionals

Rehabilitation of impaired professionals should be mandatory and based on the idea that those professionals creating problems should help to solve them. Based on an individual assessment, a Boundary Training, which is a treatment based on a combination of sex offender treatment and rehabilitation of disruptive professionals [10] is undertaken. The decision of whether an offender is allowed to return to work should be based on a comprehensive assessment (performed by forensic experts) and the legal status of the case. In any case, return should only be allowed under strict monitoring. Those professionals who have committed pedophilic offenses are to be banned from returning to any work involving children and juveniles. Laws and policies should be established to ensure this.

Awareness of the Risk

Currently, sexual offenses within institutions are considered as one-off cases and consequently no action is taken. However, a more general problem exists of disbelief – helping professionals are seen as empathetic, if not 'good people', and in general, people cannot imagine that they may have a dark side. This is addressed as the hermeneutic problem (i.e. a problem of awareness, acknowledgement and understanding) when dealing with this issue. The appropriate response must be grounded on evidence-based facts, and interventions have to be implemented from a victims' perspective. The aim is to protect patients and victims from any further abuse and to prevent this from happening in the first place.

Professional Sexual Misconduct Affects both Women and Men

This book is about violence against women as a risk factor in their health overall. This chapter on abuse in doctor-patient relationship therefore focuses particularly on affected women. However, a considerable bias exists among scientists by simply not asking the male population about their experiences related to sexual violence, in particular within the health care system. For male victims of sexual abuse it is often extremely difficult to find adequate help. While recognizing that women are more frequently victims of sexual violence, it is necessary to emphasize the need of all victims of sexual abuse to get adequate support and help. Often female therapists, including female physicians, consider themselves as responsible for only female victims – men are seen largely as the perpetrators. However, there are also male survivors and they are in need as well.

A further important question is whether therapy should be provided by male or female therapists. But this is not the key point. Rather, it is critical that therapists are well trained and sensitive to the issues of sexual violence and trauma-focussed therapy. And, most importantly, women should always have the right and the opportunity to choose a female or a male therapist.

Sexualized violence by professionals affects both women and men, and both men and women have the right to be treated adequately and get the support they need, independently of their sex.

References

1 Council on Ethical and Judical Affairs: Physicians with Disruptive Behavior. Washington, American Medical Association, 2000.
2 AMA Council on Mental Health: The Sick Physician. JAMA 1973;223:684–687.
3 WPA Madrid Declaration on Ethical Standards for Psychiatric Practice. August 25, 1996 and Amendments. http://www.wpanet.org.
4 ABIM Foundation, ACP-ASIM Foundation, and European Federation of Internal Medicine: Medical professionalism in the new millennium: a physician charter. Simultaneously published: Ann Intern Med 2002;136:243–246/Lancet 2002;359:520–522.
5 Wertz RW, Wertz DC: Lying-In: A History of Childbirth in America. New Haven, Yale University Press, 1989, pp 122.
6 Rush F: The Best Kept Secret. Sexual Abuse of Children. Englewood Cliffs, Prentice-Hall, 1980.
7 Van der Kolk BA: Afterword; in Courtois CA, Ford JD (eds): Treating Complex Traumatic Stress Disorders. New York, Guilford Press, 2009, pp 455–466.
8 Krug EG, Dahlberg LL, Mercy JA, Zwi AB, Lozano R (eds): World Report on Violence and Health. Geneva, World Health Organization, 2002.
9 Taleb NN: The Black Swan. The Impact of the Highly Improbable. New York, Random House, 2007.

10 Tschan W: Missbrauchtes Vertrauen. Sexuelle Grenzverletzungen in professionellen Beziehungen, ed 2. Basel, Karger, 2005.
11 Wilpers D, Veenstra G, van de Wiel HBM, Weijmar Schultz WCM: Sexual contact in the doctor-patient relationship in the Netherlands. BMJ 1992;304: 1531–1534.
12 Coverdale JH, Thomso AN, White GE: Social and sexual contact between general practitioners and patients in New Zealand: attitudes and prevalence. Br J Gen Pract 1995;45:245–247.
13 Brodbeck J: Bedingungen und Folgen sexueller Übergriffe in der Psychotherapie; masters thesis, Fribourg, 1994.
14 Finkelhor D: Child Sexual Abuse. New Theory and Research. New York, Free Press, 1984.
15 Abel GG, Osborn CA, Warberg BW: Professionals; in Marshall WL, Fernandez YM, Hudson SM, Ward T (eds): Sourcebook of Treatment Programs for Sexual Offenders. New York, Plenum, 1998, pp 319–335.

Werner Tschan, MD
Psychiatrist
PO Box 475
CH–4012 Basel (Switzerland)
E-Mail tschankast@bluewin.ch

Special Aspects of Violence

Workplace Harassment Based on Sex: A Risk Factor for Women's Mental Health Problems

Lilia M. Cortina · Emily A. Leskinen

Departments of Psychology and Women's Studies, University of Michigan, Ann Arbor, Mich., USA

Abstract

An estimated one out of every two women is sexually harassed during her working life, making it perhaps the most widespread form of violence against women. 'Sexual harassment' (also known as 'sex-based harassment') encompasses three categories of conduct: gender harassment, unwanted sexual attention, and sexual coercion. The more women encounter these harassing behaviors on the job, the more they report symptoms of depression, anxiety, and posttraumatic stress; increased use of alcohol and drugs; and disordered eating. Other cognitive and emotional correlates include negative mood, self-blame, reduced self-esteem, emotional exhaustion, anger, disgust, envy, fear, and lowered satisfaction with life in general. These patterns apply even to victims of milder forms of harassment (e.g., gender harassment) and to victims who do not attach the 'sexual harassment' label to their experiences. Connections between sex-based harassment and mental health remain significant even when controlling for women's experience of other life stressors, other dimensions of the job, personality traits, and sociodemographic factors. This research has been heavily based in the US, but studies in other nations have produced similar results. In short, sex-based harassment on the job remains a serious problem for women worldwide, threatening their mental health and economic survival.

Copyright © 2013 S. Karger AG, Basel

An estimated one out of every two women is sexually harassed during her working life, making it perhaps the most widespread form of violence against women [1–3]. With this abuse come costs to women's mental health. This is the focus of the present chapter.

Regarding the parameters of this chapter, our emphasis is sex-based harassment on the job. Although related, academic sexual harassment (i.e., among students in school) is beyond the scope of this article. Second, we primarily review studies from the year 2000 to the present, including only methodologically rigorous investigations. Much of that work took place in North America, but there is no reason to believe that these findings are unique to this context – they should generalize to other parts of the world. Finally, sex-based harassment is most commonly a male-on-female phenomenon. A few studies have also included the perspective of male victims[1], but these are a minority, so our chapter will focus on women's experiences.

Social science has traditionally referred to this phenomenon as 'sexual harassment'. However, experts now believe that 'sex-based harassment' is a better construct label, placing more emphasis on sex (i.e., being female or male) rather than sexuality or desire [4, 5]. We alternate between the two terms – sexual harassment and sex-based harassment – to be consistent with prior research and legal language while also encouraging revision of that language.

What Is Sex-Based Harassment?

Workplace sex-based (or sexual) harassment was first misperceived as sexual attraction gone awry: inappropriate or coercive sexual advances from male bosses toward female subordinates, springing from 'natural' feelings of sexual desire. The last two decades, however, have witnessed considerable advances in our understanding of this abuse. It is now recognized as a form of employment discrimination based more on gender than sexuality: 'sexual harassment is a kind of sex discrimination... not because it is sexual... but precisely because it is a technology of sexism. That is, it perpetuates, enforces, and polices a set of gender norms that seek to feminize women and masculinize men' [6, p. 696] [see also 4].

More specifically, sexually harassing conduct disparages, degrades or humiliates a working woman based on her sex [4]. This encompasses (at least) three related dimensions of behavior [7]. Sexual coercion is the most widely recognized form of sex-based harassment, but it is also the rarest. It entails threats or bribes to make the conditions of a woman's job dependent on her compliance with sexual demands (e.g., threatening termination unless she performs sex acts). Related to sexual coercion is unwanted sexual attention: sexual advances that are unwelcome, unreciprocated, and unpleasant to the target (e.g., unwanted touching or kissing, pressure for dates or sex, expressions of sexual interest despite discouragement).

The third type of sex-based harassment, gender harassment, is the least recognized but most common. This refers to behaviors that do not convey sexual interest; instead they communicate insulting, degrading, or contemptuous attitudes about one gender [5, 7]. Examples of gender harassment include jokes that insult women's professional

---

[1] A variety of terms appear in the literature to refer to harassed persons, including 'victims', 'targets', and 'survivors'. The term 'victim' has received feminist criticism for portraying women as helpless, passive, and without agency. The concept of 'target' fails to capture some of the most common forms of sexual harassment, which entail non-targeted behaviors in the ambient environment (e.g., sexualized calendars, graffiti, overheard jokes of a lewd nature). 'Target' also fails to connote the abusiveness that characterizes more severe harassing conduct. A third option is 'survivor,' but that term would be too dramatic for many instances of sexual harassment – for instance, it seems excessive to suggest that one 'survives' being the butt of a sexist joke. Despite its faults, we rely on the term 'victim' in this chapter, for lack of a better word.

competence (e.g., 'women don't belong in law enforcement'), terms of address that demean women ('honey' or 'girlie') or disparage them ('whore'), and lewd depictions of women in the ambient environment (such as graffiti, cartoons, and sexualized images on calendars or computers).

Disentangling the relationships among sexual coercion, unwanted sexual attention, and gender harassment, Lim and Cortina [8, p. 484] explained that 'unwanted sexual attention, as the name suggests, represents unwelcomed, unreciprocated behaviors aimed at establishing some form of sexual relationship. One could argue that sexual coercion is a specific, severe, rare form of unwanted sexual attention, involving similar sexual advances coupled with bribery or threats to force acquiescence'. Gender harassment, in contrast, expresses animosity rather than sexual interest. Gender harassment sometimes involves sexually crude conduct (for instance, calling a colleague a 'dumb slut' or spreading sexually degrading rumors about her), but the goal is to insult and reject the woman, not engage her sexually. In colloquial terms, the difference between unwanted sexual attention/coercion versus gender harassment is analogous to the difference between a 'come on' versus a 'put down' [7]. All of these behaviors, however, comprise forms of sexual (or sex-based) harassment.

Sexual coercion, unwanted sexual attention, and gender harassment refer to behaviors, not legal constructs, but they do have legal parallels. Sexual coercion is termed 'quid pro quo' harassment under United States (US) law, whereas unwanted sexual attention and gender harassment can constitute illegal 'hostile environment' harassment. We limit our discussion of legalities to the US context, but note that many other countries also have laws or policies on sexual harassment (for reviews, see MacKinnon and Siegel [9]). Moreover, sex-based harassment in any form – be it illegal or legal – can jeopardize women's mental health.

Implications for Women's Mental Health

The 1980s saw the first systematic research into mental health correlates of sex-based harassment on the job, demonstrating it to be a significant source of distress in women. Initial studies, however, were limited by their narrow operationalization of harassment, use of non-standardized mental health measures, and/or reliance on samples of convenience. In the early 1990s, researchers still lamented the paucity of rigorous empirical attention to sexual harassment correlates. This situation changed dramatically over the next 20 years, as scientists documented the myriad ways in which sex-based harassment links with women's mental health (in addition to their occupational and physical health), following the model proposed by Fitzgerald et al. [10]. These investigations have primarily relied on surveys of working adults, who self-report on actual lived experiences in real-world organizations.

Table 1. Summary of research (from 2000 to the present) on mental health correlates of sexual harassment

Study	Sample	Depression, anxiety, or general distress	Symptoms of posttraumatic stress	Alcohol or substance use	Other psychological correlates
Barling et al. [25], (2001)	292 female in-home care workers				✓ fear, negative mood
Bergman and Drasgow, [26] (2003)	22,469 US military women	✓			
Bond et al. [27], (2004)	108 nonfaculty university employees	✓			
Buchanan and Fitzgerald, [28] (2008)	91 African-American working women		✓		✓ life satisfaction
Çelik and Çelik [18], (2007)	622 female nurses in Turkey	✓			✓ general mental health
Collinsworth et al. [29], (2009)	1,218 women litigants; 86 women referred for psychiatric evaluation	✓	✓		
Cortina et al. [30], (2002)	184 Latina working women	✓			✓ life satisfaction
de Haas et al. [19], (2009)	3,001 male and 1,295 female Dutch police officers				✓ burnout, emotional exhaustion
Dutra et al. [31], (2011)	54 women in the US military		✓		
Estrada and Berggren [20], (2009)	326 women in the Swedish military	✓			
Freels et al. [32], (2005)	868 male and 999 female university employees			✓	
Gettman and Gelfand [33], (2007)	394 professional US women	✓			
Gradus et al. [34], (2008)	3946 female veterans in the US	✓		✓	
Harned and Fitzgerald [35], (2002)	419 US military women; 239 US military men; 1,218 women litigants	✓			✓ disordered eating, self-esteem, self-blame

Table 1. continued

Study	Sample	Depression, anxiety, or general distress	Symptoms of posttraumatic stress	Alcohol or substance use	Other psychological correlates
Harned et al. [36], (2002)	22,372 women in the US military	✓			
Langhout et al. [37], (2005)	13,743 women in the US military	✓			
Leskinen et al. [5], (2011)	9,725 women in the US military; 1,425 women attorneys	✓			
Lim and Cortina [8], (2005)	833 female court employees; 1,425 women attorneys	✓			✓ life satisfaction
Munson et al. [38], (2000)	216 female university employees				✓ life satisfaction
Nielsen et al. [21], (2010)	2,349 Norwegian men and women	✓			
O'Connell and Korabik [39], (2000)	214 female university employees	✓			✓ negative mood
Parker and Griffin [40], (2002)	262 female police; 315 male police	✓			
Richman et al. [11], (2002)	1,098 female and 940 male university employees	✓		✓	
Richman et al. [12], (2006)	1,086 full-time and 71 retired university employees			✓	
Rospenda et al. [13], (2009)	2,151 men and women in the US	✓		✓	
Schneider et al. [41], (2001)	46 undergraduate women	✓			✓ anger, envy, disgust
Shupe et al. [42], (2002)	124 Hispanic and 207 non-Hispanic female factory workers	✓			
Street et al. [43], (2007)	3,946 men and women US veterans	✓	✓		
Vogt et al. [44], (2005)	495 Gulf War I veterans	✓	✓		

Table 1. continued

Study	Sample	Depression, anxiety, or general distress	Symptoms of posttraumatic stress	Alcohol or substance use	Other psychological correlates
Vogt et al. [45], (2011)	592 men and women US veterans	✓			
Wasti et al. [22], (2000)	336 Turkish and 359 American women	✓	✓		✓ life satisfaction
Wislar et al. [46], (2002)	1,005 women and 875 men university employees			✓	
Weatherill et al. [47], (2011)	658 women US Marine recruits	✓	✓		
Woods et al. [48], (2009)	105 African-American working women		✓		
Woodzicka and LaFrance [24], (2001)	50 female job interviewees				✓ fear

A check mark (✓) indicates that the study found a significant relationship between sexual harassment and that mental health correlate.

Associations between sex-based harassment and victims' mental health are many. Table 1 presents a comprehensive summary of all rigorous investigations of this topic, from 2000 to the present, appearing in the peer-reviewed literature. The findings are striking: The more women encounter sexual harassment on the job, the more they report symptoms of depression, stress and anxiety, and generally impaired psychological well-being. Some research has also connected sex-based harassment to victims' abuse of alcohol and drugs [11–13]. One study further found, based on a large national random sample of US women, that 1 in 5 self-identified sexual harassment victims met criteria for a DSM-IV diagnosis of Major Depressive Disorder, and one in ten described symptoms consistent with Posttraumatic Stress Disorder (PTSD) [14]. Other psychological correlates of harassment include negative mood, disordered eating, self-blame, reduced self-esteem, emotional exhaustion, anger, disgust, envy, fear, and lowered satisfaction with life in general.

Several investigations have now summarized these findings meta-analytically, documenting clear and consistent relationships between sexual harassment experiences and women's mental ill health [15–17]. To provide an illustrative example, Willness et al. [17] meta-analyzed 41 studies, finding that increases in sex-based harassment relate to increases in victims' psychological conditions (i.e., symptoms of anxiety, depression, sadness, negative mood, and reduced psychological wellbeing). Willness et al. [17] also reported a moderate correlation between sexual harassment experiences and PSTD symptoms. This result pushes the boundaries of what has traditionally been considered 'trauma' when diagnosing PTSD according to DSM-IV criteria; the implication is that those criteria ought to be broadened. Willness et al. [17] further found a small but significant association between sex-based harassment and global life satisfaction.

Connections between sexual harassment and mental ill health remain significant even when controlling for women's experience of other stressors (general job stress, sexual and physical assault outside the workplace); other dimensions of the job (occupational level, years of employment with the organization, workload, decision latitude, distrust of the organization); personality traits (neuroticism, narcissism, negative affectivity), and other sociodemographic factors (age, race, level of education). This research has been heavily based in the US; that said, studies in other nations have produced similar results [18–22]. Most of this work has been cross-sectional in nature, but longitudinal investigations have demonstrated that negative harassment outcomes persist over time [11, 12]. A few researchers have also induced mild harassment experiences in experimental contexts, yielding stronger causal conclusions about emotional outcomes [23, 24].

It is important to note that the mental health correlates of sexual harassment are not limited to so-called 'severe' harassing conduct. Gender harassment is often assumed to be a milder and subtler form of harassment, because it has no explicit, sexually predatory component to it (unlike unwanted sexual attention or sexual coercion). However, when women have 'only' encountered gender harassment on the job, with no concomitant unwanted sexual advances, they still show significant decrements in professional and psychological well-being [7].

Even when women acknowledge having faced unwanted sex-related behavior at work, fewer than 20–30% typically label that conduct 'sexual harassment'. One should not assume, however, that absence of labeling reflects absence of distress. That is, women exposed to such behaviors report very similar mental health problems, including PTSD, whether or not they attach the 'sexual harassment' label to their experiences [3].

Conclusion

As this chapter makes clear, sexual harassment on the job remains a serious problem confronting women. Not to be taken lightly, it threatens their mental health and impedes their economic survival. It is imperative that scientists continue rigorous research on this topic, informing the evolution of law and social policy, until we have eradicated this most widespread form of violence against women.

References

1 Fitzgerald LF: Sexual harassment: violence against women in the workplace. Am Psychol 1993;48: 1070–1076.
2 Ilies R, Hauserman N, Schwochau S, Stibal J: Reported incidence rates of work-related sexual harassment in the United States: using meta-analysis to explain reported rate disparities. Personnel Psychol 2003;56:607–631.
3 Magley VJ, Hulin CL, Fitzgerald LF, DeNardo M: Outcomes of self-labeling sexual harassment. J Appl Psychol 1999;84:390–402.
4 Berdahl J: Harassment based on sex: Protecting social status in the context of gender hierarchy. Acad Manag Rev 2007;32:641–658.
5 Leskinen EA, Cortina LM, Kabat DB: Gender harassment: Broadening our understanding of sex-based harassment at work. Law Hum Behav 2011; 35:25–39.
6 Franke KM: What's wrong with sexual harassment? Stanford Law Rev 1997;49:691–772.
7 Fitzgerald LF, Gelfand M, Drasgow F: Measuring sexual harassment: theoretical and psychometric advances. Basic Appl Soc Psychol 1995;17:425–445.
8 Lim S, Cortina LM: Interpersonal mistreatment in the workplace: the interface and impact of general incivility and sexual harassment. J Appl Psychol 2005;90:483–496.
9 MacKinnon CA, Siegel RB: Directions in Sexual Harassment Law. New Haven, Yale University Press, 2004.
10 Fitzgerald LF, Drasgow F, Hulin CL, Gelfand M, Magley VJ: Antecedents and consequences of sexual harassment in organizations: a test of an integrated model. J Appl Psychol 1997;82:578–589.
11 Richman JA, Shinsako SA, Rospenda KM, Flaherty JA, Freels S: Workplace harassment/abuse and alcohol-related outcomes: the mediating role of psychological distress. J Stud Alcohol 2002;63: 412–419.
12 Richman JA, Zlatoper KW, Ehmke J, Rospenda KM: Retirement and drinking outcomes: Lingering effects of workplace stress? Addict Behav 2006;31: 767–776.
13 Rospenda KM, Richman JA, Shannon CA: Prevalence and mental health correlates of harassment and discrimination in the workplace: results from a national study. J Interpers Violence 2009;24: 819–843.
14 Dansky BS, Kilpatrick DG: Effects of sexual harassment; in O'Donohue W (ed): Sexual Harassment: Theory, Research, and Treatment. Needham Heights, Allyn & Bacon, 1997, pp 152–174.
15 Chan D, Lam C, Chow S, Cheung S: Examining the job-related, psychological, and physical outcomes of workplace sexual harassment: a meta-analytic review. Psychol Women Q 2008;32:362–376.
16 Hershcovis MS, Barling J: Comparing victim attributions and outcomes for workplace aggression and sexual harassment. J Appl Psychol 2010;95; 874–888.
17 Willness C, Steel P, Lee K: A meta-analysis of the antecedents and consequences of workplace sexual harassment. Personnel Psychol 2007;60:127–162.
18 Çelik Y, Çelik S: Sexual harassment against nurses in Turkey. J Nurs Scholarship 2007;39:200–206.
19 de Haas S, Timmerman G, Höing M: Sexual harassment and health among male and female police officers. J Occup Health Psychol 2009;14:390–401.
20 Estrada AX, Berggren AW: Sexual harassment and its impact for women officers and cadets in the Swedish armed forces. Milit Psychol 2009;21:162–185.
21 Nielsen M, Bjørkelo B, Notelaers G, Einarsen S: Sexual harassment: prevalence, outcomes, and gender differences assessed by three different estimation methods. J Aggress Maltreat Trauma 2010;19: 252–274.
22 Wasti S, Bergman ME, Glomb TM, Drasgow F: Test of the cross-cultural generalizability of a model of sexual harassment. J Appl Psychol 2000;85:766–778.
23 Schneider KT, Tomaka J, Palacios R: Women's cognitive, affective, and physiological reactions to a male coworker's sexist behavior. J Appl Soc Psychol 2001;31:1995–2018.
24 Woodzicka JA, La France M: Real versus imagined gender harassment. J Soc Issues 2001;57:15–30.
25 Barling J, Rogers A, Kelloway E: Behind closed doors: in-home workers' experience of sexual harassment and workplace violence. J Occup Health Psychol 2001;6:255–269.
26 Bergman ME, Drasgow F: Race as a moderator in a model of sexual harassment: an empirical test. J Occup Health Psychol 2003;8:131–145.
27 Bond MA, Punnett L, Pyle JL, Cazeca D, Cooperman M: Gendered work conditions, health, and work outcomes. J Occup Health Psychol 2004;9:28–45.
28 Buchanan NT, Fitzgerald LF: Effects of racial and sexual harassment on work and the psychological well-being of African-American women. J Occup Health Psychol 2008;13:137–151.
29 Collinsworth LL, Fitzgerald LF, Drasgow F: In harm's way: factors related to psychological distress following sexual harassment. Psychol Women Q 2009;33:475–490.

30 Cortina LM, Fitzgerald LF, Drasgow F: Contextualizing Latina experiences of sexual harassment: preliminary tests of a structural model. Basic Appl Soc Psychol 2002;24:295–311.

31 Dutra L, Grubbs K, Morland L, et al: Women at war: implications for mental health. J Trauma Dissoc 2011;12:25–37.

32 Freels SA, Richman JA, Rospenda KM: Gender differences in the causal direction between workplace harassment and drinking. Addict Behav 2005;30:1454–1458.

33 Gettman HJ, Gelfand MJ: When the customer shouldn't be king: antecedents and consequences of sexual harassment by clients and customers. J Appl Psychol 2007;92:757–770.

34 Gradus JL, Street AE, Kelly K, Stafford J: Sexual harassment experiences and harmful alcohol use in a military sample: differences in gender and the mediating role of depression. J Stud Alcohol Drugs 2008;69:348–351.

35 Harned MS, Fitzgerald LF: Understanding a link between sexual harassment and eating disorder symptoms: a mediational analysis. J Consult Clin Psychology 2002;70:1170–1181.

36 Harned MS, Ormerod AJ, Palmieri PA, Collinsworth LL, Reed M: Sexual assault and other types of sexual harassment by workplace personnel: a comparison of antecedents and consequences. J Occup Health Psychol 2002;7:174–188.

37 Langhout R, Bergman ME, Cortina LM, Fitzgerald LF, Drasgow F, Williams J: Sexual harassment severity: assessing situational and personal determinants and outcomes. J Appl Soc Psychol 2005;35:975–1007.

38 Munson LJ, Hulin C, Drasgow F: Longitudinal analysis of dispositional influences and sexual harassment: effects on job and psychological outcomes. Personnel Psychol 2000;53:21–46.

39 O'Connell CE, Korabik K: Sexual harassment: the relationship of personal vulnerability, work context, perpetrator status, and type of harassment to outcomes. J Vocation Behav 2000;56:299–329

40 Parker SK, Griffin MA: What is so bad about a little name-calling? Negative consequences of gender harassment for overperformance demands and distress. J Occup Health Psychol 2002;7:195–210.

41 Schneider KT, Tomaka J, Palacios R: Women's cognitive, affective, and physiological reactions to a male coworker's sexist behavior. J Appl Soc Psychol 2001;31:1995–2018.

42 Shupe EI, Cortina LM, Ramos A, Fitzgerald LF, Salisbury J: The incidence and outcomes of sexual harassment among Hispanic and non-Hispanic White women: s comparison across levels of cultural affiliation. Psychol Women Q 2002;26:298–308.

43 Street AE, Gradus JL, Stafford J, Kelly K: Gender differences in experiences of sexual harassment: data from a male-dominated environment. J Consult Clin Psychol 2007;75:464–474.

44 Vogt DS, Pless AP, King LA, King DW: Deployment stressors, gender, and mental health outcomes among Gulf War I veterans. J Trauma Stress 2005;18:115–127.

45 Vogt D, Vaughn R, Eisen S, et al: Gender differences in combat-related stressors and their association with postdeployment mental health in a nationally representative sample of US OEF/OIF veterans. J Abnorm Psychol 2011;120:797–806.

46 Wislar JS, Richman JA, Fendrich M, Flaherty JA: Sexual harassment, generalized workplace abuse and drinking outcomes: the role of personality vulnerability. J Drug Issues 2002;32:1071–1088.

47 Weatherill RP, Vogt DS, Taft CT, King LA, King DW, Shipherd JC: Training experiences as mediators of the association between gender-role egalitarianism and women's adjustment to Marine recruit training. Sex Roles 2011;64:348–359.

48 Woods KC, Buchanan NT, Settles IH: Sexual harassment across the color line: Experiences and outcomes of cross- versus intraracial sexual harassment among Black women. Cultur Divers Ethnic Minor Psychol 2009;15:67–76.

Lilia M. Cortina, PhD
Departments of Psychology and Women's Studies, University of Michigan
530 Church Street
Ann Arbor, MI 48109–1043 (USA)
Tel. +1 734 647 3956, E-Mail lilia.cortina@umich.edu

Special Aspects of Violence

Violence against Women and Suicidality: Does Violence Cause Suicidal Behaviour?

Karen M. Devries · Maureen Seguin

Department of Global Health and Development, London School of Hygiene and Tropical Medicine, London, UK

Abstract

Suicide is usually conceptualized as a men's issue. In this chapter, we present evidence on prevalence of suicidal behaviour in women, an overview of selected theories to explain women's suicidal behaviour, evidence on the correlation between violence and suicide, and a review of selected longitudinal research on the topic. Prevalence is high, with data from women in 10 different, mainly low and middle income countries suggesting that between <1 and 12% of women have ever attempted suicide. Women have been historically neglected in suicide research, but more modern theoretical developments emphasising the role of trauma in the production of adverse mental health outcomes underline the potentially important role women's experiences of violence could play in suicidal behaviour. Women who report experiencing various childhood sexual abuse and intimate partner violence are at higher risk of attempting suicide versus women who have not experienced violence, and longitudinal studies suggest that the relationship is a causal one. Because violence exposure can increase risk of suicide, interventions to reduce suicidal behaviour and improve mental health among women must adopt a gendered perspective and address women's experiences of violence.

Copyright © 2013 S. Karger AG, Basel

Why Is Suicide Important to Study in Women?

Suicide is thought of as a predominately male problem [1]. Completed suicides are more likely in men globally, but in many parts of the world, women also complete suicide at rates almost equal to men [2]. Besides completed suicides, non-fatal suicidal behaviours, such as suicide attempts, are far more common among women than men in Europe and the USA [3]. Though suicide attempts are considered less serious, they are a strong risk factor for eventual suicide completion [4].

Women's non-fatal suicidal behaviour has been especially neglected in low and middle-income countries [5]. In the WHO Multi-Country Study (MCS) on women's health and domestic violence against women, a survey of 15 sites in 10 mostly low and middle income countries, the self-reported lifetime prevalence of ever

Table 1. Prevalence of suicidal behaviour in women

Country	% of women, ever attempted suicide
Brazil, Pernambuco	6.3
Brazil, Sao Paulo	8.8
Japan, Yokohama	1.7
Namibia, Windhoek	5.6
Peru, Cuzco	9.1
Peru, Lima	12.0
Samoa (national)	3.3
Serbia, Belgrade	1.8
Tanzania, Mbeya	0.8
Tanzania, Dar Es Salaam	0.8
Thailand, Nakhonsawan	5.1
Thailand, Bangkok	5.9

attempting suicide ranged from less than 1% of women in two settings in Tanzania up to 12.0% of women in one setting in Peru (table 1) [6]. The survey was conducted from 1999 to 2003.

Why Do Women Commit Suicide? A Theoretical Overview

We know suicidal behaviour among women is common, but why? Both completed suicide and suicidal behaviour are hypothesized to occur as a result of external and internal influences. Emile Durkheim's sociological explanation of suicide, *Le suicide* [7], had tremendous influence on subsequent studies of suicide [8, 9]. This work has been criticized for ignoring women's suicidal behaviour, and has arguably contributed to a lack of consideration of gender in this field of research [3].

Durkheim argued that suicide rates could be explained by social rather than individual factors, and demonstrated that rates were higher in societies which were less cohesive [10]. Durkheim viewed social structure as governed by two forces: regulation and integration. Regulation refers to the degree of external constraints on individuals, while integration refers to the degree to which collective morals are shared.

According to Durkheim's scheme, exposure to excessive or deficient levels of either integration or regulation results in suicides in a population [7]. Low integration yields 'egoistic suicide,' which is characteristic of societies in which individuals are not well integrated into the social norms of society. Sufficient integration allows individuals to find meaning in their lives, which discourages suicide. Conversely, overly strong social integration leads to 'altruistic suicide'. This type of suicide arises when an individual feels that it is their duty to kill themselves, for instance, a soldier sacrificing himself to protect others. 'Anomic suicide' results from deficient social regulation. This type of suicide is found in societies which are undergoing rapid change, causing the degradation of shared norms and social cohesion.

The fourth type of suicide described by Durkheim is 'fatalistic'. Largely neglected by Durkheim, this type of suicide results from excessive regulation. Individuals more likely to commit this type of suicide are those 'persons with futures pitilessly blocked and passions violently choked by oppressive discipline' [7, p. 276].

Durkheim's fourth category of suicide, 'fatalistic suicide' has been used more recently to discuss women's suicides. Aliverdinia and Pridemore [11] theorize that Iranian women who choose self-immolation as method of suicide do so in order to protest appalling family conditions. The excessive regulation of women's public behaviour and physical domestic violence found in some Iranian provinces offer women a bleak future, yielding an attitude of pessimism and fatalism. This attitude is further encouraged by women's exclusion from social and economic rights, making them solely dependent on the family for their identity. High levels of domestic violence, along with the burden of bearing and raising a large number of children, reinforce feelings of fatalism. More generally, Aliverdinia and Pridemore [11] connect the oppression of women to the resulting female suicide rate. Fatalistic suicide frees women from seemingly hopeless circumstances. They also draw attention to sexual violence as a risk factor for fatalistic suicide. Some populations within Iran view women who have been sexually victimized as deserving the punishment of death. These women can be coerced into committing suicide due to the alienation to which they are subjected by their family and community.

Psychological Approaches

Martin Seligman first proposed his theory of learned helplessness in 1975 [12]. According to this theory, helplessness can result from the perceived absence of control over the outcome of a situation. An individual learns to behave helplessly in a certain situation after perceiving that they can do little to control an outcome. Thus, women experiencing domestic violence give up the belief that they can escape the abuse; they perceive that they have no control over their abuser or their lives [13]. The theory predicts that trauma damages one's ability to perceive their effectiveness in being able to control what happens to them [13]. Similar to persons facing a terminal illness, some victims of IPV may believe that their partner will inevitably kill them, and so choose to kill themselves instead.

The interpersonal theory of suicide adds the idea of acquired capability to our understanding of violence and suicide. This orientation is based on three constructs: perceived burdensomeness, failed belongingness, and acquired capability [14]. Perceived burdensomeness is the idea that one's flaws are not only detrimental to the self, but also to friends, family, and society at large. Failed belongingness is the experience that one is alienated from others; not integrated within family or a social group.

Though necessary, these two components are insufficient to result in suicide. A person must also acquire the capability to end their own life. The theory holds that only those individuals who have endured enough pain to have become habituated are capable of killing themselves. Experiences with pain, including that associated with intimate partner and other forms of violence, counter and may overcome the profoundly powerful instinct of self-preservation. Otherwise stated, an abused woman may become equipped with the capability to end her own life because she is familiar with pain. The pain associated with suicide is not an obstacle for someone who is familiar with pain [14, 15].

Biology of Trauma and Suicide
Various explanations of women's suicidal behaviour centre on the link between traumatic experiences and eventual suicide. The physiological response to trauma includes a range of changes in body chemistry, which are designed to help us minimize the danger associated with exposure to stressors. Exposures to the most common forms of violence against women, intimate partner violence and childhood sexual abuse, tend to occur over a period of time [16]. Prolonged experience of stress responses can lead to semi-permanent and permanent changes in brain structures involved in regulation of emotional responses and cognitive functioning.

Particularly when exposures to violence occur during childhood, exposures to trauma could result in problematic attachment to parents and a variety of early life difficulties. There is emerging evidence from longitudinal studies, and twin studies [17, 18], which suggests that these early violence exposures can alter the ability to cope with exposure to subsequent stressors, and the ability to form safe, healthy attachments to others such that the risk of eventual adverse mental health outcomes increases [19, 20]. These same mechanisms may explain why children whose mothers have experienced intimate partner violence are similarly at risk for later suicidal behaviour [6]. Mothers who are experiencing chronic fear and stress and consequent physiological changes are likely less able to provide the same kind of caring and supportive environment that will enable children to develop healthy attachments and internal regulation processes.

Adult exposures to violence and other traumatic events could also increase the risk of suicide in a similar way. The stress response, and the ongoing fear and isolation that can result from experiences of physical, sexual and psychological violence, can increase feelings of hopelessness and helplessness and biological responses that often precede suicidal behaviour [21, 22]. Many of the other sequelae of severe physical and sexual abuse may also contribute independently to suicidality. Anxiety, depression, post-traumatic stress disorder, and physical injuries which may cause pain or restrict movement can also have secondary mental health effects which can lead to suicidal behaviour [5, 23–25].

Suicidal behaviours tend to cluster in families, and there is evidence that this is at least partly heritable. However, new evidence suggests that part of this intergenerational transmission of suicidal behaviour may be related to intergenerational transmission of violence exposures. Brodsky found, in a longitudinal study of suicidal parents and their offspring, that parents who had themselves experienced childhood sexual abuse (CSA) were more likely to have offspring who would go on to experience CSA and who would be diagnosed with major depressive disorder earlier in their lives [26]. Few of the CSA cases in children were familial, indicating that instead, a risky environment was somehow transferred to the offspring.

Gendered Model of Suicide
Sociological, psychological and biological factors all interact to influence an individual's suicide risk, and gender impacts every level of this interaction. Women are more likely than men to find themselves in a marginalized position within a given society, to be excluded from participation in aspects of society, and to have less control over their own health and well-being. Violence against women is socially sanctioned to a greater or lesser extent in most societies, and women are subject to intimate partner violence and childhood sexual abuse at rates that are far higher than men. This has a psychological and biological effect. The normality of violence against women makes it difficult for women in many settings to disclose their experiences, receive social or professional support, and for men to stop using violence. In addition to the stress response, other sequelae of violence may lead to increased stress, fear, and isolation, all of which will increase hopelessness and helplessness, and thus could potentially impact on suicide rates.

Are Women Who Have Experienced Violence More Likely to Report Suicide Attempts?

A body of theory suggests that violence may cause suicide, because of 'excessive regulation', habituation to physical pain, and the development and neurobiological effects of experiencing traumatic events. But do women who have experienced violence report more suicide attempts? Evidence from a variety of settings suggests that they do. Although most data on the topic is from US and European studies, emerging evidence suggests the relationship is similar in more globally representative settings.

Table 2 displays data from an analysis of the WHO MCS [6]. The study shows the independent contributions of childhood sexual abuse, non-partner sexual violence that occurs after age 15, non-partner physical violence that occurs after age 15, intimate partner violence, and having a mother who experienced IPV to a woman's likelihood of making a suicide attempt. These findings are controlled for a range of demographic factors as well as a woman's score on the Self Report Questionnaire-20 (which indicates a probable common mental disorder) [27].

Table 2. Exposure to violence and odds of lifetime suicide attempts in women

	n	Childhood sexual abuse/forced sex*	Non-partner sexual violence*	Non-partner physical violence*	Intimate partner violence*	Mother experienced IPV*
		aOR (95% CI)	aOR (95% CI)	aOR (95% CI)	aOR (95% CI)	aOR (95% CI)
Brazil, Pernambuco	1,406	1.58 (0.86–2.90)	0.79 (0.34–1.81)	1.81 (1.02–3.23)	2.22 (1.26, 3.90)	1.53 (0.93–2.54)
Brazil, Sao Paulo	1,136	1.72 (0.95–3.10)	1.34 (0.66–2.69)	1.75 (1.08–2.85)	2.29 (1.37–3.85)	1.18 (0.72–1.93)
Namibia, Windhoek	1,261	1.29 (0.54–3.04)	1.10 (0.48–2.50)	2.07 (1.13–3.77)	1.57 (0.88–2.80)	2.14 (1.24–3.70)
Peru, Cuzco	1645	1.89 (1.21–2.94)	1.01 (0.65, 1.59)	1.50 (1.04, 2.17)	2.59 (1.45, 4.62)	1.47 (0.99, 2.18)
Peru, Lima	1,272	2.16 (1.42, 3.27)	1.00 (0.58, 1.70)	1.60 (1.06, 2.40)	2.99 (1.77, 5.04)	1.47 (0.98, 2.20)
Samoa (national)	1,438	2.79 (0.84–9.29)	1.61 (0.76–3.42)	2.05 (0.96–4.40)	1.82 (0.88–3.72)	1.51 (0.81–2.82)
Thailand, Nakhonsawan	1,140	1.07 (0.40, 2.90)	0.45 (0.10, 2.07)	1.06 (0.43, 2.58)	2.16 (1.15, 4.06)	1.18 (0.66, 2.09)
Thailand, Bangkok	1,379	1.82 (0.87, 3.82)	0.95 (0.41, 2.18)	2.25 (1.11, 4.56)	2.30 (1.29, 4.10)	2.16 (1.28, 3.63)

*Controlled for demographics, each other form of violence in table, and probable common mental disorders.

Across these settings, intimate partner violence has the largest and most consistent relationship with lifetime suicide attempts after accounting for demographics, common mental disorders, and other forms of violence. Intimate partner violence increased the odds of a reported suicide attempt between one and a half to three times across sites.

Women who reported experiencing childhood sexual abuse themselves, or having a mother who experienced intimate partner violence, were also more likely to report a suicide attempt in all settings, although this association did not always reach statistical significance. Notably, in a model which includes both child and adult exposures to violence, more distal childhood violence experiences independently predict suicide attempts even accounting for adult violence exposures.

Interestingly, adult exposure to sexual violence from non-partners was not consistently positively associated with suicidal attempts across sites, and the relationship did not reach statistical significance in any site. The effects of this exposure, which was generally more rare, may simply have been overwhelmed the effects of the other forms of violence considered in the model. Non-partner physical violence was related to suicide attempts across all sites, and reached statistical significance in all but two of the sites. Domestic abuse by family members has been implicated in suicides in some Asian settings [28, 29].

Do Experiences of Violence Cause Suicide Attempts?

Even though violence experience is associated with suicide attempts, it is often difficult to establish that the violence preceded the suicide attempt, and that other factors did not cause both the suicide attempt and the violence. Longitudinal studies, which follow people over time, have been conducted and are predominantly from high income settings. There is much more evidence available about childhood sexual abuse and later suicide attempts than other forms of violence against women in relation to later suicide attempts. Table 3 outlines selected longitudinal studies examining the relationship between CSA and incident suicide attempts or completed suicides in studies which included female populations (most analyses present data on male and female participants together).

Studies of exposure to CSA and later suicidal behaviour show a clear and strong relationship. Those women who experienced CSA are far more likely than their non-abused counterparts to report later suicide attempts in almost all studies outlined in table 3. This provides good evidence of a plausible causal relationship between experience of CSA and suicidal behaviour.

Studies looking at the relationship between IPV and incident suicide attempts are outlined in table 4. Two of the studies include USA adolescents who are experiencing dating violence. While this is an important experience of violence for young women in countries where dating relationships occur, this may not adequately represent the experiences of women in other settings who experience violence from intimate partners.

In any case, all studies examining women's experience of violence from intimate/dating partners and incident suicide attempts find that violence increases the odds of an incident suicide attempt, lending support to the idea that violence from intimate/dating partners is causally related to subsequent suicidal behaviour.

Conclusion

Women's suicidal behaviour is a topic that must be taken seriously. Evidence from a range of low, middle and high income settings confirms that women experiencing various forms of violence are at a higher risk of suicide than women who do not experience violence, and review of longitudinal evidence suggests that this relationship may be causal.

Table 3. Longitudinal studies on childhood sexual abuse and incident suicide attempts

	Population	Finding effect estimate (95% CI)
Brezo et al. [30]	564 female Quebec residents, Canada, recruited in kindergarten, 1985–1988, followed for 18 years	Single attempt: aOR = 1.5 (0.8–3.0) Repeated attempt: aOR = 3.3 (1.4–7.9) Early onset: aOR = 1.7 (0.8–3.5) Late onset: aOR = 2.6 (1.2–5.6)
Brown et al. [31]	334 males, 305 females from New York State, USA, recruited in 1975 aged 1–10	Any suicide attempt: OR = 5.71 (1.94–16.74) In adolescents: OR = 3.54 (0.90–13.88) In young adults: OR = 6.15 (1.48–25.81) Repeated suicide attempts: OR = 8.40 (1.86–38.06) In adolescents: OR = 15.76 (2.14–116.65) In young adults: OR = 3.34 (0.30–37.37)
Cutajar et al. [32]	State record linkage study, Victoria, Australia. CSA cases documented between 1964 and 1995 by Victorian Institute of Forensic Medicine (provides forensic examination for all of Victoria)	Completed suicides in women: RR = 40.38 (24.97–65.31); 6 of 2,201 CSA+
Enns et al. [33]	7076 men and women, representative cohort, Netherlands, aged 18–64, followed for 3 years	In full sample-with or without baseline suicide ideation: aOR = 2.62 (1.36–5.03) In people with no baseline suicide ideation: aOR = 0.32 (0.03–3.01)
Fergusson et al. [19]	1265 men and women, Christchurch health and development study, recruited at birth in 1971, follow-up until age 25	Adjusted B (SE): 0.49 (0.14), p<0.001
Melhem et al. [34]	365 adult offspring from 212 probands with mood disorders. Mean follow-up time = 2.4 years (1–6 years); 84% female	Coefficient = 1.63 (0.69–2.57), se = 0.48, p = 0.001
Plunkett et al. [35]	Cohort 1–5 years, n cases = 55, n controls = 67 cases from hospital records, controls matched on age, sex, SES recruited from schools in same geographic area	Cohort 1 (5 years): RR = 4.9 (1.7–13.7)

OR = Odds ratio; aOR = adjusted odds ratio; RR = risk ratio; B = beta-coefficient; SE = standard error.

In order to successfully prevent suicidal behaviour among women, we must explore strategies to reduce and prevent violence against women. Women who have experienced violence may need tailored interventions which address the changes that come with prolonged exposure to trauma in order to prevent future suicidal behaviour. Women who have been identified as experiencing suicidal behaviour must not be

Table 4. Longitudinal studies on physical and/or sexual intimate partner violence and incident suicide attempts

Study	Population	Finding effect estimate (95% CI)
Ackard et al. [36]	Project Eat sample is 55.6% of original cohort, 694 male and 822 female middle and high school students Wave 1 = 1999 Wave 2 = 2004	Female: aOR = 3.20 (0.97–10.59), p = 0.057
Chowdhary and Patel [37]	Goa cohort, India, 1563 married women aged 18–50 recruited from population register of Aldona Primary Care Centre	Physical violence, lifetime: aOR = 7.97 (1.75–36.37) Past 3 months: aOR = 6.56 (1.19–35.99) Sexual violence, lifetime, aOR = 10.91 (2.01–59.30) Past 3 months: aOR = 12.91 (2.32–71.80)
Roberts et al. [38]	2,206 female, 2,237 male in Add Health who had romantic partnership between wave 1 = 1,995 and wave 2 = 1 996	Female: β = 0.12 (0.02–0.22)

aOR = Adjusted odds ratio; β = beta-coefficient.

medicated and sent back into potentially violent situations, which are contributing to their suicidal behaviour in the first place. Interventions which address unequal gender norms and violence against women should be tested to see if they reduce women's suicidality. Adopting a gendered perspective may be key to ensuring women's mental health.

References

1 Kushner HI, Sterk CE: The limits of social capital: Durkheim, suicide, and social cohesion. Am J Publ Hlth 2005;95:1139–1143.
2 World Health Organization: Estimates of Numbers of Deaths by Sex, Cause and WHO Region for 2002: Revised Global Burden of Disease (GBD) 2002 Estimates. Geneva, World Health Organization, 2004,
3 Canetto SS: Women and suicidal behavior: a cultural analysis. Am J Orthopsychiatry 2008;78: 259–266.
4 Tidemalm D, Langstrom N, Lichtenstein P, Runeson B: Risk of suicide after suicide attempt according to coexisting psychiatric disorder: Swedish cohort study with long term follow-up. BMJ 2008;337: a2205.
5 Vijayakumar L, John S, Pirkis J, Whiteford H: Suicide in developing countries. 2. Risk factors. Crisis 2005;26:112–119.

6 Devries K, Watts C, Yoshihama M, Kiss L, Schraiber LB, Deyessa N, Heise L, Durand J, Mbwambo J, Jansen H, Berhane Y, Ellsberg M, Garcia-Moreno C: Violence against women is strongly associated with suicide attempts: evidence from the WHO Multi-Country Study on Women's Health and Domestic Violence against Women. Soc Sci Med 2011;73: 79–86.

7 Durkheim E: Suicide: A Study in Sociology. London, Routledge & Kegan Paul, 1951.

8 Curtis C: Sexual abuse and subsequent suicidal behaviour: Exacerbating factors and implications for recovery. J Child Sex Abuse 2006;15:1–21.

9 Kushner HI: Women and suicidal behavior: epidemiology, gender and lethality in historical perspective; in Canetto SS, Lester D (eds): Women and Suicidal Behavior. New York, Springer, 1995.

10 Kawachi I, Kennedy B, Lochner K: Long live community: social capital as public health. Am Prospect 1997;8:56–59.

11 Aliverdinia A, Pridemore WA: Women's fatalistic suicide in Iran: a partial test of Durkheim in an Islamic republic. Violence Against Women 2009;15: 307–320.

12 Seligman MEP: Helplessness: On Depression, Development, and Death. San Francisco, Freeman, 1975.

13 Walker LEA (ed): The Battered Woman Syndrome. New York, Springer, 2009.

14 Joiner TE, Orden KAV, Witte TK, Rudd MD: The Interpersonal Theory of Suicide: Guidance for Working with Suicidal Clients. Washington, American Psychological Association, 2009.

15 Joiner T, Sachs-Ericsson NJ, Wingate LR, Brown JS, Anestis MD, Selby EA: Childhood physical and sexual abuse and lifetime number of suicide attempts: a persistent and theoretically important relationship. Behav Res Ther 2007;45:539–547.

16 Garcia-Moreno C, Jansen H, Heise L, Watts C: WHO Multi-Country Study on Women's Health and Domestic Violence against Women: Initial Results on Prevalence, Health Outcomes and Women's Responses. Geneva, World Health Organization, 2005.

17 Kendler KS, Karkowski LM, Prescott CA: Causal relationship between stressful life events and the onset of major depression. Am Psychiatry 1999;156: 837–841.

18 Kendler KS, Thornton LM, Prescott CA: Gender differences in the rates of exposure to stressful life events and sensitivity to their depressogenic effects. Am J Psychiatry 2001;158:587–593.

19 Fergusson DM, Boden JM, Horwood LJ: Exposure to childhood sexual and physical abuse and adjustment in early adulthood. Child Abuse Neglect 2008;32:607–619.

20 Dube SR, Anda RF, Felitti VJ, Chapman DP, Williamson DF, Giles WH: Childhood abuse, household dysfunction, and the risk of attempted suicide throughout the life span. Findings from the adverse childhood experiences study. JAMA 2001;286: 3089–3096.

21 Kamali M, Oquendo MA, Mann JJ: Understanding the neurobiology of suicidal behavior. Depression Anxiety 2001;14:164–176.

22 Yoshihama M, Horrocks J, Kamano S: The role of emotional abuse in intimate partner violence and health among women in Yokohama, Japan. Am J Publ Hlth 2009;99:647–653.

23 Ellsberg M, Jansen HAFM, Heise L, Watts C, Garcia-Moreno C: Intimate partner violence and women's physical and mental health in the who multi-country study on women's health and domestic violence: an observational study. Lancet 2008;371:1165–1172.

24 Joe S, Stein DJ, Seedat S, Herman A, Williams D: Prevalence and correlates of non-fatal suicidal behaviour among South Africans. Br J Psychiatry 2008;192:310–311.

25 Naved RT, Akhtar N: Spousal violence against women and suicidal ideation in Bangladesh. Women's Health Issues 2008;18:1–11.

26 Brodsky BS, Mann JJ, Stanley B, Tin A, Oquendo M, Birmaher B, Greenhill L, Kolko D, Zelazny J, Burke AK, Melhem N, Brent D: Familial transmission of suicidal behavior: factors mediating the relationship between childhood abuse and offspring suicide attempts. J Clin Psychiatry 2008;69:584–596.

27 Beusenberg M, Orley J: A User's Guide to the Self-Reporting Questionnaire (SRQ). Geneva, Division of Mental Health, World Health Organization, 1994.

28 Ahmed K, van Ginneken J, Razzaque A, Alam N: Violent deaths among women of reproductive age in rural Bangladesh. Soc Sci Med 2004;59:311–319.

29 Kumar V: Burnt wives – a study of suicides. Burns 2003;29:31–35.

30 Brezo J, Paris J, Vitaro F, He´bert M, Tremblay RE, Turecki G: Predicting suicide attempts in young adults with histories of childhood abuse. Br J Psychiatry 2008;193:134–139.

31 Brown J, Cohen P, Johnson JG, Smailes EM: Childhood abuse and neglect: Specificity of effects on adolescent and young adult depression and suicidality. J Am Acad Child Adolesc Psychiatry 1999; 38:1490–1496.

32 Cutajar MC, Mullen PE, Ogloff JRP, Thomas SD, Wells DL, Spataro J: Suicide and fatal drug overdose in child sexual abuse victims: a historical cohort study. Med J Aust 2010;192:184–187.

33 Enns M, Cox B, Afifi T, De Graaf R, Ten Have M, Sareen J: Childhood adversities and risk for suicidal ideation and attempts: a longitudinal population-based study. Psychol Med 2006;36:1769–1778.

34 Melhem N, Brent D, Ziegler M, Iyengar S, Kolko D, Oquendo M, Birmaher B, Burke AK, Zelazny J, Stanley B, Mann JJ: Familial pathways to early-onset suicidal behaviour: familial and individual antecedents of suicidal behaviour. Am J Psychiatry 2007;164: 1364–1370.

35 Plunkett A, O'Toole B, Swanston H, Oates RK, Shrimpton S, Parkinson P: Suicide risk following child sexual abuse. Ambulatory Pediatr 2001;1: 262–266.

36 Ackard D, Eisenberg ME, Neumark-Sztainer D: Long-term impact of adolescent dating violence on the behavioral and psychological health of male and female youth. J Pediatr 2007;151:476–481.

37 Chowdhary N, Patel V: The effect of spousal violence on women's health: Findings from the Stree Arogya Shodh in Goa, India. J Postgrad Med 2008; 54:306–312.

38 Roberts TA, Klein J, Fisher S: Longitudinal effect of intimate partner abuse on high-risk behavior among adolescents. Arch Pediatr Adolesc Med 2003;157: 875–881.

Karen M. Devries
Department of Global Health and Development
London School of Hygiene and Tropical Medicine
15–17 Tavistock Place, London, WC1H 9SH (UK)
Tel. +44 20 7958 8164, E-Mail karen.devries@lshtm.ac.uk

Violence against Women Suffering from Severe Psychiatric Illness

Marta B. Rondon

Departamento de Clinica Medica, Seccion de Psiquiatria y Salud Mental, Universidad Peruana Cayetano Heredia, Lima, Peru

Abstract

People suffering from severe mental illness (SMI), which is defined conventionally in terms of certain diagnoses (such as schizophrenia, bipolar disorder, other psychoses, drug and alcohol dependence and some forms of personality disorder), duration of illness and intensity of contact with services, are perceived by the general public and health providers as dangerous and violent. However, the limited research in the field shows that they are only slightly more likely than the general population to engage in violent acts [1–3], but they are victimized more often than other groups [4]. As is the case with women in general, women suffering from SMI are more affected than men by different forms of violence during their life course [5]. Exposure to violence, accounted for by stigma and discrimination in addition to the multiple factors that trigger, facilitate and perpetuate gender based violence, has symptomatic and behavioral correlates in the affected women.

Copyright © 2013 S. Karger AG, Basel

Convention on the Rights of Persons with Disabilities: Protection from Violence is a Right

The recently approved and ratified Convention on the Rights of Persons with Disabilities (CRPD) [6] recognizes the special vulnerability of persons suffering from mental illnesses, and it acknowledges that women and girls with disabilities are subject to multiple discriminations, therefore requiring special protection from States parties (Article 6) to enjoy their fundamental freedoms and human rights such as freedom from exploitation, violence and abuse.[1]

The inclusion of an article that addresses the special needs of women with disabilities results from a theoretical and empirical consideration of how gendered stereo-

---

[1] Article 16: States parties shall take all appropriate legislative, administrative, social, educational and other measures to protect persons with disabilities, both within and outside the state, from all forms of exploitation, violence and abuse, including their gender-based aspects.

types coincide with stereotypes of persons with disabilities to harm and discriminate against them in compounded ways, thereby recognizing the intersection of both gender and disability stereotypes in the case of women with disabilities. 'In addition to the multiple discrimination women with disabilities have to experience, they face the problem of a double invisibility as women and as disabled persons' [7]. This invisibility stems from 'rolelessness' [women with mental disability have no social or familial participation] and interacts with stigmatization in perpetuating violence against women suffering from severe mental illness.

Stigma and Its Relation to Violence

The high risk for victimization of people suffering from mental illnesses or exhibiting aberrant or deviant thought and behavior starts with stigmatization: mental illness becomes a 'trait which is deeply discrediting' which serves the purpose of identifying and setting the deviant or stigmatized person apart from 'people like us'. He or she becomes 'the other', one who is not to be treated like me, or entitled to the same rights and freedoms I enjoy [8].

Stereotyping of people, perceiving their common traits and building categories is a normal process that allows us to simplify and organize information. It becomes problematic when we move in rigid negative stereotypical terms ('a generalized view or preconception of attributes' or characteristics possessed by, or the roles that are or should be performed by members of the particular group, e.g. women, lesbians, adolescents) [9] and act in a discriminatory way. This is often experienced by women identified as suffering from mental illness [10] who simultaneously experience the stereotypical attitudes towards women and towards people with severe mental illness: inferior, less intelligent, passive, emotional *and* prone to violence.[2]

Women experience stigma and discrimination differently than men. For example, public discourses and policies surrounding pregnant women who use licit and illicit drugs are particularly 'judgmental, blaming, and unsympathetic' [11] because of the perceived transgression of their role as caregivers.

Devalued persons are more easily stigmatized and discriminated against. Stigma against mentally ill people is widespread and shared by perpetrators of physical and sexual violence who target their violence against individuals who are known to be weak, isolated and dependent, and who, furthermore, lack the ability to communicate

---

[2] The Convention on the Elimination of Discrimination against Women committee recommends that States parties provide information on disabled women in their periodic reports, and on measures taken to deal with their particular situation, including special measures to ensure that they have equal access to education and employment, health services and social security, and to ensure that they can participate in all areas of social and cultural life. General Recommendations, CEDAW Committee, see Recommendation 18, available at http://www.un.org/womenwatch/daw/cedaw/recommendations/recomm.htm#recom18 [last visited Feb. 14, 2012].

effectively with law enforcement, be it due to their cognitive difficulties, their lack of credibility or both.

The generalized public perception that men and women with mental disorders are unreliable, impulsive and violent is central to the stigmatizing image of the mentally ill and contributes to discrimination, as it is easier to condone forced legal action and coerced treatment, as well as seclusion, when violence is involved. The presumption of violence may also provide rationalization to violent and bullying attitudes towards the mentally ill [12], particularly when psychotic features are involved.

However, fear of violence alone does not account for the high rates of victimization of women with SMI [13].

Gender Perspective

Stereotypical gender roles give rise to special stigmatization of deviant women: their 'madness' encompasses their inability to function as ideal wives and mothers and the risk of aberrant sexuality. Sexuality of women is a central preoccupation in the behavior of mentally ill women [14] as female sexual expression is only acceptable if it conforms to the ideal of heterosexuality in adulthood, preferably with reproductive intent and in the context of a stable relationship. Other expressions are considered dangerous, and the privilege of the strong partner in a relationship.

Sexual expressions by people with mental disorders are frowned upon. Women whose sexuality is different (and hence 'dangerous') may be labeled mentally ill, and subject to treatment. Psychiatry and psychiatric treatment may become one of the instruments for social control of women's sexuality [15], unless practitioners are familiar with and strictly adhere to ethical guidelines.

The feminist perspective on violence as the result of a differential in power elucidates why so many women with mental illnesses are subject to heinous violence from the state, the health care professions and their families alike [16, 17]. Gender determines the differential power and control men and women have over the socioeconomic determinants of their health and life, social position and exposure to specific mental health risks, among which violence is paramount [18, 19].

The feminist approach to disability, which complements and transcends the social perspective that underlies the CRPD,[3] situates the experience of disability in a context of rights and exclusions, helps understand the intricate relationship between bodies and selves and aims to denaturalize disability by challenging the view that femaleness is a natural form of physical or mental deficiency or constitutional unruliness [20]. Disability-feminism rejects the homogeneous category of 'women' and

[3] CRPD: This social model of disability poses an alternative to the medical model of disability, asserting that persons with disabilities are disadvantaged not because of their impairments, but as a result of the limitations imposed by social, cultural, economic, and environmental barriers.

focuses on the essential effort to understand just how multiple identities intersect. This analysis rejects an approach that obscures other identities and categories of cultural analysis – such as race, ethnicity, sexuality, class, and physical or intellectual ability.

Magnitude of the Problem

Surveys show that having a disability is correlated with higher exposure to violence for both sexes, although women with disabilities are twice as vulnerable [14]. It is estimated that rates of violence against women range from 33 to 83%, varying with the type of disability [21]. Mental disability is correlated with higher vulnerability to physical and sexual assault, with 51–97% of women specifically asked about experiences of physical and sexual violence endorsing it [22].

Studies have shown that 17–50% committed patients had perpetrated violence in the past 6 months to 3 years, and 2–13% outpatients had committed violent acts [23]. The rates of victimization of psychiatric patients, however, are much greater: some studies will show up to 35% reporting that they had suffered an act of violence in the past year alone [24].

In a qualitative study on the experience of violence by women with schizophrenia [25], participants described the double stigma of being diagnosed with schizophrenia ('bottom of the totem pole') and perceiving that society deemed them acceptable victims of violence. In this study, stigma was perceived as label (a discrediting brand) used to dismiss what they say, shedding doubt on whether their complaints were grounded in reality or came from their hallucinations, as a marker of belonging in the lower end of a hierarchy, which meant that they would be disowned by their families and communities and condemned to poverty and unemployment. Stigma also stood in the way of being listened to when they were ready to disclose their violent histories and forced them to lower their own personal expectations for the future.

Special Populations

Victimization in Prisons
Wolff et al. [24] found that among 5,728 inmates surveyed (564 women), 1 in 12 inmates suffering from mental illness, compared to 1 in 33 not suffering from it, reported victimization. The rates of sexual victimization were three times as high among women with mental disorders as among men (23.4 vs. 8.3%).

Girls and Women with Intellectual Disabilities
Women with intellectual disabilities (mental retardation) are considered either childlike or oversexed and, in spite of their increasing integration in communities, do not

generally receive proper sexual education and protection from sexual abuse. Thus, they are more vulnerable to different types of sexual abuse [25]. There is a wide range in the estimation of sexual abuse rates in this population. This fact underlines the clandestine and subtle nature of these crimes. Estimates vary from 25 to 85% of the mentally retarded population being subject to sexual abuse [26]. This is a rate 4–10 times higher than the general population. Some of the explanations for this striking fact are the great dependencies of the patient on authority figures, their powerlessness in a discriminatory society, ignorance of sexuality and sexual abuse, and emotional and social insecurities.

In this population, more than 80% of the victims are girls and women, and the overall majority of perpetrators are men, especially service providers (28%), natural or step-family members (19%), and acquaintances, babysitters or dates [27].

Partner Violence against Women with Disabilities

Partner violence against women with disabilities is a much understudied topic, even if it is already known that men are the main perpetrators of violence against women with mental disabilities. The view that these individuals are asexual may partially account for this. Other explanations would be related to poor access to health care [28], to the difficulties that women with mental problems have in communicating violent experiences, and to the attitudes of hopelessness and frustration of health providers [13].

An explanation of partner violence against women with disabilities should examine relationship, victim and perpetrator factors. Among the former, intimate partner violence (IPV) seems to be related to dependence and duration of relationship, although there is little empirical evidence of the latter. A higher educational level may provide some independence and, thus, be protective.

Among the factors of the woman, socioeconomic status is recognized as a risk factor as are low educational level and older age. The perpetrator's characteristics include the need to have control over 'their sexual property' and the use of alcohol and drugs. Feminist theory posits that women with disabilities are doubly vulnerable, being the subordinate gender and disabled, particularly in traditional, openly patriarchal groups and in cases where the partner embraces a patriarchal ideology [29].

The Brownridge's survey of 5,027 women shows that indeed women with disabilities have a higher odds ratio of suffering IPV. However, lower educational level, poverty, unemployment and alcohol use failed to explain the elevated rate of IPV. 'Patriarchal dominance and sexually proprietary behaviors were strongly linked to increased odds of violence for women with and without disabilities. Moreover, controlling for these perpetrator-related characteristics accounted for the elevated risk for violence against women with disabilities [29].

Criminal Victimization of Women with Severe Mental Illness

De-institutionalization has fueled some studies on how dangerous patients with chronic mental illness are when living in the community and a couple of studies about their risk of suffering from violent crime. The study by Walsh et al. [30] showed that people with SMI have a prevalence of victimization (16–18%) of more than twice the general population according to the British Crime Survey. Homelessness, substance abuse and a history of violence were related to risk of victimization. Men with SMI had a higher risk than women with SMI, but women had a higher risk than the general population.

In another study of 936 chronic patients living in the community (48.4% women), the rate of completed or attempted violent crime was 11.8 times higher than that of the general population, as measured by the National Crime Victimization Survey. The rate of personal theft was 140 times higher in people with SMI. More women than men were victims of completed violence, rape/sexual assault, personal theft, and motor vehicle theft. Significantly more men than women were victims of robbery [31].

Consequences of Victimization of Women with SMI

Abuse may constitute a 'stressor' triggering symptomatic manifestations in vulnerable women, fueling continued crises and a more severe prognosis. There is also the possibility that certain psychotic manifestations, such as bizarre behavior, hallucinations and delusions in the context of posttraumatic stress disorder may be misdiagnosed as schizophrenia [31].

Women suffering from SMI who are victimized have higher rates of substance use disorders, HIV infection and homelessness [32].

It is possible that certain characteristics of schizophrenia (compared to other severe mental conditions) predispose to repeated trauma. A French study found that women with schizophrenia had slightly more episodes of sexual trauma before onset of symptoms and that sexual trauma was linked with greater symptom severity and higher risk of addiction than in the case of bipolar patients [33].

From the point of view of the health provider and the therapeutic alliance, Rice [25] has observed hopelessness and frustration, as well as an effort to ignore the history of traumata, as there is so little that can be done currently to help these women.

The relationship between patient and provider is compromised due to the experience of the woman of being sexually abused or exploited by a mental health provider. The patient doctor relationship entails an advantageous position for the therapist, allowed by the patient on the expectation of respect and trust [34]. All sexual contact between a mental health provider and a patient is a breach of the trust and bound to increase the anguish of the patient.

Future Research

The magnitude of violence in different contexts has to be studied using large samples. This research would be more useful if perpetration is studied alongside with victimization in the same sample, helping us to understand the relationship between being bullied and/or abused and resorting to violent behavior.

The protective and risk factors for violence in women with mental disability (for instance, is younger age a protective or a risk factor?) need to be better characterized, so that preventive interventions can be designed. One area of special interest is the overlap of PTSD symptoms with other disorders and their management.

Finally, it is important to design and test interventions to protect severely ill women from further victimization.

References

1. Marzuk P: Violence, crime, and mental illness. How strong a link? Arch Gen Psychiatry 1996;53:481–486.
2. Noffsinger SG, Resnick PJ: Violence and mental illness. Curr Opin Psychiatry 1999;12:683–687.
3. Link B, Stueve A: Evidence bearing on mental illness as a possible cause of violent behaviour. Epidemiol Rev 1995;17:172–181.
4. Hiday VA, Swartz MS, Swanson JW, et al: Criminal victimization of persons with severe mental illness. Psychiatr Serv 1999;50:62–68.
5. Rice E: The invisibility of violence against women diagnosed with schizophrenia: a synthesis of perspectives. Adv Nurs Sci 2008;31:E9–E21.
6. Convention on the Rights of Persons with Disabilities, G.A. Res. 61/611, U.N. Doc. A/RES/61/611 (Dec. 6, 2006) available at http://www.un.org/disabilities/convention/conventionfull.shtml.
7. Arnade S, Haefner S: Gendering the comprehensive and integral Int'l Convention on the Protection and Promotion of the Rights and Dignity of Persons with Disabilities 10 [Disabled Peoples' International 2006] available at http://v1.dpi.org/lang-en/resources/topics_detail?page=446 (last visited Feb. 23, 2012).
8. Goffman E. Stigma: Notes on the Management of Spoiled Identity. Harmondsworth, Penguin, 1963.
9. Cook R, Cusack S: Gender Stereotyping: Transnational Legal Perspectives. Philadelphia, University of Pennsylvania Press, 2010.
10. Gray AJ: Stigma in psychiatry. J R Soc Med. 2002; 95:72–76.
11. Canadian Women's Health Network: Understanding stigma through a gender lens. 2009. Available at http://www.cwhn.ca/en/node/41610.
12. Stuart H: Violence and mental illness: an overview. World Psychiatry 2003;2:121–124.
13. Goodman L, Rosenberg S, Mueser K, Drake R: Physical and sexual assault history in women with serious mental illness: prevalence, correlates, treatments and future research directions. Schizophr Bulln 1997;23; 685–696.
14. Burin M: La familia: sexualidades permitidas y prohibidas; in Burin M, Meler I (eds): Genero y familia: poder, amor y sexualidad en la construcción de la subjetividad. Buenos Aires, Editorial Paidos, 1998, pp 87–91.
15. Burstow B: Electroshock as a form of violence against women. Violence Against Women 2006;12: 372–392.
16. Garcia-Moreno C: Violence against women: consolidating a public health agenda; in Sen G, GA, Östlin P (eds): Engendering International Health: a Challenge of Equity Cambridge, MIT Press, 2002.
17. Jewkes R: Intimate partner violence: causes and prevention. Lancet 2002;359:1423–1429.
18. Sen G, Ostlin P, Goerge A: Unequal, Unfair, Ineffective and Inefficient, Gender Inequity in Health: why it exists and how we can change it. Final Report to the WHO Commission on Social Determinants of Health, 2007, p xii.
19. Rice E: Schizophrenia and violence: the perspective of women. Issues Ment Health Nurs 2006;27:961–983.

20 Ortoleva S: Recommendations for Action to Advance the Rights of Women and Girls with Disabilities in the United Nations System; 2011, available at http://www.fokuskvinner.no/PageFiles/4493/Stephanie_Ortoleva_Addressing_the_Rights_ofWoen.pdf. Last visit February 5, 2012.
21 Schaller J, Fieber JL: Issues of abuse for women with disabilities and implications for rehabilitation counseling. J Appl Rehabil Couns 1998;29:9–17.
22 Ritsher J, Coursey R, Farrell E: A survey on issues in the lives of women with severe mental illness. Psychiatr Serv 1997;48:1273–1282.
23 Choe J, Teplin L, Abram K: Perpetration of violence, violent victimization, and severe mental illness: balancing public health concern. Psychiatr Serv 2008;59:153–164.
24 Wolff N, Blitz C, Jing Shi MS: Rates of sexual victimization in prison for inmates with and without mental disorders. Psychiatr Serv 2007; 58:1087–1094.
25 Rice E: Schizophrenia and violence: the perspective of women. Issues Ment Health Nurs 2006;27:961–983.
26 Pincus S: Sexuality in the mentally retarded patient. Am Fam Phys 1988;37:319–323.
27 Sobsey D, Doe T: Patterns of sexual abuse and assault: sexual exploitation of people with disabilities [special issue]. Sexuality Disability 1991;9:243–259.
28 Barrett KA, O'Day B, Roche A, Carlson B: Intimate partner violence, health status, and, health care access among women with disabilities. Women's Health Issues 2009;19:94–100.
29 Brownridge D: Partner violence against women with disabilities: prevalence, risk and explanations. Violence Against Women 2006;12;805–822.
30 Walsh E, Moran P, Scott C, Mckenzie K, Burns, Creed F, Tyrer P, Murray R, Fahy T: Prevalence of violent victimization in severe mental illness. BJP 2003;183:233–238.
31 Teplin L, MacCleland G, Abram K, Weiner D: Crime victimization in adults with severe mental illness: comparison with the national crime victimization Survey. Arch Gen Psychiatry 2005;62:911–921.
32 Burnam MA, Stein JA, Golding JM, Siegel JM, Sorenson SB, Forsythe AB, Telles CA: Sexual assault and mental disorders in a community population. J Consult Clin Psychol 1988;56:843–850.
33 Darvez-Bornoz JM; Lempérière T, Degiovanni A, Gaillard P: Sexual victimization in women with schizophrenia and bipolar disorder. Soc Psychiatry Psychiatr Epidemiol 1995; 30:78–84.
34 Madrid Declaration on Ethical Standards for Psychiatric Practice: Yokohama, World Psychiatric Association, 2005. Available at http://www.wpanet.org/detail.php?section_id=5&content_id=48, last visit June 16, 2012.

Marta B. Rondon
Departamento de Clinica Medica, Seccion de Psiquiatria y Salud Mental
Universidad Peruana Cayetano Heredia
Avenida Honorio Delgado 430, Urb. Ingeniería
Lima 31 (Peru)
E-Mail mbrondon@gmail.com

Conclusions

Violence against Women and Mental Health

Claudia García-Moreno[a,1] · Anita Riecher-Rössler[b]

[a]Department of Reproductive Health and Research, WHO, Geneva, and [b]Center for Gender Research and Early Detection, University of Basel Psychiatric Clinics, Basel, Switzerland

Abstract

This chapter provides a brief overview of the book contents and highlights the policy and programmatic implications. The book provides substantial evidence of the pervasiveness of violence against women across the world. The first section includes a global overview of the prevalence and consequences of violence against women and various regional perspectives from Europe, Latin America, the Middle East, South Asia, and South Africa. All of the chapters highlight how social, cultural and economic factors, particularly gender inequality and women's low status in society, are root causes of this violence and affect women's mental health directly as well. The chapters in the second section of the book document the burden of mental ill health among women who have experienced different forms of violence – sexual abuse in childhood, intimate partner violence (IPV), sexual violence; similarly with violence in different settings such as in conflict and among migrants and refugees. Other chapters address violence against women with severe psychiatric illness, sexual abuse perpetrated on patients by health professionals and suicide and intimate partner violence. In spite of this evidence, most mental health policies and programmes do not systematically include consideration of violence issues. Furthermore, mental health services are sorely lacking in low and middle income countries. This is a call for more awareness, for changes in the system and integration of violence issues into mental health policies and into the training curricula for mental health care providers. Increased attention to the primary prevention of all forms of violence is also urgently needed.

Copyright © 2013 WHO*

Violence against Women: A Global and Prevalent Problem

The first section of the book provides clear evidence of the high prevalence of violence against women across the world. The chapter by García-Moreno and Stöckl provides a global overview of different forms of violence against women, with a focus on intimate partner violence; it also looks at how this violence impacts negatively on women's health

---

[1] The author is a staff member of the World Health Organization. The author alone is responsible for the views expressed in this publication and they do not necessarily represent the decisions, policy or views of the World Health Organization.

*All rights reserved. The World Health Organization has granted the publisher permission for the reproduction of this chapter.

and wellbeing. The next 5 chapters in this section provide different regional perspectives on violence: the chapters by Madi Skaff on the Middle East, Niaz on South Asia and Gaviria on Latin America illustrate quite clearly the highly gendered nature of this violence; they highlight how social, cultural and economic factors, particularly gender inequality and women's low status in society, are root causes of much of the violence they experience and also directly affect their mental health. Jewkes, in her chapter, presents findings from a longitudinal analysis of data among young women aged 15–24 in South Africa and documents the increased incidence of depression and PTSD among those who have experienced physical and/or sexual intimate partner violence. Helweg-Larsen illustrates the value of different registration systems in Denmark in identifying gaps in the data collection and in bringing attention to the underreporting of intimate partner violence. Together all of these chapters point to the pervasiveness and the high prevalence of violence against women, particularly intimate partner violence and rape and other forms of sexual violence by any perpetrator. Wherever it has been studied, violence against women is common. It takes many forms, however, physical, sexual and emotional/psychological violence against women by male intimate partners and ex-partners and sexual assault, rape and other forms of sexual violence are common throughout the world. Studies from around the world have confirmed that women suffer violence most commonly in the hands of partners and ex-partners. Other forms of violence like murders in the name of honor, female genital mutilation and other harmful traditional practices are limited to certain countries and regions, although they can also be encountered in other regions particularly among immigrants. Other forms of abuse such as trafficking and harassment have also been found to have important mental health impacts as illustrated in the chapters by Kastrup and by Cortina and Leskinen.

The chapters in this book also bring attention to the multiplicity of settings in which women experience violence, including the home; during conflict, displacement and other emergencies; and in the context of health care. Sexual abuse against patients by health professionals is an issue that is very rarely discussed. And as Tschan argues in his chapter on abuse in doctor-patient relationships, it is one that the medical establishment often connives to keep hidden.

A common theme in many of the chapters is the role of gender inequality, discrimination and other socio-cultural and economic factors in perpetuating violence against women. These very same factors also have direct relevance to mental health. Biological, social, and emotional factors all interact to shape women's risk of both violence (child sexual abuse, intimate partner violence, sexual assault) and mental health problems. Gender stereotypes are pervasive and difficult to change and this includes the denial of women's agency in health systems and the general undervaluing of women and neglect of their mental and general health, as pointed out by Rondon. Furthermore, violence against women is socially sanctioned to a greater or lesser extent in most societies.

Evidence is also provided that in many settings this violence remains something shameful, not openly reported or talked about and deeply embedded in the cultural and social norms. The acceptability of violence against women makes it difficult for women in many settings to disclose their experiences, seek social or professional support, and for men to stop using violence. In addition to traumatic stress responses, other sequelae of violence (such as social stigma) may lead to increased stress, fear, and isolation, all of which will increase hopelessness and helplessness, and thus increase the impact on women's mental health including suicide rates, as noted by Devries and Seguin.

The Convention on the Elimination of all Forms of Discrimination against Women (CEDAW) has now been ratified by the majority of Member States. Under the human rights treaties governments have obligated themselves to be bound by, they have the responsibility to prevent, investigate and punish all forms of violence against women.[2] Meeting this responsibility requires specific and targeted government action through the health sector as well as other sectors, such as justice and education, to name a few. For many governments violence against women is still a low priority, in spite of the growing number of reports, agreements and recommendations that identify addressing violence as one of the key interventions for improving women's health and well-being.

Violence Against Women: A Risk Factor for Women's Mental Ill Health

The second section of the book clearly documents that violence against women is strongly associated with mental health problems. These associations are multiple, overlapping and additive at times. Each of the chapters describes in detail how different forms of violence and abuse are associated with mental ill health.

The chapters in this section document the strong associations found between different forms of violence and mental health. Overall, adult women in the general population who have experienced intimate partner violence and rape have a much higher prevalence of depression, posttraumatic stress disorder (PTSD), problem drinking and other substance misuse, suicidal thoughts and attempts. Intimate partner violence has also been shown to be associated with antenatal and postnatal mental disorders, eating disorders, functional symptoms, and the exacerbation of psychotic symptoms.

Oram and Howard review the prevalence of violence among women with mental disorders and present evidence that suggests a causal relationship between intimate partner violence and mental disorder. They note that in a systematic review of 134 studies when comparing the mean lifetime prevalence across various healthcare settings, studies conducted in psychiatric clinics and obstetrics and gynecology clinics recorded the highest prevalence of physical violence (30–50%) and sexual violence (30–35%), while the highest mean lifetime prevalence of psychological violence was reported by studies conducted in psychiatry clinics and emergency departments (65–87%).

Much of the available evidence is cross-sectional, but the limited longitudinal data suggest that the association between violence and mental health is bidirectional, with mental disorders increasing the odds of experiencing intimate partner violence and

---

[2] CEDAW General Recommendation 19.

experiencing violence increasing the odds of developing a mental health problem. Other data find a dose-response effect showing that the more severe the violence the more likely that it is associated with severe mental health problems.

The chapter by Devries and Seguin looks at the relationship of intimate partner violence and sexual violence with suicidal behavior (attempts and completed suicides). They point out that women's nonfatal suicidal attempts have been especially neglected in low- and middle-income countries and importantly they point to the fact that children whose mothers have experienced intimate partner violence are similarly at risk for later suicidal behavior. This link between a woman's mental health and her ability to bond and to provide the caring and supportive environment that will enable children to develop healthy attachments and internal regulation processes is of critical importance. It has important policy implications for prevention of subsequent violence and mental health problems.

The chapter by Rondon focuses on violence against women with serious mental disorders and mental disabilities. She points out that mental disability is correlated with higher vulnerability to physical and sexual assault, referring to a study where 51–97% of women with mental disabilities reported experiences of physical and sexual violence.

MacMillan and Wathan look at the long-term mental health consequences of experiencing sexual abuse during childhood and highlight that children's exposure to sexual abuse remains under-recognized and underdetected. They also identify cognitive-behavioral therapy for sexually abused children with symptoms of posttraumatic stress disorder as showing the best evidence for reducing subsequent impairment.

In summary, violence against women in all its forms is a major public health concern that is associated with a range of mental health problems. There is a high prevalence of intimate partner violence victimization among people with mental disorders, but violence is underdetected by mental health professionals. Also, there is a limited evidence base on interventions to address the intimate partner violence experienced by people with mental disorders. However, a growing awareness about the possibility of intimate partner violence, sexual violence, child sexual abuse and other forms of violence in women seeking mental health services may start to address problems of poor identification and care healthcare professionals are trained to respond safely, as proposed by Oramand Howard.

Policy and Programmatic Implications

The evidence of the high prevalence of violence against women and girls and of the strong associations between violence and mental health problems highlights the urgent need to address violence against women in mental health care policies, programmes and services.

In spite of the current and growing evidence presented in this book that violence against women is an important factor affecting women's mental health, this is not an issue that is systematically considered or has been integrated into mental health policies and programmes. In addition, mental health services are usually a neglected sector of the public health system, particularly in low- and middle-income countries, where mental health care is too often seen as a 'luxury'. The limited services that are available tend to focus on care for people with severe psychiatric disorders such as schizophrenia and other psychotic disorders and much less on the common mental disorders like depression, anxiety and post-traumatic stress disorder. The majority of women who experience depression and PTSD do not have access to any form of mental health care.

The discrimination and disadvantages in terms of access to and control over resources that women face in many societies has an impact on their mental health. In addition, as women increasingly join the labor force, while still having the main responsibility for household and childcare duties, many face the double or triple burden of responsibility. The inability to leave an abusive partner or an abusive situation, such as in the case of women who have been trafficked and/or been displaced, impact directly on women's mental health and also contribute to the prevalence of violence against women. Mental health policies need to take these issues into account and identify situations that can increase women's vulnerability and risk of mental problems.

To address violence against women and mental health calls for actions at many different levels. Some important actions to focus on include:
1 Preventing violence against women
2 Developing gender-sensitive mental health policies that address gender-based violence
3 Ensuring adequate health care through:
    - Integrating issues of gender-based violence into the training and curricula of mental health care providers
    - Training of primary health care providers on the management of common mental disorders such as depression and anxiety
    - Enabling referral to specialized mental health care as needed.
4 Strengthening research and data collection

Preventing Violence against Women
The prevention of violence against women would clearly contribute to reducing the global burden of mental health. As exemplified by Jewkes in the first section, among their sample of young women aged 15–26 years in South Africa, 16% of depression during the follow-up period could have been avoided in the absence of exposure to physical or sexual partner violence and about 15% in the absence of emotional abuse. The prevention of violence requires complex multisector interventions to address factors that are associated with the presence of violence or conversely protect women from such violence at different levels, from individual factors such as alcohol misuse to social factors such as norms that condone or even foster such violence.

While there is still limited evidence on what works to prevent violence against women from happening in the first place, a 2010 review by the WHO [WHO, 2010] synthesized the evidence of what works to prevent intimate partner violence and sexual violence against women and identified several promising strategies. These range from interventions to prevent child abuse and neglect, such as home visiting and parenting interventions, and school-based programmes to prevent dating violence, to strategies to increase women's economic status and other aspects of empowerment, such as through microfinance and a gender awareness and empowerment curriculum. Other strategies relate to interventions to reduce the availability of alcohol and those to change gender norms through work with boys and men and community-based interventions [see WHO, 2010, for more details on what works to prevent intimate partner violence and sexual violence against women].

Developing Gender-Sensitive Mental Health Policies that Address Gender-Based Violence
As highlighted by Devries and Seguin and several other authors in this book, women are more likely than men to find themselves in a marginalized position within a given society, to be excluded from participation in aspects of society, and to have less control over their own health and well-being. Violence against women is socially sanctioned to a greater or lesser extent in most societies, and women are subject to intimate partner violence and childhood sexual abuse at rates that are far higher than men. This has a psychological and biological effect. Furthermore, the normality of violence against women makes it difficult for women in many settings to disclose their experiences, and receive social or professional support.

Mental health care policies should have a gender perspective and systematically take into account the different social situations of women and men and how this impacts differentially on their ability to enjoy good mental health and to protect themselves from ill health. Specifically, they should address gender-based violence. Oram and Howard recommend integrating routine enquiry about violence into the standard uptake form in mental health services; however, the efficacy of this needs to be evaluated. Ultimately knowing and understanding more about a woman's situation should contribute to increasing the effectiveness of whatever therapy is being proposed. Treatment and care options will most likely need to be adapted and tailored to take into consideration the changes that result from prolonged trauma as in the case of sexual abuse during childhood or intimate partner violence. For example, women who have been identified as having suicidal behaviour must not be medicated and sent back into potentially violent situations, which are likely contributing to their suicidal behavior in the first place, as discussed in the chapter by Devries and Seguin.

Services must be available at the primary care level and must be acceptable and affordable to women. Awareness of what services are available and when and how to seek help is also important.

Integrating Issues of Gender-Based Violence into Training and Curricula of Mental Health Care Providers
There is an urgent need to integrate issues of gender-based violence (e.g. intimate partner, child abuse, sexual violence by any perpetrator) into the training and training

curricula of mental health professionals (psychiatrists, psychologists, psychotherapists, social workers, others) at both undergraduate and postgraduate levels. Multiple strategies are needed to increase awareness of issues of gender-based violence among mental health providers, be they at primary health care level or in specialized services.

Providing an Adequate Health Care Response
While prevention is important, many women are and will be already in abusive situations and need care and support that can help reduce the recurrence of this violence and/or mitigate its harms and consequences. Early identification and an appropriate response are of critical importance, yet they are not readily available in most settings, particularly in low and middle income countries. Early identification could be enhanced by the systematic inclusion of issues of violence in assessing mental health conditions, particularly depression, PTSD and other anxiety disorders, suicidal behavior, self-harm, eating disorders, sleeping disorders, and problems with alcohol and other drugs. All of these have been found to be associated with intimate partner violence, sexual violence and child sexual abuse. Sexual harassment in the workplace is also associated with depression and anxiety as Cortina and Leskinen document in this book. This has important implications for the care provided to these women.

The World Health Organization has developed the mental health GAP action programme, in order to scale up services for mental health in low-resource settings. Evidence-based clinical guidelines for management of the most common disorders have been developed to increase the knowledge and capacity of primary health care providers to handle the most common mental disorders such as depression, and anxiety. New guidelines are under development for disorders and problems specially related to stress, such as PTSD. All of these are of great relevance in responding to the mental health consequences of violence against women.

Some women will need referral to more specialized services and this may prove challenging in many settings, but an important part of the mental health burden related to violence could be addressed with improved mental health care at primary health care level.

Strengthening Research on Mental Health and Violence against Women
Most of the evidence on the associations between women's experience of violence and mental health comes from cross-cutting studies where it is not possible to demonstrate causality or to fully understand the temporal relationships of the associations. There is a need for more longitudinal research in order to fully understand the burden of mental health that is related to violence.

There is a need for studies of psychological interventions that are specific to the populations of women affected by violence and to evaluate the provision of some of these interventions by nonspecialists. There is also a need for more research on how to change social norms and attitudes related to gender-based violence. Researchers, advocates and health care professionals must work together to develop culturally appropriate, effective intervention.

Further research is also needed to improve our understanding of child sexual abuse experienced by children in low and middle-income countries and global strategies for prevention of this form of abuse.

Concluding Remarks

In 2006, the World Psychiatric Association (WPA) approved the 'Consensus Statement on Interpersonal Violence against Women', which had been developed by the WPA Section on Women's Mental Health, as well as the 'International Consensus Statement on Women's Mental Health', developed by the International Association for Women's Mental Health (IAWMH) [Stewart, 2006]. These consensus statements have been approved by all psychiatric associations (130+) which belong to the WPA, but much more needs to be done to implement them.

In May 2012, the World Health Assembly, at its 65th session, adopted resolution WHA 65.4 – The global burden of mental disorders and the need for a comprehensive, coordinated response from health and social sectors at the country level – and called on WHO to develop a comprehensive mental health action plan. The draft action plan would propose actions to address the health, social and economic burden of mental disorders by adopting a comprehensive and multisectoral approach involving coordinated services from the health and social sector, with an emphasis on promotion, prevention, treatment, care and recovery, and with due attention to the principles of equity, human rights, evidence and user empowerment. It would also seek to implement strategies for mental health promotion and protection, including actions to prevent mental disorders and suicides, and to strengthen information systems, evidence and research for mental health. This plan offers the opportunity to integrate and address issues of gender-based violence and other gender-related issues that particularly affect women into mental health policies and services. There is a need for more research on the attitudes of men and women regarding gender-based violence and how these attitudes may be changed; also, researchers, advocates and health care professionals must work together to develop culturally sensitive interventions.

References

WHO/LSHTM: Preventing Intimate Partner Violence and Sexual Violence against Women. Taking Action and Generating Evidence. Geneva, World Health Organization, 2010.

Stewart DE: The International Consensus Statement on Women's Mental Health and the WPA Consensus Statement on Interpersonal Violence against Women. World Psychiatry 2006;5:61–64 (see also www.iawmh.org).

Dr. Claudia García-Moreno
Sexual Health, Gender, Reproductive Rights and Adolescence
Department of Reproductive Health and Research, World Health Organization
20 Ave Appia, CH–1211 Geneva 27 (Switzerland)
E-Mail garciamorenoc@who.int

Author Index

Bachelet, M. VII

Cortina, L.M. 139

Devries, K.M. 148

García-Moreno, C. XII, 1, 167
Gaviria, S.L. 24

Helweg-Larsen, K. 54
Howard, L.M. 75

Jewkes, R. 65

Kastrup, M. 118

Leskinen, E.A. 139

MacMillan, H.L. 96
Madi Skaff, J. 12

Martin, S.L. 86

Niaz, U. 38

Oram, S. 75

Parcesepe, A.M. 86

Riecher-Rössler, A. XII, 167
Rondon, M.B. 159

Sartorius, N. X
Seguin, M. 148
Stavrou, V. 107
Stöckl, H. 1

Tschan, W. 129

Wathen, C.N. 96

Subject Index

Addiction, *see* Substance abuse
Afghanistan, *see* South Asia
Alcohol abuse, *see* Substance abuse
Armed conflict, *see* War-related violence against women

Bangladesh, *see* South Asia
Bhutan, *see* South Asia
Bipolar disorder, violence against women impact 7
Burma, *see* South Asia

Caribbean, *see* Latin America
Central America, *see* Latin America
Child sexual abuse
   definition 97
   epidemiology
      rates 97, 98
      risk factors 98, 99
   identification 101
   mental health impact
      adults 100, 101
      children and adolescents 100
      overview 99, 100
   overview 96, 97
   prevention 103
   prospects for study 103, 104
   treatment 101–103
Cognitive behavioral therapy, post-traumatic stress disorder management 102, 111
Consensus Statement on Interpersonal Violence against Women 174
Convention against Transnational Organized Crime 125
Convention on the Elimination of All Forms of Discrimination against Women 125

Convention on the Rights of Persons with Disabilities 159, 160

Denmark, *see* Europe
Depression, *see also* Suicide
   child sexual abuse association 100
   sexual harassment association 144
   sexual violence association 90, 91
   South Africa and intimate partner violence 65, 66
   violence against women association 7
Doctor-patient abuse, *see* Professional sexual misconduct
Dowry murder, South Asia 41
Drug abuse, *see* Substance abuse

Egypt, *see* Middle East
Europe, violence against women
   data sources 57, 58
   intimate partner violence
      identification by different data sources 58–60
      mental health impact 57, 62, 63
      prevalence 55–57, 60, 61
      trends 61, 62

Fatality, *see* Mortality
Female genital mutilation
   Middle East 17
   reproductive health impact 8
Finland, *see* Europe
France, *see* Europe

Honor killing
   Middle East
      complications 18

Honor killing (cont.)
    legal background 16, 17
    prevalence 16
    social background 16
  South Asia 41
Human immunodeficiency virus, violence against women association 8
Human trafficking
  cultural aspects 124
  health consequences
    mental health 122, 123
    physical health 122
  overview 119, 120
  prevention of violence against women 125, 126
  social consequences 123
  South Asia 41

Immigration, *see* Refugee
India, *see* South Asia
Injury, violence against women 6
International Association for Women's Mental Health 174
Intimate partner violence
  disabled women 163
  Europe
    identification by different data sources 58–60
    mental health impact 57, 62, 63
    prevalence 55–57, 60, 61
    trends 61, 62
  Latin America 29–33
  mental health impact relationship, *see also* specific mental disorders
    interventions 80–82
    overview 7, 78, 79
    screening in healthcare settings 79, 80
    South Africa, *see* South Africa
  mortality 5, 6
  physical injury 6
  prevalence 4, 5, 76–78
  reproductive health impact 7, 8
  South Asia 39, 40
Iran, *see* Middle East
Iraq, *see* Middle East
Ireland, *see* Europe

Jordan, *see* Middle East

Kuwait, *see* Middle East

Latin America
  education of women 26, 27
  health status of women 28, 29
  interventions 34, 35
  intimate partner violence 29–33
  magnitude of violence against women 25
  patriarchical culture and stereotypes 26
  political and social violence 33, 34
  prospects for study 35, 36
  workload of women 27, 28
Lebanon, *see* Middle East

Maldives, *see* South Asia
Mental illness, *see also* specific disorders
  gender perspective 161, 162
  prospects for violence studies 165
  severe mental illness, criminal victimization and consequences 164
  stigma and relation to violence 160, 161
  violence
    exposure and perpetration impact 162
    intellectual disability 162, 163
    intimate partner violence 163
    prisons 162
    as risk factor 169, 170
    victim populations
Mexico, *see* Latin America
Middle East
  attitudes regarding violence
    judicial system 20
    men 19, 20
    women 19
  complications of violence against women 15, 16
  countries 13, 14
  female genital mutilation 17, 18
  honor killing
    legal background 16, 17
    prevalence 16
    social background 16
  interventions 20–22
  prevalence of violence against women 15
  prospects for study 20
  war-related violence against women
    Iraq 18
    Lebanon 18, 19
    Palestine 18
  women's rights 14, 15
Mortality, *see also* Dowry murder, Honor killing, Suicide

children of intimate partner violence victims 8
violence against women 5, 6, 33

Nepal, see South Asia
Norway, see Europe

Oman, see Middle East

Pakistan, see South Asia
Palestine, see Middle East
Platform of Action of the Fourth World Conference on Women 49
Poland, see Europe
Policy
   gender-sensitive mental health policy 172
   health care response adequacy 173
   prevention of violence against women 171, 173
   research strengthening 173, 174
   training and curricula development for mental health care providers 173
Population attributable fraction 79
Posttraumatic stress disorder
   child sexual abuse association and treatment 100, 102
   health care response adequacy 173
   human trafficking 123
   sexual harassment association 144, 145
   sexual violence association 89, 90
   South Africa and intimate partner violence 65–67
   violence against women association 7, 78
   war-related violence against women 108, 110, 111
Pregnancy
   South Asia and violence during pregnancy 41
   violence against women impact 7
Prevalence, violence against women
   child sexual abuse 97, 98
   geographic distribution 3, 4
   global perspective 167–169
   intimate partner violence in Europe 55–57, 60, 61
   intimate partner violence overview 4, 5, 76–78
   Middle East 15, 16
   overview 2, 3
   professional sexual misconduct 132, 133
   sexual violence 87, 88

Professional sexual misconduct
   consequences for victims 134
   definition 131, 132
   handling
      curriculum 135
      rehabilitation 136
      reporting 135
      support 135, 136
   myths and facts 129–131
   path to offense 133, 134
   prevalence 132, 133
   risk awareness 136, 137
   sex of victims 157

Qatar, see Middle East

Rape, see Sexual violence
Refugee
   burden on women 118, 119
   cultural aspects 124
   empowerment 125
   health consequences
      mental health 122, 123
      physical health 122
   prevention of violence against women 125, 126
   sexual violence 120, 121
   social consequences 123
   treatment
      access to care 124
      barriers 124, 125

Saudi Arabia, see Middle East
Schizophrenia
   criminal victimization and consequences 164
   violence against women impact 7
   violence by women 162
Sexual harassment
   definition 140, 141
   mental health impact 141–145
   overview 139, 140
   South Asia 42
Sexual violence, see also Child sexual abuse
   definition 86
   mental health impact
      depression 90, 91
      factors affecting
         prior sexual assault 91, 92
         relationship with perpetrator 92
         severity of sexual assault 92

Sexual violence (cont.)
    social reactions 92
  interventions 93
  posttraumatic stress disorder 89, 90
  substance abuse 88, 89
  suicide 91
  prevalence 87, 88
  refugees 120, 121
  South Asia 40, 41
South Africa, intimate partner violence and mental health
  adolescent women
    alcohol abuse 72
    depression 68–70
    suicide 70–72
  depression 65, 66
  overview 65, 66
  population-based research 66, 67
  posttraumatic stress disorder 65–67
  prospects for study 73
  suicide 65
South America, *see* Latin America
South Asia
  discrimination and violence risk 42
  domestic violence risk factors 44, 45
  dowry murder 41
  honor killing 41
  human trafficking 41
  interventions
    challenges 45–49
    global initiatives 49
    nongovernmental organizations 49
    prospects 51
    women's organizations 50, 51
  intimate partner violence 39, 40
  overview 39
  Pakistan and violence against women 42–44
  sexual harassment 42
  sexual violence 40, 41
  violence during pregnancy 41
Spain, *see* Europe
Sri Lanka, *see* South Asia
Substance abuse, violence against women association
  alcohol abuse in South Africa 72
  child sexual abuse association 100, 152
  overview 7
  sexual violence association 88, 89
Suicide
  biology of trauma and suicide 151, 152
  child sexual abuse association 100, 152, 155
  gendered model 152
  prospects for study 154–156
  psychological theories 150, 151
  rationale for study in women 148, 149
  sexual violence association 91
  South Africa and intimate partner violence 70–72
  types in women 149, 150
  violence and suicide attempts
    causation 154, 156
    reporting by women 152–154
Sweden, *see* Europe
Switzerland, *see* Europe
Syria, *see* Middle East

Tibet, *see* South Asia
Trafficking, *see* Human trafficking

United Arab Emirates, *see* Middle East

War-related violence against women
  community engagement 114
  counseling 113, 114
  integrated approach to psychosocial interventions 111, 112
  Middle East
    Iraq 18
    Lebanon 18, 19
    Palestine 18
  overview 107–109
  psychosocial support linkage to education, medical care, and economic strengthening 112, 113
  review of psychosocial support interventions
    findings 110, 111
    methodology 109, 110
Workplace harassment, *see* Sexual harassment

Yemen, *see* Middle East